Cultured Grugs

Cultured Grugs

—Dispatches From America in Collapse—

a collection of essays by

John "Borzoi" Chapman

Antelope Hill Publishing

First printing 2021
Printed in the United States of America

Cover art by sswifty
Edited by Margaret Bauer

The publisher can be contacted at
Antelopehillpublishing.com

ISBN-13: 978-1-953730-17-6 Paperback
ISBN-13: 978-1-953730-79-4 Hardback
ISBN-13: 978-1-953730-18-3 EPUB

"We have struggled on, and on we must still go.
We may have to smash things.
Then let us smash.
And our road may have to take a great swerve,
that seems like a retrogression.

But we can't go back."

— D.H. Lawrence,
Studies in Classic American Literature

Contents

Preface

Cultured Grugs, my collection of essays written since 2018, is a work that was only made possible by the extremely online addiction to cultural gawking. Readers will find the work is timeless, not in the sense that its proof stands the tests of time but that the work simply has *no sense* of time. Where Western civilization once held notions of continuity and progression, technology's obliterating influence on what cannot be computed has made it so that whatever may be called history and culture finds itself chewing the cud of the past, spitting it up, and regurgitating it again. Any attempt to untangle the decade past us now by future historians will find themselves more enamored by the personalities of hyperreal politicians than anything that really even happened.

These essays are a snapshot of that time during the late 2010s when the cringe-inducing Great Awokening had ossified into the culture and when the nominal opposition to it came in the form of message board cults and reality star heroes. Civilization never seemed more post-apocalyptic.

The project of our civilization is a finished one. A young Francis Parker Yockey, twenty-three years old at the time with the annihilation of Europe in the Second World War now begun, penned an essay on "Life as an Art" during his studies at Notre Dame University. Explicating his neo-Spenglerian philosophy, he declared the Western project to be finished, writing:

> *But the present form of our world-knowledge leaves no doubt that the Western Soul has in this field closed its cycle of development, and that the*

future of development of this soul is not in religion, philosophy, art and science, but in the field of technical, economic, and political activity. The WESTERN SOUL HAS BECOME FINALLY EXTROVERTED. It has entered the last stage.

We are now living in the detritus of this final stage, its destiny hijacked by hostile aliens, will-to-power pederasts, and small-souled sycophants. The Caesarism of the future has skipped right to its Elagabaluses, leaving its peasants and déclassé dissidents to pick through the flotsam and jetsam of the West and become Jonathan Bowden's "cultured thugs." There is no school for culture however, rendering education a foolish and schizophrenic errand in a time when the avenues of discovery are being swiftly snipped. Man and grug can only learn now in between failed e-dates, the simulated pump of the gym, and the omnipresent despair of staring at a screen. What he learns is like the pioneers on a dark continent comparing notes and maps, weighing each madman's claims of gold and monsters against one another.

As I write this preface, the United States is entering a great uncertainty thanks to its 2020 election. Its winner, Joe Biden, promises a "very dark winter." Spirits and demons more easily enter a world in its down-turning, when the lines of definition become so blurred that the veils of realities become lifted. Yeats once wrote "the centre cannot hold," but few would have imagined that center could be the membrane of a world safer from devil rulings. This book may end up being less of a collection of disconnected essays but a travelogue in the darkness of the world to come.

Within this book readers will find familiar essays but also new ones. Some of the older essays have been edited for clarity due to their previously hyperlinked nature not being conducive to the medium of the printed word. I have endeavored to keep the essays intact outside of those examples, even if I must suffer to see perceived imperfections.

There is no overall "point" as it were to this book other than to be a safari of schizophrenic and radical right-wing thought, insofar it means anything to be right-wing in the psychotic panopticon of this collectively neurotic fever dream. Further it has the dubious distinction of being an "e-book," a troubling situation that is usually comorbid with serious cries for help. These are unfortunate burdens that one must bear. In this day and age, when the DMV plays the role of the Sovereign's (wo)man, a handbook on how to be a dissident would be supremely more useful. This will have to do.

Thanks are in order as this book was only made possible by a handful of people. First to my beautiful wife who not only bears my children and my difficult nature, but whose work and assistance in the home life has been the only thing that has allowed me to collect, write, and edit these essays. Second to the very fine people of Antelope Hill Publishing who have given this writer a chance that almost no other publishing company would. Finally to my parents who have always encouraged me to write and will likely never read this book unless disaster has finally befallen me.

Every wise man is a religious man at heart, both to hedge his bets and to find his necessary transcendence. I am a religious man and prayer does not come easy, but I do offer up one prayer to God: leave a light on so we can find our way back home, because as far as I can see, tonight is dark and the stars do not shine.

John Chapman
Borzoi Boskovic
Edward Chang
2021

Cultured Grugs

"Truthfully, in this age those with intellect have no courage and those with some modicum of physical courage have no intellect. If things are to alter during the next fifty years then we must re-embrace Byron's ideal: the cultured thug."

— Jonathan Bowden

"grug stand among cave ruins

grug rebel against new ways

grug ride tiger"

A curious phenomenon of the internet: more people are certainly aware of Julius Evola, but arguably not many more people have read him than the ones who read him before.

The problem with intellectuals is they try to impress people who don't matter.

Essays published in

—The American Sun—

The Last Flight of the White Man

The American Sun, October 2018

> *"How then am I so different*
> *From the first men through this way?*
> *Like them, I left a settled life*
> *I threw it all away*
> *To seek a Northwest Passage*
> *At the call of many men*
> *To find there but the road back home again"*
> — Stan Rogers, "Northwest Passage"

> *"Nah, I'm just a white guy."*
> — Beebo

F. Scott Fitzgerald in *This Side of Paradise* called summer "only the unfulfilled promise of spring…a sad season of life without growth," but, like a bolt from the blue, one stolen plane and one young man's life changed all of that. On August 10th, 2018, underneath an auspicious clear sky a young man by the name of Rich Russell, Beebo to friends and family, took to the air in a stolen Bombardier and carried with him the shattered hopes and failed dreams of a million silent white men. There was something magical about that weekend in the way people connected with that perplexing event, and though nearly two months have passed now since that day, the feelings are still as raw and real as they were the day the Skyking took to the air and made his final plunge into Keton Island, burning brightly for one final time.

We truly believed we had witnessed the last flight of the white man.

America loves its folk heroes, but in the glitz and glam that are glommed on by the separated millions of a fractured nation, there aren't many to look to anymore. Where folk heroes like Johnny Appleseed once manifested America as an unspoiled promised land, now the folk heroes of the 21st century are men like the Killdozer who manifested the simmering violence of a nation that is triggered by endless indignities of a perpetually petty bureaucracy. Remove the Killdozer tank though and he's a man with many grudges. We can sympathize, but we can't empathize. Maybe some can, but the situation is too absurd. It's a good folk tale, but it doesn't speak to the human condition. Rich, for one moment, seemed to be relegated to that role of an American curiosity, but as the details of that fateful flight leaked out his spirit drew millions to be near to him. Rich was special. Rich was different.

Rich became a martyr. And every real white man of my generation understood that immediately.

Psychopaths with fancy pieces of paper will scoff at every word I write about this, but that's fine. It's not for them I write and they aren't my people anyway. They even barely qualify as such. They're social climbers for widely discredited institutions. At best they can only imagine the little lives in little houses from the top of their crumbling little summits. If you're still with me this far, you either already know what I'm going to say or you're eager to actually understand.

The Snark Set likes to sneer at notions of whiteness when they know full well what it is; if the admissions office of the University of Michigan and every Human Resources rep in this country know what whiteness is, then you with your $100k ticket to perpetual box wine parties and SSRI-stares with your cat certainly know what it is. This is not open to discussion. This isn't about parrying the disingenuous and bad faith rhetorical gotcha-questions, however. To understand what truly happened to cause so many total strangers to connect with the curious event of the Sea-Tac airport you have to first admit there is whiteness. You then have to admit there's a lot of trouble and tension going on with it. And Rich embodied it and carried it on with him.

There's something genetic, cultural, and spiritual that drove men like Rich's ancestors to go "yes, I'll climb into this God-forsaken man-made vessel and launch myself to the unknown ends of the earth at risk of life and limb." They traipsed the world for God, king, country, and family, for the spoils of war and the bounties of the earth no matter what it took to get to them and no matter who they needed to kill to have them. And in that great capacity for both evil and good, an awe-inspiring world was made. A world we are privileged in our whiteness to watch fall apart before our very eyes, like the farmers outside the city of Rome watching barbarian soldiers trample the crops and powerless to stop the ruin ahead. There really is madness and melancholy in our way of being. Nowadays the *Wanderer Above the Sea of Fog* by Caspar Friedrich feels like a clarion call to us, we feel an intense sense of longing in the painting, but it was created by a depressive who was largely forgotten by his death. His resurgence only came later. We all know this is the fate that awaits us, with immortality feeling so impossible to achieve. Our ancestors could channel that madness and throw themselves at the wilderness and the wild tribes of the earth, but what is left for us to explore? Born too late to explore the earth, born too soon to go to the stars, but born just in time to wonder how the hell we feel so lost, sad, and angry in such a bountiful society.

I paint a picture that makes it sound like every white man has in him to be one of the Great Men history, but there are actually few white men who can be that and fewer still who strive to be Great Men, even if the spark is there. For most what remains is either their children or what Stan Rogers called "a lonely cairn of stones." Those who haven't been utterly degenerated and degraded by a world that straight-faced intellectuals seriously try and explain is now a better place are almost always very humble people. What they want is simple. Home and hearth. Wife and child. This is not a future for many of them now.

Rich, it will be noted, was married. To what his own chaos was, I cannot attest. The devil here is not in the details as the results remain the same. It's simply important to note that often times these simple desires aren't enough to save white men like the Skyking. What he must've seen through that windshield in the light of the dying day may have been some reflection of a better life.

All the mental health services in the world would have never saved him. I predicted at the time in a tweet thread that in light of his death people will likely try to speak about mental illness without even really speaking about it. Just another fundraising drive for people who peddle pharmaceutical panaceas without the wisdom to apply the medicine in anything approaching responsibility. I then made a prediction that they will probably just ignore it because Rich was claimed by the undesirables. I was correct on the latter. He could've been on pills that would balloon up his weight and maybe kept him on a steady simulacrum of normality at best. Or he could've ended up another OD in the crisis the media doesn't really talk about in proportion to the amount of people it's affecting, strangely enough. It's okay though, the Sacklers who pumped the poisonous rot into white communities have just the cure with their own medicine for their medicine.

Truth is, the game was rigged from the start. Rich had a glimpse of that. He was afforded the clear-eyed lucidity that is granted to holy fools. In fact it seems almost like divine providence that we even got the tapes, but it's likely they would have gotten out one way or the other. Had we not heard him in his own words, unedited and unabridged, we would have never grieved for him. We've had men crash planes for foolish reasons, he could've been just another Sunday story. But when people heard those words, he became in those moments a generation's howling anguish.

Rich may not have had a full understanding of what he was going through and would have likely denied it. He didn't want to hurt anyone. He didn't want to trouble anyone. He didn't want to be a problem. Why would anyone think like that? Why do thousands say they understand it too? That's the prison white men find themselves in. The problem with no name that cannot be named. Your choices end up being that you either grit your teeth or you check out completely and terminally.

Jordan Peterson has been an inspiration for many men seeking clean and orderly domiciles and the maintenance of pristine phalluses, but Peterson would have failed him too. Just like every instance where he's dumbstruck by simple questions that challenge his house-of-cards liberalism or just outright refuses to answer the questions he knows the answers to, there's nothing of value he could have told Rich that would have saved his life because Rich embodied the deep-seated damage of a whole generation of white men. If Peterson could have even said anything, Rich would have probably just smiled, thanked Mr. Peterson, and walked away unhelped. Difficult questions require difficult answers, none of which the gatekeepers of polite society can ever offer for the sake of their own social standings and salary.

There was never a future for someone like Rich, absorbing messaging that he was slated for planned obsolescence in the fake and gay "Superior Future." His own words show how aware he was of this on that gut level. He described his own job as "I lift a lot of bags. Like a lot of bags. So many bags." The kind of job that will eventually go to a fat bisexual Latinx with a degree in Queer Latin-American Studies, before they too are peacefully sunset by a robot gayer than them. Whether or not he knew he was opting himself out of a raw deal, we knew immediately. And so we all lost our minds a little bit that day. We all remembered we were just guys with a couple of screws loose.

What touched so many people was the sincerity in Rich's voice. Listen to his voice and you know the kind of guy he was, one would always be out of step with the New Normal. I have my own criticism of my fellow millennials, but a lot of what was said about them is and was always so absurd that it doesn't even merit refutation. Guys like Rich fell behind and will continue to fall behind. If you want to trust a plan, that's the plan you can trust to happen. Just look to the conditions.

Material conditions? Shit.
Health conditions? Shit.
Mental conditions? Shit.
Spiritual conditions? Shit.

Twitter is an amazing place in it reflects the collective Ids of the diverse groups that populate it. It is here you will find no end to the genocidal intent that inevitably emerges when people are neighbors and aren't really certain why. And as every issue that plagues white folks becomes more and more apparent, the cheering of their demise gets louder and louder. The conditions that are tearing through people of my generation, from the economics to the narcotics paint a dark picture of the future, made grislier by the hooting and hollering that accompanies it. All of this has been bottled up in our collective unconsciousness for too long. And before this the bursts of rage were reprehensible murders.

Not with Rich. Because of the guy he was, he achieved the transcendental liberation that the saints receive when faced with their demise willingly without a shred of doubt in their hearts. We are no longer a religious age so we forget this, and thus for the thousands, possibly even millions, who were learning this and learning about Rich it became a religious experience for them too.

Snarky reactions don't make it any less true. Man is driven towards religion and faith because of our ultimate smallness in the great and grand scheme of things. Deprive them, they'll find it elsewhere. Rich embodied the Everyman quality many feel and thus he became an unknowing vessel for people's own failed hopes and dreams. They sailed off into that evening sky, doing one last barrel roll of defiance just to see if it could be done at all.

It's not for nothing that more and more look to non-fiction in their entertainment as the fiction produced now less and less resembles their lives. Fiction can be about anything you want it to be, but at the end of the day for it to be real at all it has to be real to our lives. So now deprived of the true feeling of religious expression, his first God, and now deprived of stories to be inspired by and to aspire to, his second god, the white man has no catharsis. There is no purging of the deep turmoil of his soul. He is trapped inside of a night that has no end.

Hence Rich as a vessel and martyr.

People looked to him and saw the guy who was failed by society, but unlike the exploding evil that pops off every couple of months, he never wanted to hurt anyone. He was the guy who can't even be allowed to go along to get along as it isn't even enough anymore. A guy that the people in power just want to see move more quickly to the exit sign. A guy like us, like our brother or the friend they couldn't save. A guy who just wanted to see a baby orca.

I'm an older millennial. For me, Rich was like one of my own little brothers. And this time I couldn't save my little brother. For many of you though, Rich was your older brother, and though he's gone you still want to do him proud. White men, sons and fathers, may have taken their last flight, but you're still here, alone and fighting. So clench those teeth, dry those tears, and make your older brother proud.

The last white men took off that fateful day on August 10th, 2018. This was 100 years to the day that it became clear that the Germans would lose the Battle of Amiens, and thus lose the Great War, setting in motion the historical forces that would lead to everywhere we are and the condition we are now in. History is made in the great moments but it is lived through the smaller, more painful ones. Rich carried all of that fear, anxiety, pain, and dread with him and he crashed it right into a sparsely populated island, hurting no one else and killing only himself. He even apologized to the people who had to clean up the mess he left behind in his death. I can't think of anything nobler than that. I can't think of anything whiter than that. The last white man died that day in the last frontier of the continental United States, charting a course to the end and guided by the same crazy determination that drove his forefathers into that land. And in that wreckage, burning through what remains of the last white man, a beloved hero and a make-shift saint, the flames are rising higher and higher. They never stopped burning, however. They were never extinguished. Time has stopped in this moment and the world watches with bated breath to see if a phoenix will emerge from what remains or if the rains of history will douse the flame and scatter the ashes away inside of a gentle wind.

Sinners in the Hands of an Angry Broad

The American Sun, March 2019

*"They **deserve** to be cast into hell; so that divine justice never stands in the way, it makes no objection against God's using his power at any moment to destroy them."*

— Jonathan Edwards, "Sinners in the Hands of an Angry God"

"lol white tears"
— black twitter

In the 18th Century, the Christian world that had been sucker-punched by the Enlightenment found new footing. Known as the Great Awakening, the first one mind you, a religious revival began to sweep across the Anglo world as a new fervency rekindled its own fire and regained its sense of urgency to remind people of the fallen state of the world and themselves. In the midst of this, a Yankee theologian from East Windsor, Connecticut, approached the pulpit of his Congregationalist parishioners and began to speak. He did not scream. He did not bleat. He did not pound a Bible and deliver a sermon with sulfur-laden pathos. Jonathan Edwards merely explained calmly, methodically, and point-by-point that "*there is nothing that keeps wicked men at any one moment out of hell, but the mere pleasure of God.*" That sermon, *Sinners in the Hands of an Angry God* is a classic piece of American theology but its legacy may lie more outside the shuttered doors of hollowed churches and inside the dark Satanic degree mills that churn out Human Resource representatives by the thousands every year.

When I first started to write this, Michigan had only just received its first proper snow of the season, a queerly late phenomenon, and with that January snow it carried with it thoughts of whiteness and death. It seemed fitting then that on that first snowy weekend that I would finally finish a three month slog through the future classic of all freshman orientation classes, *White Fragility* by Robin DiAngelo. Like Jonathan Edwards before her, DiAngelo will join that exalted class of American clerics for it will be through her that nothing will keep wicked whites at any one moment out of racism but the mere pleasure of the new gods.

Robin DiAngelo, it seems to me, is probably not a real person but more of a postmodern Prometheus, stitched together in a lab from the parts of lesser cat-ladies. One need only look at her bio to sense the gravitas of these credentials. She is *"an academic, educator, and author working in the fields of critical discourse analysis and whiteness studies. She formerly served as a tenured professor of multicultural education at Westfield State University"* and boasts of being a two-time recipient of *"the Student's Choice Award for Educator of the Year from the School of Social Work."* Most importantly, however, to the invisible executives of Globohomo, Inc., *"DiAngelo has been a consultant and trainer for more than twenty years on issues of racial and social justice."*

You see, DiAngelo isn't your run-of-the-mill boring and square academic, hidden behind stacks of ancient tomes as she writes dissertations titled *"The Neo-Kantian Perspective Of Stalin's Five Year Plan And Its Implications In The Development of Queer Liberation Theory."* Oh no no no no, why lock one's self up in the Ivory Tower So White when there's workers to terrorize and checks to cash that Woke Capital is begging to write to you.

You may have heard that *White Fragility* is an academic book. It is not. While you may scan the back of the book and find numerous questionable citations (the persistent problems of replicability and academia covering each other's tracks), to actually read the book is to discover that DiAngelo's extra fat pamphlet reads more like the diary of an oversocialized Congregationalist preacher. In page after page, DiAngelo recounts countless anecdotes of things-that-totally-definitely-happened where white employees resisted their company-mandated diversity seminars, the resistance being an insidious venom that DiAngelo calls "white fragility." Among the personal anecdotes that DiAngelo expects you to take seriously about how unserious white people are about their inherent racism is a text conversation she had with another bourgeois friend of hers who found a black New Orleans neighborhood "sketchy" or the time that a German woman at one of her seminars insisted she wasn't racist because as a little girl she saw the black American soldiers and thought they were *so handsome* (she fails to mention if this woman was blonde-haired and blue-eyed too). I'm not making this up. It's in the book:

> *I was working with a small group of white participants when a woman I will refer to as Eva stated that because she grew up in Germany, where she said there were no black people, she had learned nothing about race and held no racism. I pushed back on this claim by asking her to reflect on the messages she had received from her childhood about people who lived in Africa…She was furious and said she had been deeply offended by our exchange and did not 'feel seen'…However, I also held to my challenge that growing up in Germany would not preclude her from absorbing problematic racial messages about black people. She countered by telling me that she had never even seen a black person 'before the American soldiers came.' And then when they did come, 'all the German women thought them so beautiful that they wanted to connect with them.' This was her evidence that she held no racism.*

With evidence like that it would seem fitting that Robin DiAngelo may be the most insisted upon academic currently stalking the halls of clickbait media.

But what even is white fragility?

White fragility is defined by DiAngelo as any attempt to deny racism or refusal to engage in correct racial dialogue that serves to further prop up the perceived institutional racism and inherent white supremacy of our present neoliberal capitalist society. Not sure if you have it? Why not take their handy-dandy quiz? Fittingly enough, one of the possible answers to how you've responded to being told you're racist is "sought absolution." Bless me xir, for I have sinned.

White Fragility, for the uninitiated, may be a term you only recently became acquainted with when you were called out for correcting the Sacred POC. Often used in conjunction with "white tears," the history of "white fragility" begins with DiAngelo and the incestuous circles of social science pedagogy, filtered down into Tumblr microblogs run by white fourteen-year-olds and their obese woke idols, and then filtered back up academia and the media industrial complex. What was once niche and novelty becomes, as all things do in the culture of the last men, the morally-imperative mainstream.

These pet ideologies, always seriously unopposed, eventually reach their apotheosis in the form of college orientation books. Anyone who has been through these oxymoronic educational seminars knows that whatever the pet ideology that is currently in fashion, that will be the book that will be the required reading. Thousands of parents every year willingly surrender their young to penal re-education without the slightest curiosity as to what new programming will replace eighteen years of love and care. *White Fragility* will join those ranks, ensuring thousands of more young women hate their weak white fathers, if they even have such a thing. Such as it is in Dark Age America.

What's interesting, however, is that this book isn't for us. By "us" I mean the cadre of extremely online posters who chose Internet Racist as their MMORPG class and grind N-word threads one letter at a time. In fact, if you take that above quiz what you will find is that you may score as having very little white fragility or even none at all. It's the funny little phenomenon of the far-right and the neoliberal left racing to see how much of the center they can destroy. The book is quite clearly designed for those who are apolitical or invested in having a managerial or bureaucratic role in the system, to break them on the spoked wheel of woke and render them pliable for further instruction, with the added benefit that those seeking status get to psychologically terrorize the

American kulak.

The notion of progressive leftism as being a religion unto itself is not any kind of new observation. Colleges are the monasteries where neoliberalism's vanguard have proper bona fides first burnished. The neoreactionary sphere has long called the present system we reside under the Cathedral due to its firm commitment to fashionable dogmas taken on faith and wishes while others have called the persistent inquisition of the left the "Church of No Salvation." Where Christianity offers the road to salvation in faith, penance, and redemption, the left's own inverted church offers only perpetual mortification and groveling with not an end in sight. What was once a rhetorical description of the left's religiosity has now been fully embraced in *White Fragility* and been made more explicit.

Beyond the example of "seek absolution" in the quiz above, what you will find in the pages of the book itself is what it means to be "doing the work" of unpacking your own white supremacy. To quote from *White Fragility*:

> *The final advice I offer is this: 'Take the initiative and find out on your own.' To break with the conditioning of whiteness—the conditioning that makes us apathetic about racism and prevent us from developing the skills we need to interrupt it—white people need to find out for themselves what they can do. There is so much excellent advice out there today—written by both people of color and white people. Search it out. Break with the apathy of whiteness, and* **demonstrate that you care enough to put in the effort**. *(Emphasis mine)*

Like all clerical bureaucracies, once one begins to don the robes of the magicians' Higher Mysteries, one changes their knowledge from the exoteric to the esoteric. In practice, this is meant to keep you perpetually off-kilter, always unable to challenge the decrees of these new clerics, since it means that only they know what is truly going on, forcing more people to defer to them. At the same time though, they'll fall back on platitudes like "*It's not my job to educate you*," partly because they really don't know what they're talking about, partly because doing so would give the game away, but also because it gives them a status over the uninitiated. It leaves the uninitiated vulnerable to be abused because their ignorance is on display, and they lack the time or ability to take the time and ingest the knowledge of their sacred tomes. Finally, it allows them to see who is worthy enough to eventually join them, who will have the constitution to prostrate and make eunuchs of themselves for this new religious order.

Where the soft-spoken Jonathan Edwardses of the world would calmly lay out the reasons for their congregation's damnation and how one may even have a hope to escape such an eternal fate, these acolytes of the inverted age issue abusive missives behind cloak-and-dagger to keep people frantically searching for an absolution they will never find or receive. This is the reality of what Vaclav Harvel called the post-totalitarian ideology in *The Power of the Powerless*:

[A] *labyrinth of influence, repression, fear and self-censorship which swallows up everyone within it, at the very least by rendering them silent, stultified and marked by some undesirable prejudices of the powerful...*

I pondered for a long time what the value even was in reading a work like this. This is a problem that many in our circles run into where the thought of even trying to engage their ideas is as ludicrous as trying to engage someone who doesn't believe in the correct shape of the earth. I realized that is the brilliance of what they do. Their entire body of work is based on exhaustion and avoidance, of nobody having any time for it and ceding more of the battlefield to a cavalcade of the aggrieved in cat-step formation. They thrive on dismissal because they aren't even attacking us, they're attacking the average people who were left behind or missed the memo.

I've sent excerpts of the book to those types of average people and I've heard the bewildered tones in their voices. Like a priest who knows his congregation all too well, DiAngelo knows and understands her mark. She takes such delight in abusing them, as can be seen when DiAngelo's literary agent DMCA'd the screenshot I took of this anecdote she recounts:

> *A cogent example of white fragility occurred during a workplace anti-racism training I co-facilitated with an inter-racial team. One of the white participants left the session and went back to her desk, upset at receiving (what appeared to training team as) sensitive and diplomatic feedback on how some of her statements had impacted several of the people of color in the room. At break, several other white participants approached me and my fellow trainers and reported that they had talked to the woman at her desk, and that she was very upset that her statements had been challenged. (**Of course, "challenged" was not how she phrased her concern. It was framed as her being "falsely accused" of having a racist impact**.) Her friends wanted to alert us to the fact that she was in poor health and "might be having a heart-attack." Upon questioning from us, they clarified that they meant this literally. These coworkers were sincere in their feat that the young woman might actually die as a result of the feedback. **Of course when news of the women's potentially fatal condition reached the rest of the participant group, all attention was immediately focused back onto her and away from engagement with the impact she had on the people of color. As professor of social work Rich Vodde states, "If privilege is defined as a legitimization of one's entitlement to resources, it can also be defined as permission to escape or avoid any challenges to this entitlement."** (Emphasis mine)*

Bask in this. Bask in the indignation that the American kulak tried to escape from her NKVD interrogator.

I screenshot many books to provide commentary and have never been DMCA'd. I'm not the first person to do this. I will not be the last person to do this. I have never run into this issue before. That it happened in a book like *White Fragility* and that this specific passage was the one that was DMCA'd should speak to their cognizance of just how fundamentally unlikeable they are. That they go hand-in-hand with the corporate structure is frankly no surprise. These incomprehensible and scaled-up power structures that require diversity indoctrinations are dependent upon the sniveling status-seekers and oversocialized psychopaths to maintain order and compliance and these are the roles that people like Robin DiAngelo and her sycophants are meant to fill-in. They're meant to find nice, normal people, and abuse them of their own personal dignity, to ensure that there is not an ounce of rebellion left inside of the American worker. They are meant to be stretched on the rack of human resources, and such torture must be left in the hands of people all-too-eager to practice.

The error of these maltheistic annihilationists in the Church of No Salvation, when properly understood and taken apart, is that they want to make these people uncomfortable so that they can both abuse them for fun and profit but also create a few more ravenous acolytes of their eldritch cult. When you do not have the truth on your side, when everything you do is in the service of your own noble lie, the only warriors you'll ever find on your side are fanatics, and like the blood tax paid by Christian sons under the Ottoman's devshirme system, it will be rendered unwillingly. There is no hope or salvation or love in the prostration they expect, only willful subjugation.

This will not be a pleasant thing to say, but this may ultimately be necessary. People should be made uncomfortable. They should feel a little pain. The softness and false bravado of American society is inching towards its well-deserved collapse and at that moment the division will occur. Molon labia mindset and beer gut swagger will be put to the test and made to put-up or shut-up. The choice will be put forward for those who want to live and those who want to lie down and wait to die. This can never be a thing for those who do not love life and its truths, and want to see it prevail. The works of *White Fragility* provide that opportunity, to show them that there's nowhere left to run to and no they're never going to leave you or your children alone.

Read this, and read it to people who resist you like you're Cassandra. Let them see just how damned they are, how much people like Robin DiAngelo want power and want power over them, how the foundational work for the next Inquisition is already being built, how voting for Donald Trump isn't going to save them when they have to sit in on these diversity seminars led by women who aborted their only children and want to torture yours. Let them see Lovecraft's twisted church ladies in all their ugliness and let them see how they spill out in these sermons of revenge. Make them open their eyes and stand by their side when they frantically clutch at you looking for answers. They need to understand that we don't have the government, we don't have academia, and we don't even have the businesses. We have nothing and we are nothing. We have each other though, and that's enough to start.

That which bonds together, clings together, will not be made fragile.

PissEarth, 2025

The American Sun, December 2018

"If much in the world were mystery the limits of that world were not, for it was without measure or bound and there were contained within it creatures more horrible yet and men of other colors and beings which no man has looked upon and yet not alien none of it more than were their own hearts alien in them, whatever wilderness contained there and whatever beasts."

— Cormac McCarthy,
Blood Meridian, or the Evening Redness in the West

"*BORN TO DIE*

WORLD IS A FUCK

鬼神 *Kill Em All 1989*

I am trash man

410,757,864,530 DEAD COPS"

PissEarth, 2025

It is cliché at this point to speak of how horrified you are at the detritus of our postmodern world. There is, of course, a certain kind of thrill in digging beneath the pallid white corpses of decency to see what strange and mutated life is writhing beneath, just so you can scoop it up and toss it in the faces of your friends. However, it has become rote and formulaic to look at just another story of neoliberal capitalism functioning in its just-as-planned absurdity and pull out the clown horn to signal to your friends how far we've fallen and how far left there is to get to hell. Our receptors for rage-flavored dopamine need something more, our *haterade* must be topped off. So I come to you as a prophet and I offer you a vision of the world to come.

I offer you, PissEarth, 2025.

When one hears the name PissEarth, it may conjure up images of ammonia-scented oceans of fetid yellow water, ebbing and flowing in tide under a blood-moon in a night-sky bereft of stars, while little islands of human refuse taper across like logs of flotsam and jetsam. The spirituality of such a world is not that far off. The seers who are blind know that they were blessed to have lost their sight. You, too, may find yourself in such a state, like Oedipus staring wistfully at the golden pins after his terrible, horrible, no-good very bad lunch date with the shepherd. Like Oedipus, you're all tainted motherfuckers.

You must understand, I do not tell you these things to hurt you, but to warn you that this new world *wants* to hurt you. It will. Oh, believe me it will. PissEarth, 2025 is accelerated humanity, and there is no more room for obsolete units that think in terms of the abolished humanity. They will not return you for store credit or sit you up in Dorothy McGillicuddy's Home for Antiques. Anything less than total depravity of your spirit, dispossession of your body, and annihilation of your mind would be a mercy. I say 'you' because if 'you' are still reading this past the first 150 words, then you are already a member of the abolished.

Everything you hate, everything you fear, everything that disgusts you inside, all of that will come quite naturally to PissEarth, 2025. A totalistic reality wholly assumed with no history. What you see now as the "slippery slope" will simply be the waterslide into a community piss-pool everyone will be baptized in. You will never gawk, never sigh and point at just how far we've come. You'll be amazed at the efficiency of it all when it whittles down the Buddha's Four Noble Truths down to just the very First one.

"I teach suffering."
— some Indian who sat under a tree

Let us be clear. There is Clown World, and there is PissEarth. When we speak of Clown World, we speak of the contradictions and absurdities that the present culture and political order are built on. We speak of a president who is able to shoot impotent missiles at a country his own citizens can't find on a map but who is powerless to stop a caravan of admixtured Aztecs wearing the hand-me-downs that Fat Bob of Fat Bob's T-Shirt Emporium wasn't able to sell. We speak of the nation grounding to a halt over whether or not little girls should be exposed to the Halloween parade hopped up on homemade HRT hobbling into their bathrooms. We speak of dozens of men who have lost gainful employment for making OKAY signs in photos because the Morris Dees newsletter fell for a prank from mischievous, anonymous frogs.

When we speak of these clownish things, we speak with a feeling that dragging these things into the light and exposing them for all the world to see will allow the light to shine in and obliterate the vampires with its cleansing sunbeams. These are all flashpoints in the broad and all-encompassing culture war that the West has found itself embroiled in, with each day yielding a brand new skirmish to deploy for, though the war is already lost. When we speak of Clown World, we speak of trying to find a way to shoo out the clowns.

PissEarth is different. PissEarth is the surrender. PissEarth is the occupation. PissEarth is the Morgenthau Plan for your shattered psyche. PissEarth is the moment this has all been building up to. Clown World ain't got nothing on PissEarth, 2025, the *real* Greatest Show on Earth.

WORLD IS A FUCK

"Get on with it," I hear you (*and the editor*) say, "You've talked enough, like you're trying to warn us from hearing out your vision, like no matter how awful it is we aren't going to look anyway. Just put me in the hurt-box, please. Just show me what sights there are to behold."

Very well. Behold, PissEarth, 2025.

Behold PissEarth, where the tech-giants have spread their privatized favelas far-and-wide, where debt-ridden PhDs hustle from gig-to-gig, chasing bounties that allow you to snitch on anyone insufficiently committed to diversity. It will become a game all unto its own, with high scores for 'scalps' that were claimed, no matter how absurd the bounties one gets. The dopamine must flow.

Behold PissEarth, where you celebrate your abortion from a mail-order kit as you make a public pledge to reduce your carbon footprint by remaining childless while Nuevo Americano rides a river of trash into your welcoming arms. Adopting enormous underprivileged families becomes the norm as a form of public atonement, and their weak-chinned fathers beam with pride and joy that their daughters are doing such a public service to the world.

Behold PissEarth, where pornographers have the social capital to demand and force aggressive men to watch pornography lest their employment and finances are endangered, mocking them for the damage it does at the same time. A thousand smirking social climbers, all in unison saying "have a fap, you'll feel better" as their malice goes unchecked.

Behold PissEarth, where procreation is a quaint novelty—every boy a girl, every girl a boy, belonging to everyone and no one, in beautiful rainbow shades of light brown to dark brown, as even the socially ostracized will respect the pronoun and they will suck the feminine penis. Then real communism can finally be tried.

Behold PissEarth, where war is abolished but skirmishes are constant and daily with little purpose to them other than the grim remains of human resistance or simple lashings of animal rage. No one is happy, but at last they are free. A friendly notification pops up in your latest smart-device, warning you of which roads to avoid for threat of most recent self-contained riot.

Behold PissEarth, with such technological wonders like the IUD that filters the microplastics out of your dick, "air purifiers" in place of trees, and artisanal soylent green but it's from free-range, cruelty-free cockroaches. Status vloggers chase clicks by dumping half their paycheck to eat dressed up prole food made for them by a group of queer hijabis who receive their funding from a nearby corporation.

Behold PissEarth, where the purpose of a lifetime of labor is to fund research into how corpulent immovable masses of flesh can have better and more revolutionary forms of sex. The research and test subjects themselves become their own programming, another screen to pass the time in your shrinking apartment.

Behold PissEarth, where every neurosis has become a fetish to be enacted in order to attain collective cummies, to be taught in schools, and to be talked about incessantly on perpetual content devices. While the fear of pedophiles will always remain as a release vale for anger, its normalization will be so thorough that vigilantism against it is arbitrary.

Behold PissEarth, where the President will be a figurehead American idol, sworn-in on a human resources manual as they pledge to do their utmost to continue the pursuit of equality before a million teeming masses yearning to breathe at all in the crowd so that they can snap selfies for their social credit score. Though the president will be known as a figurehead, and though everyone will acknowledge that tech corporations have all the power, everyone still states solemnly the importance of a hallowed or is it hollowed democratic institution.

Behold PissEarth, where the gods of the new world are men disfigured into chimeras made from the new sacred rituals and paraded out in victory for their ascendance. Where children are made to be their wards by loving and approving parents. The parents will allow their children to be "babysat" by these creatures, in order that values of acceptance be inculcated at an early age.

Behold PissEarth, where any intellectual curiosity beyond the new and revised canon will be immediately suspect, where not having a strong opinion on the most current pop culture multimedia franchise will mark you with a big red flag on your social credit score, where you will never be able to escape the perpetual content stream as the algorithms pioneered by Netflix find a way to be lodged inside your brain like some kind of mind-control slug slithering its way inside. Your future has been written by media mathematics.

Behold PissEarth, where your experience with nature is a virtual reality simulation that you share with the few people online that you've been able to light any embers of a human connection with. Though the simulation glitches and shimmers in an unnatural way, you cling to this image because that little voice in the back of your head fears what you will do if you lose even this little bit of hope's simulacrum.

I can hear you protest that this is already happening. Yes, the sprouts have sprung but they have not yet bloomed. Only when you have accepted all of these things as assumed and normal, when instead of being complacent your friends and family applaud it will you truly understand the reality of PissEarth, 2025. There will be no more pieces to point and gawk and decry that the world has gone mad. It will all be as staid as the abolished Sunday dinner.

This is what you must understand about the reality of PissEarth, 2025. Everything you joke about is assumed. Everything you satirize is simple reality. Whatever protests you think you'll register against it simply won't exist. You'll keep your head down and just try to get through this life if you have any thoughts of rebellion, because you saw what Clown World did to the ones before you. You saw what it did to your friends, your family, and your brothers. You have accepted that you are but a drop of wine in the entire piss-bucket.

Technology will improve, but your quality of life will not. Materially it will not. Spiritually it will not. Every force that champions this great progress being made will be actively trying to harm you every which way in a totalistic system, if there is any sense that you are not on board or there was a point you were never on board.

If you truly wish to understand PissEarth, 2025 on an intellectual level beyond the confetti-and-glitterbomb sermon I've laid out, then you must understand the nature of post-totalitarian ideology. Vaclav Havel lays out many of these concepts in his work *The Power of the Powerless* but elucidates the nature of PissEarth quite well in his concept of the greengrocer:

{9} *The post-totalitarian system touches people at every step, but it does so with its ideological gloves on. This is why life in the system is so thoroughly permeated with hypocrisy and lies: government by bureaucracy is called popular government; the working class is enslaved in the name of the working class; ... Because the regime is captive to its own lies, it must falsify everything. It falsifies the past. It falsifies the present, and it falsifies the future. It falsifies statistics. ...*

{10} Individuals need not believe all these mystifications, but they must behave as though they did, or they must at least tolerate them in silence, or get along well with those who work with them. For this reason, however, they must live within a lie. They need not accept the lie. It is enough for them to have accepted their life with it and in it. For by this very fact, individuals confirm the system, fulfill the system, make the system, are the system. . . . .

The difference between Havel's greengrocer and the PissEarth denizen is that the people of the former are a people trained to avoid negative stimuli while the latter have learned to love the negative stimuli. They embrace it as a mission, as a religious calling, and like Andres Serrano's Piss Christ they will strike their own perverted Christlike pose and submerge themselves wholly into these bodily fluids. They will immerse themselves and baptize themselves into a world they will lovingly embrace despite every dissonant thought, despite every horrible incident, and despite every pain that's inflicted on them. They will hate you if you try to pull them out of it.

This is the totalistic reality of PissEarth, 2025.

Okay, Yeah, That Sounds Pretty Awful.
How Do I Escape From PissEarth?

You don't. You don't escape PissEarth. You fight. You struggle. You take your Boomer father's yacht that he spent your inheritance on and like Johansen you ram that shit as far into Cthulhu's sleepy eye as you possibly can. Regardless of how it all ends. You delegitimize the system. You take everything you possibly can get from it and you rob it blind any way you can. Legally of course through any clever loophole you can find, because (*taps NSA microphone*) we're good upright citizens who don't commit any crimes and disavow any and all illegal activity.

Some seek a much more simple way to terminate this endless

suffering. Listening to the wisdom of the modern nomads, they have joined the caldera deathcult and pray earnestly five times a day in the direction of Yellowstone for one final eruption to scald away our modern sins. Along this same vein, even the insects in people suits who work unpaid overtime to bring about PissEarth, 2025 stare hopefully up at the stars, not to explore them but to pull down a meteor and simply end it all. Personally, I'm pulling for a nice little grey goo scenario, an experiment of the Han Empire run amok that engulfs, smothers, and consumes the entire world. These are understandable expressions. The trashworld citizen, who knows the world for what it is, who often sat in silence like a totemic mystic once intoned *"we are fucking up shit that cannot be easily unfucked."* It's the bleak reality of a grim future, so why not end it all with a pithy "gg, everybody."

I have another vision though. A hypnopompic one not as clear, like a dream that fades in the morning but you retain some inkling of it as you go about your day-to-day life. When I meditate I can almost see it within my mind's eye.

I can see that even in a world lit up in gasoline-doused fires, where pain is maximal, there are men who have learned to love life so much that they will defend the last dignified patch of wood with their very lives, and not a care for how little it all means. I can still see little babies being born and suckling at their mother's breasts in the dark of night as plastic meteors go down over the lonely mountains. I can see bands of foolhardy boys laugh about the stories they've heard, when technological demons once roamed the earth. I can see cold, bitter days made just a bit less uncomfortable by a fire that people learned to light by their grandfathers and great-uncles.

It must be made clear that these green dreams are not premonitions, only some slumbering notions of a better future after the inevitable long dark. Extinction is always on the table, always a possibility, and that wave of existential terror thunders inside like a beating heart in every action.

Short of a miraculous consciousness simultaneously sweeping across the great swaths of the abolished humanity, you will not stop PissEarth. It lumbers and slouches toward us, consuming everything it sees with the moral imperative of a brimstone preacher. To fight against PissEarth will be to engage in the inner jihad, to always be at war with one's self and the world as the wars of PissEarth, 2025 are maximal wars. The forever wars.

We are not the middle children of history. We are the abandoned children of history, set down in the bulrushes of a river so polluted that it's being set on fire. Like the Cuyahoga, I don't know if this one has any chance of being fixed in time to undo any of the damage. Humanity has been abolished and PissEarth is rolling out the recall. You might call this bleak, you might call this depressing, but the facts are the facts and it has become clear there are two types of people in the modern world and there will only ever be these two types of people. Those who want to live and those who want to die. Those who want to die, who have given up on life, are the denizens of PissEarth, whose own lives are simulacrum broadcast back to them by malevolent entities charging them for the privilege. Those who want to live will, to a man and woman, be banished to the outer dark and be made to fend for themselves against every hostile entity, their own just desserts for rejecting the Superior Future.

Do you love life? Do you want life for your descendants? Do you want any hope against just how bad things are going to be? Then you better learn to swim in a burning river, my man, because what else are you going to do?

The Feasts of Shame

The American Sun, January 2020

"Humiliation with a big H denies the social world of normalized encounter. In fact, it humiliates by virtue of this denial. It tells the victims that all social norms are suspended in dealings with them because they are not human."

— William Ian Miller,
Humiliation and Other Essays on Honor,
Social Discomfort, and Violence

The air was jubilant in many of those summer months of '44, the tide was turning. The Germans, the dreaded Nazi war machine, was on the retreat as the Allies in the west pushed them back town-by-town out of the fields of France. The shame of humiliating defeat and the occupation by the Germans was finally coming to a close; now would be the time of celebration. People could breathe freely in the air again. They could speak freely again. Love freely again. Be free people again. And to celebrate this joyous occasion they would have a parade—a parade of half-naked shorn women, tear-wet cheeks stained red with shame and lipsticked swastikas, and packed into lorries to the happy jeers and hollers of a blood-frenzied crowd. Within these good people of free France beat the animal hearts of a mad populace that needed to wet their beaks with revenge, to strike another creature and pin it down with primal glee. To humiliate. To remind them, you are not human.

This is not just a piece about the past. This is about the past, present, and especially about the future. This is a work of control, of pain, and of destruction. The dark side of humanity is never an easy thing, and to even glimpse into the darkness is to invite all manners of recriminations upon your character. But this is not only the necessary thing to do, it's the right thing to do.

We have to talk about humiliation.

I. Rituals of Humiliation

"To submit to an insult, to forget a humiliation, to quail before an enemy—all these are signs of a life become worthless and superfluous. But this is not at all the same thing as priestly moral, for that moral does not cleave to life at any cost of degradation, but rather rejects and abstains from life as such, and therefore incidentally from honour. As has been said already, every moral action is, at the very bottom, a piece of askesis and a killing of being."

– Oswald Spengler,
The Decline of the West

The origins of this essay lie in a manic free association Twitter thread I made about a Modern Farmer article entitled "This Trick Might Actually Get Americans to Eat Bugs" by one Dan Nosowitz. The medium of Twitter doesn't lend itself well to collecting one's thoughts, much less doing research into the myriad topics that the thread shotgunned all at once. First, we must correct a term.

The term 'humiliation ritual' has its own particular meaning that's used by, for lack of a better term but this is meant neutrally, the conspiracy-minded. That is not the scope of this work. Further, the term 'ritual humiliation' also has another meaning, often overlapping with 'humiliation ritual' and frequently denotes certain types of hazing, but not always. One could argue that many of these things are distinctions without differences, but this will be about the phenomenon of 'public humiliation' and its social and political expressions.

The piece in Modern Farmer is very strange, and has an air of unreality in how it's written. The trick, as it were, in the piece was about how insect farming can work as a middleman in livestock feed. What is bizarre about it is its framing that this is an alternative in trying to break through the American resistance to eating bugs. The question that is begging to be answered here is "why is this something that's on your mind?" Entomophagy has been something that's been near and dear to the hearts of the propaganda class, with Vice magazine writing miserable pieces about being on an exclusive bug diet entitled "This Is What Happens When You Eat Nothing but Bugs for a Week" while concluding at the end:

> It's an absolute cultural bias...but it's just a matter of educating the public, and it's important to make insects favorable for the common people.

One could devote an entire book to reading all of the articles that have been published in the last ten years trying to convince people of the delicious virtues of eating insects and digging deep into the who's who and why's why of how this is so important to them. If you read this a year after this has been published, no doubt there will be an egregious number of new pieces written about it. They certainly get upset if you begin to wonder why there's always new pieces about this, accusing the curious of cooking "up a conspiracy theory around the bug-eating trend," though the word trend probably merits a thousand quotation marks around it.

The indignant attitude when questioned plays out the same no matter what the issue is. "Why do you even care?" they ask when people question anything they do in the name of utopia, whether it's race-swaps of fictional and non-fictional characters or chemically castrating children for reasons that are unfathomable to the devil himself. The correct answer is always "I care because you care."

Without a shred of doubt, we know they care a lot about people eating insects. There is an article that is either written or re-posted every week about this. Just do an advanced search on CNN's Twitter for "bug" and look at the frequency of these articles. A dance has begun to develop every time this happens, where they clearly know the reaction they're going to get as they get mobbed and ratio'd by Twitter users screaming at the top of their lungs "I WILL NOT EAT THE BUGS!", as though they're relishing in what they would view as the people's futile resistance to their plans. They probably are delighted.

The ostensible reasons for this is for ecological sustainability. This is bunk to anyone who isn't an idiot. Populations peak. Things don't go on forever, no matter what your stupid pop songs say, and that's without getting into the issues that your problem isn't ecological sustainability but industrial instability (which is what's going to wreak havoc on the former). Californians are already living in fear of having their power shut off on them. You already know the answer to the perennial question "are things getting better or are they getting worse." The 'cult of progress' has no magical spell that is going to spirit you up a simple and non-catabolic energy source. You're not going to mitigate human and food transport costs by cockroach farming. No, this isn't about sustainability. The one thing you must always remember living in liberal societies that are run by the rootless and the cosmopolitan is that *everything* becomes counter-intuitively, so you must think counter-intuitively.

You must think counter-intuitively because of the way liberalism functions. Every ideology, every belief, and every group seeks to dominate. This is called life. This is what Carl Schmitt noted when he looked at liberalism and capitalism, that being in this world you cannot escape friend-enemy distinctions and so liberalism being the utilitarian nothingness of flexibility and freedom, it must overcome inevitable conflict by subsuming everything that would oppose it and bring it to heel. Liberalism, just like any other thing, has a will to dominate but because liberalism in its ideology is meant to be free and flexible, it must then dominate everything that opposes it, especially when it becomes tied to economics. There can never be an end to the expanding market under liberal capitalism. Like the Judge in Cormac McCarthy's *Blood Meridian*, liberalism must become a suzerain, the ruler of rulers, upon the whole of earth for *"only nature can enslave man and only when the existence of each last entity is routed out and made to stand naked before him will he be properly suzerain of the earth."*

Liberal capitalism forced open the ports of Japan by black ships and shell guns, for the Japanese were intolerant of the tolerant. This is the true essence of Karl Popper's 'The Paradox of Tolerance'. Popper's so-called paradox isn't an attempt to plug the hole in a mental child's understanding of tolerance but to make the case that anything that opposes the liberal order, but especially those who drive the liberal order, has to be rooted out and destroyed because those who stand for something are always more holistically powerful than the ones who stand for nothing but power itself. There is no vitalism in liberalism.

You must think counter-intuitively. When you see the dopamine-dispensing treats of technocapital you might think you see a world of freedom and choices, but this is merely the IV drip of product to keep you medicated to the will of others. Ask yourself, what autonomy do you truly have to be outside of this system? None. You are living in a false reality. Remember, like anything else, liberalism seeks to dominate and being the flexible nothingness it must then dominate everything. Conquerors do not invade territory to do nice things to it and especially for the people that reside there.

History bears this out.

Our history must be remembered by the light of its fires.

II. Occupied Americans

"Obviously this is a very idealised representation of war; we see a game of pure power, from which one would like to erase all trace of physical and moral suffering. Everything is done in order to pretend that humiliation is not part of the game."
— Bertrand Bardie,
Humiliation in International Relations

The chief selling point of liberalism has been that it's the most peaceful and prosperous system available to mankind, allowing the vast range of humanity to be part of a rising tide that lifts all boats, but there is nothing in this world that hasn't come with its price. Power and status do not abide by any notion of equality. So nothing in this world we live in will ever make sense to you unless you understand you live under an occupation and are thus subject to the rules of an occupation. If you do not start from there, you will fruitlessly search for multiple explanations and rationalizations for everything that the people with financial and media power—the power that matters far more than political power now—push the people to expect and accept, such as vegetarian burger schemes, bug protein, and drag kids.

For every argument that's made about ecological sustainability or making sure that "sexual minorities" are able to express who "they really are" early and often, the question has to be countered "then why are they so aggressive about it?" Why are they so eager to bring about PissEarth, 2025? All the reasons that are given are additional components to the project of total atomization of human society, but when you shed every additional layer to get to the core, the driving force of why, all you are left with is shame; the public humiliation of the conquered. It makes a vicious mockery of the conquered by denying them any bit of dignity. A bitter reminder for the vanquished of their new status in victory's triumph and delight for the victorious.

Public humiliation is intrinsically linked to status. In history, people would be disfigured, branded, or tattooed to deny them their right to simply blend in with society. They would be marked, letting people know what they did to deny them the privacy of the self. Ruining their appearance in this way kept their status low and their autonomy violated. Mass media has only served to amplify that effect, transmitting a village shame into a national shame. People are all too eager to participate in these Little Brother acts, often the only taste of the power process they'll ever have in their lives.

When the Germans lost WWII, the French women who were sleeping with German soldiers and the SS or even just friendly with them had their heads forcibly shaved and were paraded down the street. Much of it was done by previous collaborators themselves to curry favor with liberators (read: conquerors) and maintain their own fleeting sense of status. Hair, being an important thing for women, was tinged with seductive implications, with longer hair usually a sign of femininity. Denying them this denied them being good women in their essence. These shorners had power over these women, and as we are often told rape is about power, not sex. The resentment of defeat against the Germans necessitated that the nation knew *someone* would have to pay for it and *someone* would need to suffer for it and that the hierarchy of status would be restored. The whole nation would know. Wendy Webster writing on this in *The Essence and the Margin: National Identities and Collective Memories in Contemporary European Culture* states:

> In France, shearings were often conducted in front of jeering crowds outside town halls with shorn women subsequently paraded through the streets, sometimes naked. Fabrice Virgili calculated that as many as 20,000 French women were shorn. At the moment of French liberation, large numbers of women were very publicly humiliated, while extensive dissemination of visual imagery—in newspaper photographs, and on postcards—ensured that their humiliation was widely known throughout France.

The Ottoman Empire had a culture of boys, actual children, called *köçek* who crossdressed and danced in sexually provocative ways and were sexually available. These boys, who were kept as dancers *until* they grew beards, engaged in belly dances with suggestive expressions and steps described as "coquetteish" in *Made in Turkey: Studies in Popular Music* to the rapture of male audiences. The scenes described bring to mind the sights one might see at any contemporary gay pride parade or a public library.

Most accounts of pederasty in the Ottoman Empire appear to come from the people who went to see it for themselves, such as Lord Byron with the dancing boys. In the case of the *köçek*, they were banned by the Ottomans in the 19th century due to the jealous fights that would break out over the attention for these boys, though one wonders if the increasingly British Orientalist attraction to this phenomenon and their lurid accounts played a role. They were "recruited" around the age of six or seven. How a child can be "recruited" to be a dancing boy is a rhetorical mystery. There seems to be little historical record of how this came about, though it is clear that as Ottoman power and harem culture solidified that dance "recruitment" evolved into ethnic-oriented guilds. It likely developed alongside the *devshirme* system whereby one child from every 40 non-Muslim households was taken to serve in some bureaucratic or military function of the Ottoman Empire.

It is difficult to see this as anything more than a flex to let the conquered non-Muslim people know the conquerors could turn their boys into a dancing monkey, a girl, and a prostitute and there was *nothing* they could do about it. Other roles reserved for non-Muslim boys could include the role of the *tellak,* the washers in the bath houses who could also double up as sex workers for the "clients." Once the shock of the whole system wore off however, it was not uncommon for non-Muslim families to offer bribes so that their children would be picked to serve some function in the Ottoman system since it was the pathway to a better and more prestigious life, regardless of what it would entail. It was the ideology of the imperial state and the alternative was often being put-upon laborers, regardless if it meant giving over their own children as sexual playthings. There was no more shame; it had internalized itself. The temptation is strong to see parallels between that society and the one of today.

Humiliation moves from public to national to global when we look at the culture today and what the powerful and privileged institutions and media outlets push to the average American. What other answer could there be? Does anyone actually believe that the average American is in charge of their own culture? They can try to lie if they want but their cynical way of speaking about the institutions of the country and their assumption of bad whites as poor and stupid betray them. Do people who supposedly share the same culture view each other as nearly alien or speak of the other side in dehumanizing terms the way the leftist whites and Jewish people view what they call the "Trumpenproles"? These are tribal differences viewed in a war lens.

Who dreams of sexually humiliating their political opponent the way that many of these Democrats do in their anti-Trump cartoons and memes? Who engages in sadomasochistic fantasies of their political opponents, an act tinged in performative violence, other than conquerors? Normal Americans value their right to bear arms and the American culture of having the right to do as you please, shoot guns, eat red meat, have big open spaces with big houses, and have a nice, normal family. The process of humiliation is key to this, whether people want to believe that or not. They often get it backwards because their brains are poisoned by complex ideology so they complicate this with explanations. They puzzle over *why* those with power want to destroy what normal Americans value when the answer is a simple one.

Because it's something you value.

They care because you care.

There's a famous Reddit post where a white family posted their entire generational family in a large home. If you are part of the Normal American tribe, it's cute. Normal people like large families, or at the very least they are not deeply affected when they see one. If they see it, they likely won't register a single emotional thought about it.

These people instead saw an enemy tribe that needed to be conquered and humiliated.

Who speaks this way but conquerors? Nobody but a conqueror has glee when they tell someone they disagree with that their children and grandchildren are going to be brown. That's tribal warfare, and it's tribal warfare tinged in sexual violence. The Ancient Greeks had a word for the systemic sexual destruction of a tribe through its women: *andrapodizing*. This aspect of warfare has, according to *Sexual Violence in Conflict Zones: From the Ancient World to the Era of Human Rights*, "historically been central to warfare and to the creating of enslaved or other subjugated persons in antiquity."

This was considered a natural law of conquest. Xenophon is quoted as writing in *Cyropaedia*:

> *It is an eternal law among all peoples that when a city is captured among those waging war, the **bodies** and goods of those in the city are the captors' own.*

And in his recollections of Socrates in his *Memorabilia* it is seen as just that an "unjust and hostile" city is enslaved. It is just to use deception to bring down an "unjust and hostile" city. It is just to do what one will to an "unjust and hostile city." *Vae victis.* Woe to the vanquished. *Vae iniquis.* Woe to the unjust. A fitting tribute to the conquering liberal and ethnic tribes who see what the vanquished value as forfeit to them.

They want your guns because *you* value them.

They want your kids to be transgender because *you* value them.

They want your families dying from drugs because *you* value them.

They want your kids sexually available to others to flex on *you.*

They want your daughters in pornography not for profit but so that they can be filmed as subjugated to a foreign tribe for the entire world to see. There is a social dynamic within pornography where white women are "punished" in their status by sex with black men. These are violently titled videos that proliferate pornographic websites in a genre that has not been profitable, as even within the industry itself and media outlets that cover it that performers do not want to go near it. Broadcast that to the world, and the enemy world sees what they've always wanted to believe: a conquering tribe conquered themselves. That is what humiliation is.

Through media it becomes the ultimate simulation of this and is reified by making it a prestige ideology that the vanquished would become willing to give up their arms, bodies, and families for a place in the ruling ideology without a single shot fired. And for resisting parents, the supreme flex is when the children do it willingly to spite *them.*

Americans value red meat and living big and free.

So they are going to make you eat bugs and live in pods, and they're going to convince you that's what you want. You'll tell yourself you're saving the world, while they snicker knowing that they can get you believe and do anything they want. Humiliation controls in this way. They love it when you loudly proclaim "No, sir," you won't eat bugs. They're confident that your protests are helpless whines.

They don't want you disarmed, eating bugs, raising a brown grandchild in a pod space because your daughter died from drugs, and clapping for your drag queen son getting fucked in public because it's socially good. They just want to see that because they think it's a funny punishment. Cuckoos birds coming home to roost.

The twisted ways people have tried to control the dominance hierarchy and break the ones they hate or wish to control have a long history. This is nothing new.

III. Season of the Lib

"What does it indicate that our culture is not merely tolerant of expressions of pain, of tears, complaints, reproaches, gestures of rage or of humiliation, but approves of them and counts them among the nobler inescapables?"

— Friedrich Nietzsche, *The Dawn*

Understanding humiliation begins with understanding how it works. Broken down there are four elements to humiliation:

1. An individual makes a status claim
2. The status claim publicly fails
3. The humiliated is rejected by those with status
4. Finally, the humiliated's right to even claim status is rejected

The mechanisms of this need not be fully explored. Suffice to say, those who have studied the psychological effects of humiliation have it pinned to a human being's need for status when living in a society, but especially to the right to make a claim of status. It is one thing to be rejected, quite another to be told you never have the right to rise above where you were smacked down in the first place. Being denied this right damages identity and ability to function, inflicts conditions of hopelessness, worthlessness, and learned helplessness, and can perversely create the conditions of violence, where having no path for restoration, the humiliated will pointlessly and murderously lash out.

Humiliation is a powerful tool.

"Humiliation is clearly about power; that is, in a general sense power

over others," according to *Humiliation: Mental Health and Public Shame.*
Humiliation says to its target "you are less than you imagine yourself to
be." Humiliation can make them believe it. The dynamics of humiliation
are the most powerful expressions of power and control, and among the
most destructive. Where conventional punishments fail or are
insufficient, humiliation and shame return as deterrent and control. From
the dynamics of two to the border stones of an empire, humiliation is the
paperclips and chewing gum that holds together the mechanisms of
control in civilization. The final flex is the public execution, which was a
show of humiliation upon the body and the answer from the sovereign to
the challenge that crime posed to his rule. It became clear as societies
developed that power was integral for the maintenance of society and the
ability to hold and imprison was paramount to that political legitimacy.

The birth of the prison developed out of that and punishment favored
them more and more due to the unintended consequences of public
executions' spectacles—public humiliations backfire when the populace
does not fear or respect the sovereign's power. Reliance on the prison led
to two separate currents that formed in understanding them—their use
as deterrence and their use as rehabilitation. The latter was fueled by the
spirit of Christian piety, especially by Quakers whose tenets focused so
heavily on a direct relationship with God that the conditions for prisoners
to experience personal revelation commanded their reform. The problem
of crime and its necessary punishments drove countries like England to
send their prisoners across the Earth as punishment, but what do you do
when you have nowhere left to send these bodies and reform largely fails?

It was for this reason that Jeremy Bentham, the godfather of liberal
society's reflexive utilitarianism, created the idea of prison as the
panopticon and constant surveillance as its reform, deterrence, and
punishment. The panopticon was a prison whereby within its structure
the warden would be able to see what all of the prisoners were doing at
all times without the need to do the rounds. It was, in essence, a reality
TV show as punishment upon the privacy and souls of prisoners under the
auspices of keeping them safe and secure.

This wasn't a mere thought experiment for Bentham, the architect of modernity. He desperately wanted it to be deployed and believed its logical efficiencies made it a million dollar concept. Those who had met him after the failure of his Panopticon scheme noted his bitterness that it was not taken up as the money-printing scheme he believed it to be. Bentham, being the good liberal he was, had also taken the concept to its logical conclusions and believed it could also be used for factories, schools, and hospitals.

While Bentham's scheme was left fallow, piece-meal notions of Bentham's ideas would influence prisons in liberal countries like Britain, the Netherlands, and the United States. The closest attempt made at a true panopticon before the 21st century was Presidio Modelo, built by the Cuban Liberal Gerardo Machado. Fidel and Raul Castro experienced life in the panopticon, which had utterly collapsed in access to necessities and quality of life, and kept it open six years after taking power before shuttering it for good.

The Panopticon was ultimately an experiment. Michel Foucault notes this in *Discipline and Punish*:

> But the Panopticon was also a laboratory; it could be used as a machine to carry out experiments, to alter behaviour, to train or correct individuals. To experiment with medicines and monitor their effects. To try out different punishments on prisoners, according to their crimes and character, and to seek the most effective ones. To teach different techniques simultaneously to the workers, to decide which is the best. To try out pedagogical experiments—and in particular to take up once again the well-debated problem of secluded education, by using orphans. (Discipline and Punish, 203-204)

Bentham has had his revenge. Now society has become the experimental prison with all of its atomized and orphaned children. Just as liberalism, by its very nature, must tear down every border and wall for lack of a friend-enemy distinction, so must it make society into a Panopticon. Orwell, being a true English son, understood this when he wrote *Nineteen Eighty-Four*, a novel of surveillance and humiliations inflicted by a sovereign. Orwell got many things right, but missed many things in his blind side—though given what the novel focuses on this may have been unavoidable. What was missing from Orwell's work was where liberalism has the same impulses as the surveillance and totalitarianism he warned against, though inverted in its implementation.

Liberalism requires a flexible internationalism that outsources its most terrible costs but more importantly that while humiliation may sometimes be kept private under classic totalitarianism—all they ask is that you break to *them*—under liberalism it *must* be made public. The reasoning is quite simple. As liberalism denies the existence of out-groups, it is forced to turn inward and to seek the enemy within, to find and root out those that it perceives as a threat to the expansive franchise: the Paradox of Tolerance. And to find these enemies, one must always be watching and waiting. When liberalism doesn't lead to the peace and prosperity it promises then the enemy must exist within and must be observed. What Vaclav Havel called the post-totalitarian ideology—the way the ideology of Soviet bureaucracy becomes reified by individuals who help perpetuate the system—becomes the cultural norm under liberalism. This kind of surveillance is bad enough in any kind of complex society, but when it becomes a technological system it leads to extreme levels of what Kaczynski called "oversocialization"—an intense sensitivity to society's liberal morality that every person is conditioned with and a desire to inflict severe penalties on anyone who violates those rules.

Such a system is self-enforcing and beneficial to those in power. The impossible rules are by design.

The existence of these impossible rules are seen in the nonchalant way the New York Times writes of "cancel culture" among the youth, with casual references to social justice classes and seminars as simply being quite natural. Perhaps it should be accepted as such given that Americans willingly hand over their children for instruction as easily as they were taught the Catechism in their youth. Where they learned of a higher salvation however, their children are brought to a lower damnation. Shunning transgressors who violated the code of conduct was seen as enough in shame societies, but these are performative times and they require a performance. A Dionysian spectacle where the modern maenads redeem themselves by tearing apart and destroying the unclean to please a woke god. In the panopticon of liberal society, for want of being able to engage the power process, each person is fit with the torturer's tools to expose every aspect of a person's life and interfere with it on every level as what the torturer tells his victims is "that all social norms are suspended in dealings with them because they are not human," as described in "Review: On Humiliation." A chance to be seen putting someone in their place, to publicly shame them, to see their claim to status and deny it; it is more than enough of a reward, even if it's at the behest of power.

It's the kind of reward most prisoners content themselves with.

IV. Fear and Self-Loathing in America

"What did the Pilgrim Fathers come for, then, when they came so gruesomely over the black sea? Oh, it was in a black spirit. A black revulsion from Europe, from the old authority of Europe, from kings and bishops and popes. And more. When you look into it, more. They were black, masterful men, they wanted something else. No kings, no bishops maybe. Even no God Almighty. But also, no more of this new 'humanity' which followed the Renaissance. None of this new liberty which was to be so pretty in Europe. Something grimmer, by no means free-and-easy."

— D.H. Lawrence,
Studies in Classic American Literature

Harvard was established to train Puritan clergy and it never stopped.

Humiliation runs deep in the American soul. America is not a land that one thinks of when they think of cultural cringe or the self-loathing that other nations, especially Anglo, have been all too eager to revel in. The Puritans occupy the American imagination, as they should for that American soul cannot be understood without understanding the Puritans, one of history's great purity spiralers. Never has the purity spiral ascended so high and fallen so low than in their history.

The origins of the Puritans—briefly. They were England's premier turbo-Protestants of the 16th century and into the 17th century. They sought a pure church, removed from the corrupt trappings that had been imposed by man upon the (Roman Catholic) Church over the centuries, as they saw it. Though they grew in power in England, their most discontent would leave for the New England colonies and found the New World's first university, Harvard University; explicitly to train the clergy. Meanwhile those who stayed behind would eventually claim the head of King Charles I and a Commonwealth under Cromwell. That failed, and with the restoration of the monarchy the *capotains* (sans those stylish buckles unfortunately—a myth!) thought it best to ghost for America as to avoid those incoming awkward conversations with their new king, Charles II, the son of the man they executed. His brother James II/VII got the boot (for crimes and Catholicism) and the Glorious Revolution would kick-start the coming age of English liberalism. Puritanism petered out in England, but would define America for centuries to come.

Their industrious presence and misunderstood ways in America have served as an eternal mirror of the American soul. Their very name has become a byword for sexual prude, a great irony given that one in six Puritan women in New England who filed for divorce did so on grounds of impotency or that their sexual morality trials are rife with accusations of bestiality, cuckolding, and homosexuality. The more the modern American man has thought he has achieved escape velocity from the nation's Puritan anchor, the more it becomes clear he is pinned beneath it and dreaming from the depths. Puritanism decried Mary worship for worshiping her as Virgin. Puritanism relied on humbling and humiliating the heretic. Puritanism needed equality to establish the equal worthlessness of all in their depravity before God. Puritanism was performative wokeness in its restriction to the 'visible saints'. Puritanism was the original call-out culture and encouraged all to spy upon all. Dehumanize yourself and face to Harvard.

The distance between then and now is short. Too, too short. When the Puritans are thought of, they conjure images of barbaric punishments, social shunning, and scarlet letters of public humiliation. Yet on their punishments, Louis Taylor Merrill in "The Puritan Policeman" found that in the long view the Puritans were not unique in the punishments they doled out. What set them apart appeared to be the public spectacle of it with the myriad trials, accusations, and testimonies. So prevalent was this that it was very common for the tables to be turned on one another within the same trial as everyone accused the other of wrong-doing, and with the total depravity of man such as given, each would be litigated. Each would need to do the work of their humiliation. Each would snitch and spy on each other in order to create a more perfect union with the congregation and with God. The truest perception of the Puritan was as the cop.

Merrill writes ominously in 1945, the once and future Year Zero of American consciousness:

> While such censorious watchfulness had the effect of bringing a larger proportion of sinners to justice in the New England of 300 years ago, there is suggestive evidence of a not too admirable effect on the minds of folk encouraged to practice espionage upon their neighbors and even upon their relatives. It is hard to conceive in the present day the type of mind that would turn over to the magistrates a relative guilty of indulging in agnostic remarks in the family circle, when in reporting this offense to the authorities the accuser knew his action might mean the culprit would have his tongue bored with a hot iron.

All examinations of the Puritan punishment linger on the instruments of humiliation and torture such as the ducking stool, spectacles of the imagination for centuries to come. The ducking stool has no record of being used in Puritan New England, much like the majority of instruments of medieval torture that were never real. These are perpetual fantasies the American indulges in of no longer being a buffoonish monster. The American puffs up in pride at being able to point to a cartoon caricature and feel complete confidence that they are nothing as obscene and backwards as that. The petty tyranny of the truth is that at the end of this fun-house hallway is the scariest mirror of all: the plane mirror of the American soul, where light does not spread.

To know that one will always be a Puritan is the humiliation of the American soul.

Humiliation, it must be said, has a particular meaning in the context of Puritanism. Humiliation here is processional humility. Those who converted to Puritanism all had to undergo this process. You had to understand your depravity. You had to understand that nothing you could do could ever rid you or forgive you from the stain of sin so that you would realize that salvation was God's mercy and Christ was the way before you ever stood a chance of being restored. The process was religiously traumatic, and meant to be. From the Puritan perspective, the Catholic Church had enslaved humanity to notions that they could buy their way out with indulgences and receive salvation through membership and token works. To be humiliated and broken meant to open your heart to introspection and healing, to be wounded so terribly that you'd finally see that only God could restore you at His mercy.

You may have already felt a shiver go up your spine with the question, "and what do you become in this humiliation once God is dead and we have buried Him?"

Nearly everyone gets the Puritans wrong. Humiliation belonged to God, and what public shaming and punishments were done was no more or less than the norm of the time. Strict, but corrective. Some transgressions require permanent correction. What made the Puritans different was the necessity of the public confession and of being witnessed. To close your eyes to the sins of others, to keep secrets and confessions safe as long as you repented and sinned no more, was not a charity but a sinful privilege itself. Humiliate yourself before God, *and confess!* Confession was the key to this humiliation, and every manner was taken to get that confession, but where there was no confession and there was no witness, they would be set free. "Always, confession opened the way to reconciliation and restoration," according to David Hall in *A Reforming People.*

So that it was that John Buxton Marsden, English historian of the Puritans, wrote that it was only the Puritans who could have subjected

King Charles I, the regicided runner-up in the English Civil Wars, to the terms of the failed Treaty of Newport. From *The History of the Later Puritans* he writes:

> *The treaty consisted of three articles. By the first, the king was required to revoke all his declarations against the parliament, and to admit 'that the two houses had been necessitated to enter into a war in their just and lawful defence,' and that the kingdom of England had entered into a solemn league and covenant to prosecute the same. The king was naturally reluctant to admit the truth of these propositions; nor ought they to have been submitted. He willingly offered an oblivion for the past, and this should have been sufficient. This, indeed, was the only basis on which the wounds of the nation could be healed.* **To make the king assert, in effect, that he himself had been a tyrant, was an insult and a humiliation from which no sovereign could recover...To insist on these propositions was an act of needless cruelty, a triumph over a prostrate king, of which men less religious than the puritans—might have been ashamed.** *(Emphasis mine)*

The treaty's failures, among the rest of the national clamor, ultimately gave way to Charles receiving the silver medal around his neck on the headsman's block. It must be noted, of course, that when Charles was executed, the block was situated in a way that he was forced to lie down versus kneeling, a very deliberate humiliation upon the king. The purpose, after all, in a public execution is to flex political power and for those that consider themselves the lowliest before God to grasp at power and force their political opponents even lower than that must have felt righteous indeed. The meek shall inherit the earth, but beware their political ambitions.

Eleven years of Puritan rule in the Commonwealth ensued. What followed was bedlam with the readmission of Jews to England after a 350 year timeout, an attempted takeover by an apocalyptic sect known as the Fifth Monarchists who wanted to call themselves *sanhedrin* and accelerate the return of Christ, and the division of the country into military districts.

To speak nothing of the Irish. The experiment was aborted. Monarchy was restored.

The great irony of history is that less than thirty years after the Puritans left, their labor would finally come to fruition. The Glorious Revolution kicked out the final Catholic monarch and brought with it The Bill of Rights in 1689. What stands out about it is it outlawed "cruel and unusual punishment," the first time this phrase would be used in English. This phrase was never properly defined from the start, and it's been a puzzle for legal scholars and historians as to what it actually means. The barbarity of punishments? Their proportionality to crime? Both? Excessive fines and penalties would seem to offer the clue, and if that's the case then that notion has long left America as it subjects suspected heretics against liberalism to an outsourced pillory of plaintiff cases to break their bank account and force a confession in such a humiliating public display. 1689 was a very good year for any English who wanted their dignity restored.

The Salem Witch trials would begin three years later in Puritan America.

Of the Salem Witch Trials, there is not much to be said. The incident invites the opportunists, the hucksters, and the agenda-setters of the world to try and get a bit of attention, turn a quick buck, or make into a Holocaust the murders of 25 Christians from mass hysteria. It was fear and loathing in the New World frontier, the anxious proximity of a red apocalypse of natives that could explode at any moment (the frighteningly violent King Philip's War had only ended 14 years prior) and wicked land ambitions in an unraveling community that destroyed those lives in the traumatic hysteria of the American wilderness. Reverend Parris, the fourth minister the fractious and quarrelsome Salem Village had in less than two decades, sowed the seeds of what was to come through his inability to quell the rising tensions with his publicly disciplinary method of resolving disputes. The trials would involve screaming accusatory questions, coerced confessions, and searching bodies for the Devil's mark. Is this not what they knew best in the Puritan colony, however? Everyone was guilty and confession was good for the soul. Why shouldn't it have ended like this? People are fired for making okay signs like cheeky

Puritans. The distance from then and now collapses upon itself.

Such was their infamy that Nathaniel Hawthorne, descendant of the Judge Hathorne who presided over the Salem Witch Trials and its humiliations changed his name to put a great distance between him and his forebears, but he was haunted by him with every written word. *The Scarlet Letter*, a title that makes high school students now groan, being the first truly and uniquely American novel must then be a novel about public humiliation. D.H. Lawrence called it "one of the greatest allegories in all literature" in his beautiful literary criticism, *Studies in Classic American Literature*. Despite the distance he placed, Hawthorne was ambivalent toward his Puritanism. He could not embrace it, but he would not command himself to hate it like Faulkner's Quentin Compson from the humiliated South. It ran through his American bones. Its essence was his American blood-nature and his American soul. How can anyone truly hate themselves and what they are unless they themselves are humiliated? No man can hate himself without total surrender. Self-loathing is the impoverished fiefdom of broken kings and queens.

Auspiciously, *The Scarlet Letter* had been published just that spring in 1850 when Hawthorne met Herman Melville, who would go on to pen the greatest American novel about what America once was and whose ghosts linger on to haunt her corpse's orphaned children. Biblical and poetic, *Moby-Dick* chronicles the tragic end of America as a ship full of colored savages being led by insane messianic Quakers on doomed quests to take revenge and destroy the white specter "of our deepest blood-nature," as Lawrence would have described it. Melville sensed the tragic and humiliating character that lay beneath the surface of America, which it would inflict on everything it conquered, but especially its rebel brother in the South from whom America's only aristocracy (as the Norwegian author Knut Hamsun viewed it in *The Cultural Life of Modern America*) would be destroyed for the equality of the coerced confession. It was in that sensitivity to what they were that Melville saw and found his Calvinist brother in Hawthorne with the blackness and a touch of Puritanic gloom. *Moby-Dick* too, that Great American Novel, is a tale of humiliation stretched out divinely like twisted scripture as Ahab leads a microcosm of all the world in a forsaken crusade not for the inflicted wound—but because the whale bore witness to it.

We are not yet done with Harvard. Oh Harvard, Harvard, Harvard. Your students, your shipwreck survivors of the Pequod, know who you are. You may have forgotten that Puritan past, you may have thought you had become the most serene commonwealth of pure research, but Ahab's crew know what you are and they will lash you back to the prow of this broken ship to serve as figurehead as they resume the chase for the white whale. And that is *your* humiliation. And that is *your* wheel to be broken on, and may your eyes find God on the upturn. And may you ask for forgiveness for the perverse and sinful experiments you inflicted on an America you despised in its purity, like Claggart who lies entombed in your very library as a grim reminder of your "natural depravity" and perverse rule over the American soul.

"Tell me just one thing more. Why do you hate America?"

"We don't hate it," we said quickly, at once, immediately: "We don't hate it," we said. *We don't hate it* we thought, panting in the cold air, the iron New England dark. *We don't. We don't! We don't hate it! We don't hate it!*

V. Freedom Club

"It is true that primitive man is powerless against some of the things that threaten him; disease for example. But he can accept the risk of disease stoically. It is part of the nature of things, it is no one's fault, unless it is the fault of some imaginary, impersonal demon. But threats to the modern individual tend to be MAN-MADE. They are not the results of chance but are IMPOSED on him by other persons whose decisions he, as an individual, is unable to influence. Consequently he feels frustrated, humiliated, and angry."

— Theodore J. Kaczynski,
Industrial Society and Its Future

Should civilization collapse and man revert back to his blood-consciousness and spirit-nature, he'll know to treat the ruins of Harvard like a necropolis containing the souls of the eternally cursed and damned. While the CIA was more the domain of Catholics and "East Europeans ethnics," 25% of its top people had a Harvard degree. In 1954, its affiliate Boston Psychiatric Institute was the site of an experiment by Dr. Rinkel and Dr. Hyde in dosing students with LSD. By 1960, according to *A Mind for Murder / Harvard and the Unabomber* by Alston Chase, three-quarters of all of Harvard's research "was funded by the government, much of it at the behest of the Defense Department." During that time, starting just a year earlier, the godfather of CIA interrogation study, Henry Murray, sought out the most vulnerable and wounded gifted young men he could humiliate and break. For science.

Theodore J. Kaczynski, his gifted intelligence noticed early on, was sixteen years old when he arrived at Harvard University. A product of the Silent Generation, he had grown up in an uncertain world shaking off the dreadful dust of the Second World War. A world where boys like him minded their manners and respected their elders. They were told to be thankful for the sacrifices older generations had made as they grew up aware that scarcity, disease, and unwanted pregnancy still mattered and where the brand new alien threat of the nuclear bomb threatened to annihilate them at a moment's notice. He would be seventeen years old when he would be subjected to this psychological experiment from Henry Murray; the Dyad. He would be twenty years old when the experiment was finished. An experiment whose sole purpose was to see what a bright young college student could endure under persistent interrogation, badgering, deconstruction, and humiliation under the most stressful of situations.

It even had a cute and fun name: Multiform Assessments of Personality Development among Gifted College Men.

The experiment sought out college students that inhabited one extreme of either optimism or pessimism. Out of seventy volunteers, twenty-two young men were chosen to participate. Curiously, Kaczynski was the only blue-collar background in the bunch. Even more curiously, most people got the invitation to join the experiment by enrolling in a popular psychology course; a course that Kaczynski had never been in. It does not appear to be known how Kaczynski ended up in Murray's experiment, but continuing from *A Mind for Murder/Harvard and the Unabomber*: "*Murray's preliminary screening would identify him as the most alienated of the entire cohort.*"

The students brought into the experiment were tasked with writing an essay on their personal philosophy of life and the principles that best exemplified what they would wish to live by. They were then told they would be debating it with a talented lawyer. Prior to this spirited discourse however, the college students were interviewed by Murray and his cohorts which included, as reported in *A Mind for Murder/Harvard and the Unabomber*, "*intimate questions on a range of subjects from thumb-sucking and toilet training to masturbation and erotic fantasies.*"

What the participants then got was a debate, but not the kind of debate they were expecting. The debate Murray gave these gifted young men was more akin to an unannounced YouTube debate, a pre-Internet BloodSport where the talented law student would relentlessly attack the subjects and their beliefs in order to make them upset and test their resolve. According to Alston Chase who quotes Forrest Robinson, Murray's official biographer, it typically played out as such:

> As instructed, the unwitting subject attempted to represent and to defend his personal philosophy of life. Invariably, however, he was frustrated, and finally brought to expressions of real anger, by the withering assault of his older, more sophisticated opponent...while fluctuations in the subject's pulse and respiration were measured on a cardiotachometer.

The participants were recorded under bright lights with electrodes. One reported feeling like they were being fastened in an electric chair. In recall interviews the experience was played back to them with Murray calling attention to their grimaces and sputtering responses to the interrogator. Six months before the experiment was rolled out, Murray wrote in his "Notes on Dyadic Research" that his fixation was on the "degree of anxiety and disintegration" that would occur in designing the procedures for how the subjects would respond to burning under the light of the Dyadic interrogation. In the analysis of the student reactions, Murray's research team rated Kaczynski's reactions as the most extreme in their intensity and dissension. Murray's own assessment of Kaczynski's reactions: "*Overt expressions of Low Evaluations...low, underlying resentment and contempt.*"

The most common recollection to the experience was that it was very unpleasant, a statement Kaczynski made himself to his attorney. Even Kaczynski, in his "Truth vs Lies" document where he is adamant to dispel rumors, statements, and insinuations he found to be fiction and could be easily used to misrepresent him (including his usage in a book by one of Murray's students), he merely refers to the experience as unpleasant while wiggles his eyebrows about the Henry Murray Center's sealing of the documents. Quote Kaczynski:

> *The assessment arrived at by the psychologists would be very useful in determining how people saw my personality, but...the Murray Center...has refused to release any of the psychologists' conclusions to my attorneys; and most of the individual psychologists involved have declined to cooperate with the investigators, who to my knowledge have obtained no information concerning any conclusions that were drawn about me. One wonders whether the Murray Center has something to hide.*

What gives concerns about the Murray experiment having weight is that Kaczynski does not appear to have contradicted anything he told the court appointed psychiatrist, Sally Johnson after his arrest. The Truth vs Lies documents spends several hundred pages correcting assessments made about him, and even though Kaczynski wrote to the author, Alston Chase, who had exposed the experiment to the public that he was "quite confident that my experiences with Professor Murray had no significant effect on the course of my life," the document does not appear to touch on the revelations made in the book or previous Atlantic article written about it, such as Kaczynski considering a sex change or his recurring nightmares about murdering psychologists.

While at University of Michigan, after leaving Harvard, Kaczynski began to exhibit signs that bear a striking resemblance to post-traumatic stress disorder. He reported to the psychologist that was testing his competency to stand trial that in his recurring nightmares, psychologists were trying to convince him he was "sick" or outright control him until in anger he'd kill them and feel a great wave of relief and liberation wash over him. That relief would be short-lived however as the psychologists never stayed dead. Psychological problems and sexual frustrations continued to compound on top of him until he concocted a solution that made sense to him: get a sex change. Kaczynski, feeling ashamed at what he was almost driven to do and by talking to the psychiatrist about this finally came to his turning point.

> I felt disgusted about what my uncontrolled sexual cravings had almost led me to do and I felt humiliated, and I violently hated the psychiatrist. Just then there came a major turning point in my life. Like a Phoenix, I burst from the ashes of my despair to a glorious new hope; I thought I wanted to kill that psychiatrist because the future looked utterly empty to me. I felt I wouldn't care if I died.

It was only when he was able to leave society and go to the wilderness that he was able to find any respite from society's unrelenting barrage of psychic warfare. That an experiment designed to break down and belittle a person's beliefs and humiliate them before an official interrogator would include among its subjects a vulnerable teenager who would later go on to have murder and sex change fantasies is an ominous portent of society's moral arc toward its perverted justice. Kaczynski, as stated, does not appear to have commented on what he told the court-appointed psychiatrist.

Perhaps there are legal reasons for this or perhaps it's integral that he not comment on it because for Ted Kaczynski it's incumbent that his ideas not be dismissed as the ramblings of a mentally ill lunatic or one that had been made that way. Kaczynski's ideas are so lucid—and should be necessary reading—that it's extremely unlikely that the Murray experiment would have been what put the idea to be skeptical of the technoindustrial system in his head, but his statements to the court-psychiatrist Sally Johnson are extremely damning to the notion that Kaczynski was not at all affected by what Murray subjected him to.

It is a feature of humiliation that those who are subjected to it deny what is happening to them and deny what it does to them. They trick themselves into thinking they're in control, they can stop it if they want, and anyway it isn't happening, because that would be admitting their own powerlessness. And those who do admit it and survive look back bitterly on those experiences, hating themselves more than their tormentors as they interrogate themselves with the same questions over and over again: "Why didn't you stop them? Why were you so weak? Why did you let them do this to you? *Why are you so pathetic?*"

As written in his memoirs on their relationship, when his brother David asked Ted why he kept going back to the experiment, week after week, for three years, he replied "*I wanted to prove that I could take it. That I couldn't be broken.*"

VI. Zen Koan

"If you are men, how could a man's pride allow this? Even after enduring and enduring, rising up with firm resolution once the last line of what you are supposed to protect has been crossed is what it means to be a man, what it means to be a warrior. We desperately strained our ears. But from nowhere in the [Japanese Self-Defense Force] did we hear a man's voice rise in response to the humiliating order to "protect that which negates you." Now that it has come to this, with the awareness of your own power, you knew that the only path forward was the correction of the twisted logic of the nation, but the SDF has been as silent as a canary with its voice stolen."

— Yukio Mishima,
His last speech before committing seppuku

The peculiar way of modern politics is often reminiscent of gaslighting. Gaslighting, properly understood, is the psychological manipulation that induces the victim into thinking that they are the ones who are losing their minds. Its purpose is to spread a certainty of doubt through the use of lying and denial in order to destabilize the victim. Unsurprisingly, it's very well-suited for liberalism in its subtle expressions.

The destruction and implosion of the Western world is a well-worn topic, but often overlooked in the Year Zero history of post-WWII has been the breaking of Japan. Owing to the foreignness of the Japanese, the bureaucrats of the world are shockingly upfront about their plans for the recalcitrant ethnostate. In his 2004 book *The Pentagon's New Map*, for instance, former Department of Defense wonk Thomas Barnett wrote:

> *As for Japan, as much as one-third of its 2050 population would be foreign-born if they pursued the immigration rate required to stabilize their absolute number of working-age citizens.* **Simply put, that wouldn't be Japan anymore; that would be an entirely new country. I personally believe that would be a better Japan**, *because I think that insular society has so much to offer the world that letting more of that world in will let the Japanese achieve the "normal" nationhood they have sought ever since their brush with the apocalypse in 1945—such are the tides of history.*

This is a master class in humiliation via gaslighting. Thomas Barnett, a representative of an actual military occupying force that has disarmed the country it occupies, speaking casually about destroying its homogeneity and framing it as something the Japanese would want after the United States atomically "rescued" them from their own apocalypse. The thumbscrews have been turning for some time now.

Japan will always be reminded of their place in the liberal order should they ever think they've achieved some status of equality. In May of 2018, the Prime Minister of Japan Shinzo Abe, who has been trying to re-arm Japan and restore their global prestige and power since his re-election, got a mouthful of this during a dinner with the Israeli Prime Minister

Benjamin Netanyahu when he was served dessert in a shoe. The Japanese aversion and cultural taboo toward shoes would have taken five seconds of research to learn as they are not a bush tribe plucked from the aether of some lost time. People were quick to point to the cultural insensitivity of the gesture, but one thing that does not appear to have been brought up is why this idea would have even occurred to a chef like Moshe Segev. Shoes are not just poor etiquette in Japan but are also an insult to Arabs to the point that it's insulting to even be called a shoe, something Segev would certainly be aware of as an Israeli. Obama himself caused a minor diplomatic stir in 2009 when he was photographed putting his feet up on the desk while on the phone with Netanyahu. Segev and his dessert did not emerge at the dinner as a sudden and unexpected surprise kept hidden from everyone else. Diplomatic affairs are a careful kabuki performance with many unseen actors in which entire tomes of information are projected by extremely subtle, knowing gestures. What looks like a minor accident can, in truth, be a highly-calibrated message meant to be understood deeply by the parties it's directed at.

Abe understood it. Abe ate out of the shoe. The Japanese diplomats seethed, but Abe did his supplicating *dogeza* for his global masters.

It angers any person with a modicum of decency in them to see these kinds of relentless attacks on the Japanese psyche. The far-right's fascination with Japan goes way beyond an appreciation for anime and a post-ironic attraction to their women. There's something about the Japanese that is unique and different and worth preserving and protecting. It can be seen in the tea ceremony and it can be seen in their ephemeral understanding of impermanence, the zen of wabi-sabi. Even in defeat they approach it in a way that can only be described as *Japanese*. It's a very tautological essence. Fatalism often permeates the Japanese way of being with the common resignation *sho ga nai* ("it can't be helped") and expresses itself in mockingly calling the military boots and uniforms "defeat shoes" and "defeat suits," respectively. Despite latter day revisions and critique, Ruth Benedict's *The Sword and the Chrysanthemum* has proven to be remarkably resilient in explaining and understanding the Japanese in their being.

No other country in recent history has been as meteoric as the Empire of Japan. Much of that rise was due to the industrious character of the Japanese themselves, but the modern expression of that character was forged in the crucible of the kiln that the rest of the world was shoveling them into. Neighboring imperial China was fifteen years into its century of humiliation when those American black ships finally forced an isolationist nation to open its ports. The Japanese were not unaware of what was going on in the world when Commodore Perry finally made the Western breakthrough—he just had the weapons big enough to finally spook the Japanese. Furthermore, the Japanese had engaged in limited trade with China, meaning that they were aware of what national humiliations China was experiencing with the (First) Opium War in 1839-1842 and the unequal treaties that the Western powers had been imposing on them even if they did not have first-hand Japanese accounts of them.

The opium was especially troubling for the Japanese as it proved just how far the West, especially the British, were willing to go to achieve what they wanted. The British had been smuggling in opium for an entire previous century despite four separate edicts from the Chinese emperor to make and keep the trade illegal. Opium as medicine had a long history in China, but when the Dutch in the 16th century discovered you could blend it with hemp and tobacco, a product called *madak*, and make a killer drug to smoke that the history of opium in China would really begin. Its usage was confined to the coastal port cities it came in on until the first ban in 1729, though history would truly turn its course when the British East India Company obtained a full monopoly on opium in 1773 and promptly began to smuggle it into China. The East India Company found itself in a bad way financially in 1780 thanks to the American chaos of the British Empire, and began a tit-for-tat escalation of flooding China with opium any which way until the Chinese were hopelessly addicted on the raw stuff at the end of the century. It would continue to grow worse, bringing with it all of the political and social dysfunctions decadent addiction culture has, until the Chinese were made to kowtow to the British after defeat in First Opium War, all for opposing their imposed addictions.

The Japanese did not see it for themselves but they knew about the destruction opium had rained down on China, a neighbor they considered powerful even in spite of its faults, and it was a very bad omen for them. The Japanese knew the West was coming for the Asian nations, but were operating on bad information due to their isolation and had assumed that *they* would be invaded before the Chinese to the point that *daimyo* vassal Tokugawa Nariaki stated as the Opium War was starting up: *"Russia most probably will decide to invade Japan first and then go about conquering China."* The stories of the unrelenting humiliations on the Chinese prompted furtive soul-searching and explanation such as Mineta Fuko's 1849 proto-manga manuscript *Kaigai shinwa* in which he identified the social and political-wrecking power opium had, and the inability of the Chinese to oppose this due to a weak national unity and an abundance of traitors and soft-bellied cowards who let the opium in and allowed the foreigners to trade and seize as they pleased. To Fuko, the answer was clear. Close the damn ports and expel the devils! For many Japanese, the only way to hold onto their way of life, but especially their sovereignty, was to aggressively double-down on the *sakoku* closed border policy by any means necessary. Others, like the *daimyo* vassal Shimazu Nariakira, knew they would need to stop clinging to the past if they had any hope of facing the future on terms *they* could dictate rather than being dictated. In his words, *"if we take the initiative, we can dominate; if we do not, we will be dominated"*

The Westerners were coming. Time was running out.

Contact between cultures that have a technological and firepower disparity is almost always apocalyptic for the people found wanting. Unfamiliar sicknesses, colonization, enslavement, and even genocide have been the tragic destiny for many people who have been the unfortunate victims of history in every living creature's savage drive to prevail, survive, and dominate, lest it be dominated. At best they might achieve a second-class or even junior partner status if they prove capable of fighting back, being added to a larger empire even if they had been an empire themselves just the other day. Common folk have a compassionate and simple dignity for others like them, even if they are alien. Its gentleness of spirit is admirable, but the world is forged by will and power with no space for the little children of history to be left alone.

Commodore Perry sailed into Uraga Harbor on July 14th, 1853 and landed on Japanese shores. The Japanese would need to grow up. And fast.

The lead-up to this event and its aftermath would affirm many of the Japanese's most existential fears. Six days earlier, Perry fired blank shellfire to "celebrate American independence." Between then and the landing he intimidated the guard boats into backing off and gave the Japanese a white flag they would want to immediately start waving should they choose to provoke the Americans into combat. The shore landing was accompanied by the full military pomp of gun salutes and the playing of "Hail, Columbia" to a people who had no idea what a Columbia was. There is tragic symmetry that the Japanese Empire would end in unconditional surrender as it was born in it.

The Chinese echoes would continue in the immediate years to follow. Playing on the Japanese fears that what happened to China would also happen to them, the diplomat Townsend Harris negotiated a favorable treaty for the Americans by telling the Japanese how awful opium was and how dastardly the British were for smuggling it and pushing it on the Chinese; the Harris Treaty allowed America to import opium into Japan. Japan's own humiliations were now beginning, seemingly destined to follow the path of their neighbor.

The Japanese remarkably turned their fortunes around in short order. They had no choice. They knew what failure would entail. They'd seen it. They'd felt it. Beginning with the Meiji Restoration, Japan industrialized, centralized, and militarized as quickly as possible. The old ways had to die, even if they needed to be murdered. In the span of fifty years an isolationist and stubborn feudal society of rice farmers would go from experiencing the public humiliation of technological firepower to conquering their own neighbors and crushing a European power, Russia, in war.

From dominated to dominate in three generations.

With its own power came the usual cruelties of empire. Colonization, exploitation, and subjugation. Like any great power in history there is no shortage of books that can, have, and will be written about their atrocities. In their attempt to author their own destiny, however, despite the trauma of their rapid industrialization they were still unmistakably *Japanese.* For the West to be confronted with a non-European power that could actually defeat one of their own was its own worrisome enigma. The white supremacy of the West meant that competition was among people who found more similarities than differences when stacked against the black, brown, red, and yellow world. French and German might hate each other with a hellfire's passion, but they weren't alien to one another in their ways. What would it mean if they were subjugated to someone so *alien?*

Ruth Benedict's *The Sword and the Chrysanthemum,* even with its inaccuracies, did much to keep the Japanese *Japanese* after they were once again overwhelmed by technological superiority and forced into unconditional surrender in 1945. The ferocity of the Japanese fighting and their way of violence had shocked the Americans as they had never experienced anything like this from a group of people before; to this day the oldest generations retain an understandable bitterness to the Japanese for the killing and maiming they were able to inflict. It is not surprising that a 22-year-old Jewish refugee who had *just* become an American citizen that year, Beate Gordon, was given the leeway to add the most liberal interpretation of equal rights to date into the Japanese Constitution. The Potsdam Declaration had already made it clear that Japan *would* be liberalized and they didn't have a choice in the matter. What was surprising was that Emperor Hirohito was not only going to be passed over for a war crimes trial, but that he would also retain his throne. This effort was thanks purely to Douglas MacArthur, who seemed to intuitively understand that it could push a destitute and ruined country over the edge, and Ruth Benedict who had previously advised Roosevelt of this as well.

This understanding on Benedict's part came from what she had studied in the Japanese reaction to humiliation and fault. On the latter point, Benedict believed that the Japanese did not believe in lost causes. *Sho ga nai*. It can't be helped. If it is lost, abandon it. Those infamous holdouts still fighting in the jungles were exceptions, fiercely loyal to their notions of military ideology, orders, or honor, or simply unaware that the war had even been lost. The Japanese would do what they could to earn prestige in the world, but now they lost. It was over. The Emperor told them they lost. MacArthur, whether he understood it or not and whatever his intentions were, managed to avoid national humiliation.

On this Japanese way, Ruth Benedict writes in *The Sword and the Chrysanthemum*:

> It has been incredible to American occupying troops that these friendly people are the ones who had vowed to fight to the death with bamboo spears...It has not impeded that course by insisting on using techniques of humiliation. It would have been culturally acceptable according to Western ethics if we had done so. For it is a tenet of Occidental ethics that humiliation and punishment are socially effective means to bring about a wrongdoer's conviction of sin. Such admission of sin is then a first step in his rehabilitation. The Japanese, as we have seen, state the issue in another way. Their ethic makes a man responsible for all the implications of his acts, and the natural consequences of an error should convince him of its undesirability. These natural consequences may even be defeat in an all-out war. But these are not situations which the Japanese must resent as humiliating. In the Japanese lexicon, a person or a nation humiliates another by detraction, ridicule, contempt, belittling, and insisting on symbols of dishonor. **When the Japanese believe themselves humiliated, revenge is a virtue.** No matter how strongly Western ethics condemn such a tenet, the effectiveness of American occupation of Japan depends on American self-restraint on this point. For the Japanese separate ridicule, which they terribly resent, from 'natural consequences'...Japan, in her one great victory over a major power, showed that even as a victor she could carefully avoid humiliating a defeated enemy when it finally capitulated and when she did not consider that that nation had sneered at her.

When the Japanese shocked the world by defeating the Russians in 1905, they did not strip the Russians of their arms. When the Russians surrendered, the Japanese victors brought them food. The Japanese honored the gifts of the vanquished Russians. The Japanese had never felt slighted or humiliated by the Russians of 1905. They fought. The Russians lost. There was nothing to try and correct and there was no other status for them to be lowered to. All they did was lose.

The Japanese seemed destined for the worst in 1945. For them the 1920s and 1930s were full of the little dishonorable slights and ridicules that demanded revenge, demanded to be opposed because unless it's opposed your nation gets raped, torn apart, and flooded with opium by the predatory West. They could have humiliated Japan. They wanted to. According to *Bridging the Atomic Divide*, 33% of Americans wanted to see Hirohito executed; only 7% would have allowed him to be retained. Japan attacked America, there should have been even more punishment. It was enough though to make them junior partners and plant some liberal poppy seeds to keep an American foothold in Asia. It would be enough.

These competing forces on how to deal with Japan led to the numerous post-war contradictions within the country that are endlessly debated to this day, with its nationalist and communist currents battling for its defeated soul. Sadly, the seeds that were planted in 1945 have sprouted. Japan is being humiliated now with the political opiates that were smuggled into their Constitution, but at that brief moment in time when MacArthur took that famous photo with the Emperor in his feet of clay, they weren't. At that moment in time, they were allowed to save face. Those small things matter to the little children of history.

Japan is facing the demographic and spiritual crisis that liberalism and Zionism imposes on every country they infect. The Japanese, however, are among the people most deeply connected to their past through the businesses that have existed for centuries and an imperial family that is 1500 years old. Nations who remember their deep past tend to remember the pains outsiders cause, such as the way Japan's rising neighbor, China deeply remembers what was inflicted upon them.

The Israelis and the liberal order would do well to remember Ruth Benedict's warning that for the Japanese, revenge is a virtue.

VII. Komsomol Parade

"In my study of communist societies, I came to the conclusion that the purpose of communist propaganda was not to persuade or convince, not to inform, but to humiliate; and therefore, the less it corresponded to reality the better. When people are forced to remain silent when they are being told the most obvious lies, or even worse when they are forced to repeat the lies themselves, they lose once and for all their sense of probity. To assent to obvious lies is...in some small way to become evil oneself. One's standing to resist anything is thus eroded, and even destroyed. A society of emasculated liars is easy to control. I think if you examine political correctness, it has the same effect and is intended to."

— Theodore Dalrymple,
Frontpage Magazine (August 31st, 2005)

It's not for nothing that the Puritans, among the most revolutionary of Christians in their time period, would have found the rituals of humiliation to be a comfort. Revolutions seek to overturn an order, to change the way of things and thus the old hierarchy *must* come tumbling down. It simply cannot be avoided. There is no revolutionary who believes in the dignity of the man he wants to dispossess.

Religion has always been the revolutionary's sticking point because what gives a society its bones is the faith of its fathers, whatever form that may take. It proves to be a problem for revolutionaries because of religion's frequent final word on the way things are, whether it's explaining the capricious will of disinterested gods or actively following the tenets of God's Natural Law. For men to live the new ways of any revolution, any religion with influence into the way men live would need to be either fundamentally transformed or made to bend and break before the new gods of society. Revolutionaries come in as conquerors, and to establish the new order the status of the old powers must be denied. For the revolutionary, there is nothing more enjoyable than to make a mockery of those old powers and bring them low.

The French Revolution was the first to practice this on a large scale level with their attacks on the Catholic Church. Within the revolutionaries, there was tension between those who wanted an atheist revolution and those who wanted to supplant the Catholic Church with something of their own as the topic of de-christianization was a hot one. This broke out with clergy in the crossfire when the Archbishop of Paris, Jean-Baptiste-Joseph Gobel went before the National Convention and resigned his office, donned the liberty cap of the revolutionaries, and professed it was by the will of the people. This act unleashed a series of priests seeking to give up their offices with even more blasphemous words, the seizure of churches, mob mockery of the defrocked, and the transformation of Notre Dame into the Temple of Reason.

Contrary to the pageantry of the whole affair, Gobel did not do this because he was overcome by any epiphany of reason. He had been warned the night before by an atheist named Cloots and a Jew named Pereira to renounce his office. Reason, or rather its perversion, would follow however as three days later at the new "Temple of Reason," the more atheistic contingent of the revolutionaries put on a pageantry for the Cult of Reason that from description sounds like a child's church pageant done up by the infantile-minded. Unfortunately for these devotees to Reason, many others found this embarrassing. Gobel and the men who pushed him into this were executed during the Reign of Terror as the deist Robespierre felt that atheism was going a bit too far and so he put on his own festival to supplant them: the Festival of the Supreme Being. In contrast to the passionate outburst of the Festival of Reason, the one for the Supreme Being would be meticulously planned and full of pomp as Robespierre attempted to co-opt the justice-minded worldview of Christianity and sermonized on the virtue of the new civic life.

Robespierre was executed a month later.

For the Thermidorian Reaction, they'd have to sift through the rubble of what the revolutionaries had done and try to restore what they could as restoration is the key to any humiliation. The spirit of the French

Revolution would live on, not just in the horrors to come but in the *ressentiment* of the age. Ressentiment, as Kierkegaard understood it, was the leveling process of an apathetic and passionless age where men cannot rebel. This would seem counterintuitive to being a revolutionary, but others such as Gil Richard Musolf in *Structure and Agency in Everyday Life: An Introduction to Social Psychology* have noted that it could be used to initiate revolutions; the resentful often desire to humiliate those they see as having wronged them or prevented their potential. The perceived ethnic humiliation of Jews via the pogroms under the tsar would drive many of them into the arms of the Zionist and Bolshevik movements.

And it was in the Soviet Union that the anti-Christian parade of shame would be perfected.

When the Bolsheviks took power in Russia, they had nothing less in mind than a complete turnover in society and knew that only by lowering the status of the once privileged church that the rights of the people could be properly respected under their guidance and tutelage. The bitter violence of the Russian Civil War didn't help with the antipathy, but it was already the view of Lenin in "Socialism and Religion" that while private religious belief could be tolerated, any resistance to religion becoming as private as possible would need to have ruthless war declared on it. Lenin understood that this would be the inevitable outcome as for the Russian Orthodox Church to follow this would be a negation of its own beliefs and purpose. Trotsky, born Lev Bronstein, was seemingly unique among the many Jewish Bolsheviks as he reported few incidents of antisemitism in his early life and was a hardliner on the assimilation question, at least according to *Leon Trotsky: A Revolutionary's Life*. Daniela Kalkandjieva in *The Russian Orthodox Church, 1917-1948* reports he was adamant about destroying the Russian Orthodox Church despite the fact that he was cognizant of how bad it looks to have a Jew in charge of the police in a society with high degrees of antisemitism when Lenin offered him the role of People's Commissar of Internal Affairs as Robert Service records in his own biography of the man.

Trotsky's plan to destroy the church was to co-opt a small schism of modernizers in the church called the Renovationists. This plan came into place after Lenin forbade Trotsky from arresting and executing Patriarch Tikhon back in 1918 for excommunicating the Bolshevik leaders who had been Orthodox at some point or another. As Trotsky and others worked to undermine the church from within, the 1921-22 famine led the Soviets to begin confiscating church valuables, ostensibly to feed the poor though some wrote in "The Ukrainin Review, Spring 1989" that "the most important objective was to humiliate and destroy the authority of the church." Tikhon was put on public show trial during this time, going from house arrest to criminal arrest, a ploy that backfired for the Soviets internationally since Tikhon approached it and maintained his simple dignity.

This was not the first time the Soviets would go too far. The infamous Komsomol parades, much like the Festival of Reason, was meant to be a carnival that celebrated the liberation of the people from their white-and-gold chains and mocked the notions that once heavily oppressed them. As fervently as Trotsky wished to destroy the church, he understood the necessity of something that needed to take its place. While Tikhon warred with Trotsky's Renovationists who were in the process of trying to "depose" him, Trotsky began to view amusements, especially the cinema, as a way to sever people's connections with the clergy. In his July 1923 *Pravda* piece entitled "Vodka, the Church, and Cinema," Trotsky writes:

Meaningless ritual, which lies on the consciousness like an inert burden, cannot be destroyed by criticism alone; it can be supplanted by new forms of life, new amusements, new and more cultured theaters. Here again, thoughts go naturally to the most powerful—because it is the most democratic—instrument of the theater: the cinema. Having no need of a clergy in brocade, etc., the cinema unfolds on the white screen spectacular images of greater grip than are provided by the richest church, grown wise in the experience of a thousand years, or by mosque or synagogue. In church only one drama is performed, and always one and the same, year in, year out; while in the cinema next door you will be shown the Easters of heathen, Jew, and Christian, in their historic sequence, with their similarity of ritual. The cinema amuses, educates, strikes the imagination by images,

and liberates you from the need of crossing the church door. The cinema is
a great competitor not only of the tavern but also of the church. Here is an
instrument which we must secure at all costs!

Soviet cinema was still quite young and nascent at the time Trotsky penned this, but he recognized all forms of theater as having the power to change people through viewing performance. During the civil war Trotsky had used an agit-train to deliver propaganda and speeches in order to keep the hot spots engaged, and it was an example many young propagandists would follow. Trotsky and the phenotypically intriguing Platon Kerzhentsev were also keenly aware of the power of theater (Kerzhentsev was a man of the theater after all and a pioneer in Prolekult, the revolutionary artistic movement for the people), and saw the necessity in bringing theatricality to public life. Life is performance and people repeat the performances that they see.

The Komsomol was the youth league for the Communist Party and often served as the most vociferous defenders of whomever had the power and the sway within the government at the time. As Lenin stated, the war on the church would need to be ruthless if the church would not go private in all manners and matters, and the church simply would not budge without resistance. The Komsomol pursued their instruction campaign with reckless abandon, especially attacking the countryside, with every manner of belittling mockery. It's impossible to see this policy as anything except the shaming of a conquered people when they appeared in front of churches wearing mock garments, engaging in "red devotions'' and "red masses" that ridiculed rites, blasphemed Christ and the Mother of God, supplanting the religious songs with revolutionary tunes, all in a jubilant anti-religious parade they carried on through the town. The enthusiasm was strongest for Christmas and Easter parades, where they are now most commonly known as the Komsomol Christmas. The first experiment in 1922-23 involved 184 cities with the various religious figures of all the religions that had been represented in the Russian Empire being paraded around like puppet effigies until being tossed into a great bonfire to burn. *Revolutionary Dreams: Utopian Vision and Experimental Life in the Russian Revolution* reports that the Komsomol Christmas went all out with this, among the scenes of propaganda marches being *"trucks bearing clowns who mocked God, a figure of God embracing a nude woman...priests in ridiculous poses chanting parodies of church liturgy set to indecent lyrics."* The Komsomol parades would turn into these grim cavalcades over the next two years, frequently followed by an anti-religious hooliganism its air would bring.

As it turns out, even this was a bridge too far. The Soviet officials had no love for the church or its believers, but the strange carnival of boisterous blasphemy aimed at rubbing defeat in the faces of people they wanted to bring obediently into the new paradigm offended even many of the communists and calls from above were made to shut them down. The behavior of the young and empowered revelers was such an embarrassment, with vandalism of cemeteries and religious sites going hand-in-hand with public drunkenness, that Stalin is recorded in *Storming the Heavens: The Soviet League of the Militant Godless* as saying *"hooliganish escapades under the guise of so-called anti-religious propaganda—all this should be cast off and liquidated immediately."*

Stalin was consolidating his power as the new General Secretary at this time, with Trotsky being sidelined by illness. Before the Komsomol Christmas of 1924, Stalin had announced his plan for Socialism in One Country in opposition to Trotsky's Permanent Revolution with Bolshevism being exported everywhere as quickly as possible, especially in Germany. By the spring of 1925, when Stalin made his comments about the Komsomol Christmas however, all of the revolutionary movements in Germany had failed and fascist movements in opposition to liberalism and communism were on the rise in Europe. Continuing to humiliate and antagonize believers in this way was a juice that wasn't worth the squeeze. The peasantry would not get on board with any Soviet program while the Komsomol was allowed to go on being this brazen.

The Soviet Union under Stalin would pursue a somewhat different pattern, though the church and its people remained no less under some form of assault. The people would soldier on, to the consternation of the Soviet bureaucracy, that after a decade of proper education the "bad tradition" of people attending church on Easter continued to persist.

The Soviets had attempted to humiliate the soul of the Russian peasant, but by God they somehow endured. Somehow, they endured. God sees the truth, and waits.

VIII. Vae Victis

"Let the shame be on those who have made such humiliation necessary"
— Georges Clemenceau

Liberalism is an occupational force, and this is without getting into the fact that many of the people with power in this occupying force of history are primarily loyal to their ethnic own and a welfare queen ethnostate that the conquered shed endless blood and treasure for. Many will think "what are you talking about, no army conquered me or my country." You must think counter-intuitively. Carl Schmitt's critiques of liberalism get to the heart of this because there is a misconception, even among people who are illiberal, that liberalism and democracy go hand-in-hand. Liberalism is a force that reduces all people to smaller and smaller economic units, so wherever there is any resistance in the arts, in culture, in religion, in community, and especially in democracy, these must be overridden by the will of liberal rulers. As the weblog *Hesiod's Corner* notes:

> *Embrace of particular art, culture, community, religion, and nation often leads to conflict with the "other" (the enemy) which negates the peaceful consumeristic and hedonistic lifestyle that liberalism was constructed to provide.*

We simply don't see it for what it is because liberalism's conception of the political is economic at heart, and so if it is to remain that way then the people under its thumb need to be seen, but especially to feel, that they are buying what's being sold to them of their own free will and intent. Otherwise, it would be the naked piracy and domination it actually is with the way it tries to dictate how a people and their markets are to live. In order to maintain the illusion of the free and open society, it must dominate your soul and humiliate the conquered as an example and revenge.

Humiliation is associated with strong feelings of powerlessness and those who have been humiliated, according to the NCBI publication "Affective Dimensions of Intergroup Humiliation," have shown to be less likely to endorse violence, especially the political kind. It confuses the response actions of the humiliated, induces shame within them, attacks their social identities, and internalizes their sense they lack any power.

In short, it's a perfect vehicle to control a population.

Public humiliation of the Jews from the National Socialists has been well-documented by them, where-in they lay out their reasoning for why it was employed. Quoting the United States Holocaust Memorial Museum website:

> *Public humiliation under the Nazis had three primary functions. The first function was to exacerbate the suffering of Nazi victims. Second, public humiliation served to remind the German public about the risks of opposing the Nazi Party. Lastly, it functioned as a way to visible degrade victims in order to create critical distance between the Nazis and their victims. Differentiating themselves from their victims in this way made it easier for Nazis to perpetrate horrific acts of violence against people who otherwise were just like them. In 1971, the British journalist Gitta Sereny asked Franz Stangl, the commandant of Treblinka, about the purpose of humiliating victims: "Why, if they [the Nazis] were going to kill them [the victims] anyway, what was the point of all the humiliation, why the cruelty?" Stangl replied: "To condition those who actually had to carry out the policies. To make it possible for them to do what they did."*

It's a lesson they understood quite well themselves as people like Jakub Berman, after the defeat of the Germans, established the Ministry of Public Security (read: secret police) in communist Poland, an organization so staffed to the gills with agents of terror that they had one for every 800 Poles. The terror unleashed by the Ministry could be analyzed by the numbers—at least 300,000 arrests, at least 6000 death sentences—but it is much easier to understand the preponderance of Jews in the Soviet apparatus (noted by Nikita Khrushchev in his memoirs no less) as the chance to enact a humiliating terror on people who they perceived did not do enough to protect them or participated in violence.

Certainly, their descendants are willing to acknowledge some of this, such as Jacob Mikanowski in his New York Times' opinion piece "My Grandfather, The Secret Policeman," and explain it away as being useful idiots for Stalin who believed that if you put Jews in positions of the secret police and security that they could curb other people's "nationalist deviations." Why this would be a conclusion Stalin would come to is anyone's guess, but with Jews like Julia Brystiger, tasked with destroying the Catholic Church in Poland, and Jozef Swiatlo, a torturer of prisoners who was instrumental in destroying the nationalist Home Army and arresting the men who would be ritualistically humiliated and convicted in the show Trial of Sixteen, it would seem they proved themselves more than adept to Stalin's challenge. This period of Polish history would end with the rise of Władysław Gomułka, whose form of socialism appealed explicitly to Polish national sentiments and who would, for seemingly no rational reason whatsoever other than obviously base and animalistic antisemitism, allow a purge of Jews in Poland from the military and positions of power to take place. This would ultimately drive out the majority of remaining Jews in Poland.

This is the retaliation effect that Phil Leask describes in the NCBI journal "Losing trust in the world: Humiliation and its consequences" that may occur when the humiliated are given power. In this way, it reveals that empathy can be conditional and can be conditioned *out*. Some could view the terms of the Treaty of Versailles as a humiliating imposition on the German people. Certainly it was viewed as humiliating to those who lost, but what's always more illuminating are the intentions of the victors. France's *revanchism* (literally revenge) was born in the humiliating defeat of 1870-1871 when the upstart Prussians single-handedly ended the Second French Empire by capturing their emperor and unified the

German state in the Hall of Mirrors in the French Palace of Versailles. This moment would define the French psyche for the next 48 years as the peace talks for the World War I Treaty of Versailles would open on the exact same day the German Empire had been proclaimed in the exact same place. Like Japan, the Second German Reich had a tragic symmetry ending in the same place and the same day where it had begun.

While the spirit of explicit *Revanchism* ebbed and flowed in French politics, the wound of their loss and how that wound was inflicted was a chronic sting in their nation's consciousness. *"Never speak of them; never forget them!"* was Prime Minister Leon Gambetta's reminder to the population when it came to the loss of Alsace-Lorraine. Internally they debated how to restore themselves as the liberal Third Republic had expanded the colonial empire of the Second French Empire, a poor consolation prize to many for losing the lands that were once part of France. Some of them saw the liberal empire as a distraction from taking back what was theirs. Some of them wondered if they could placate Germany's colonial ambitions by trading territories to get back Alsace-Lorraine. Others saw a much more ingenious use for the African territories they'd conquered in the form of biopower against their most hated enemy.

Charles Mangin was the architect of France's usage of African troops against the Germans. His vociferous advocacy of it did not come from any well-spring of *liberté, égalité, fraternité* however but from the "demographic disparity" between France and Germany and to have the absolute crushing manpower to prevent a repeat of France's humiliating defeat. Mangin was born in Lorraine and four-years-old when his home was annexed by the Germans in that defeat. His family were among the 5,000 of French citizens living in Alsace-Lorraine who were forced to leave their ancestral homes and go to France's imperial possession of Algeria, where instead of being seen as a dumping ground for the refugees of a national disgrace it was seen as the promised land where national regeneration would begin. This may have had more to do with the imperial-minded Opportunist Republicans who were granting the Jews in Algeria French citizenship during wartime and making arguments that the only way for France to oppose rising Prussia now was to develop an African empire and demographically overwhelm them, such as the argument put forth by the Jewish ambassador to the United States Prevost-Paradol. This was a rather curious argument to the nationalists who just wanted Alsace-Lorraine back and the republicans who were anti-colonial by their tradition. The Opportunist Republicans had the power however, and more than enough French were willing to go along with it, *revanche* sharpening their teeth.

Charles Mangin lived his whole life, save those first four years, in the French Third Republic in that milieu of empire and vengeance. From the age of nineteen on he'd be a military man in the Republic's empire, climbing up through the ranks and being exposed to the fighting ways of the colonized subjects. In 1899, H.G. Wells published a book entitled *The Sleeper Awakes* in which the world in the year 2100 has African policemen putting down worker unrest and riots in European cities. It is unknown if Mangin read the novel. He certainly had an affinity, however, for the local African customs as he received 30 days detention five years prior for currying favor with the African foreign legionnaires by giving them slave girls, as reported in *The March to the Marne: The French Army 1871-1914*. It's not hard to see that he was consumed by revenge, by plans to recapture Lorraine, and to inflict a maximal amount of pain onto a conquered Germany by throwing an endless supply of what he considered to be primitive men against them. He started a firestorm of controversy in 1909 that would last up to the war by first bringing up the topic of using African troops to fight wars in Europe with falling birthrates and natural warriors as his main arguments, at least according to *Race and War in France: Colonial Subjects in the French Army, 1914—1918*. The Germans were vocally horrified by it, calling it a war crime, which must have only encouraged the French to pursue the policy. Protests only hardens the hearts and sharpens the steel of the vengeful.

Mangin certainly wanted to see their lands divided and subjugated to these savage troops. The French were quite deliberate with this, having specifically segregated the Senegalese from everyone else, especially French women, so that they could be unleashed purely as a bioweapon. *A*

More Unbending Battle records that the African troops had a reputation for taking no prisoners and for cutting off body parts of the men they fought, dispelling any notion that this war would be fought in any honorable European spirit. The Germans would not be worthy of that. Some may rationalize that it was just desserts to the Germans for the Rape of Belgium. This is the kind of messy history that makes it easier for many to accept occupying the German lands with colored soldiers. According to "The 'Black Horror on the Rhine': Race as a Factor in Post-World War I Diplomacy," Mangin delighted that the Moroccans on the Rhine were "doing marvelously; the Germans are very much afraid of them," letting these Germans know exactly what their place in the world was and what their status would be. Even through 1918 the French were preparing to send in a million African troops against Germany as further shock troops to break them. It was not necessary, however. The United States broke Germany first.

The occupation of Germany and the sense of national humiliation has to be understood in a context lost to most modern readers. Germany had managed to forge itself together through blood and iron after millions of Germans had been disunited for centuries and often kept that way by the European powers as all of the German-speaking peoples in Europe united together would always have the ability to alter or direct the balance of power. Like Japan, it got into the imperial game late but it got in there strong, doing its best to keep up and be on an equal footing with the other Great Powers. It even managed to acquire overseas territories of its own in a world where the United Kingdom had dominion over at least a quarter of the earth. The defeat it was rendered stripped it of its equal status with the Great Powers, stripped it of its colonies, and stripped it of its freedom to determine its own destiny as it was sliced up, occupied, and dictated to. While every European empire of the 20th century would follow the long and bloody path of decolonization, Imperial Germany was unusual in that it was forcibly decolonized purely for the victors' gain and in order to keep it from being a threat to the new order. For many Germans, and for one charismatic one in particular, they were in not much a better state than the Irish or the Indians. They had gone from colonizers to colonized, and were now beneath the status of colonial African soldiers who were conscripted specifically to be fierce cannon fodder.

There is no evidence that the French were explicitly intent on engaging in some kind of German genocide from race-mixing—the number of Rhineland bastards born from the occupation was relatively low—and the liberal rationalizations they provided past demographics and cannon fodder was that this was a "civilizing mission" of the unwashed, but they certainly knew what they were doing by being the first to bring colonial troops into Europe. They were violating their own standards and upending the gentlemen's agreement of European imperialism to leave colonial subjects in the colonies, all for the cheap and destructive thrill of seeing their most hated foe humiliated worse than they had been as revenge. The tragedy and humiliations of the First World War killed so much in the European spirit, and would cement the grip the racially-erratic New World colonies would have over the Old World. That malevolent spirit of the Rhineland occupation lives on to the present day as the occupiers of Europe, and their bureaucratic toadies, delight to inflict this same shame through racial domination upon the conquered. Liberals become giddy at the thought that old white people are punished with brown children—an admission that they too do not see this as something to celebrate but that brown bodies are a tool of biopower to humiliate.

All these roads, it seems, converge on this terrifying now.

All these roads converge on being overwhelmed by the entire global world, giving up space, meat, and families, so that they can take up the role of the celebrated servile.

Eat the bug.
Live in the pod.
Buy the dress for your mulatto grandson.
It's what you deserve.
It's who you are now.
You can be no more.

IX. Go as a Great Wave of Cool Water

"Warrior spirit is characterised by direct, clear and loyal relations, based on fidelity and honour and a sound instinct for the various dignities, which it can well distinguish: it opposes everything which is impersonal and trivial...In dealing with relationships, not only man-to-man, but also State-to-State and race-to-race, it is necessary to be able to conceive again of that obedience which does not humiliate but exalts, that command or leadership which commits one to superiority and a precise responsibility."

— Julius Evola, *Metaphysics of War*

Humiliation is a powerful impulse, and its effects touch us at every step. Where cultural humiliation was once more abstract, like a cultural miasma that one was swimming through, social media has transformed it into an immediate performance. Articles are written that are designed to induce your outrage and weaken your defenses because of its feelings of inevitability in their victory. Guy Debord in *The Society of the Spectacle* warned that the authentic social life would be replaced by its representation in images, and that people would be defined by their relationship to that image. People would consume that image, perform like that image, wish to be like that image.

Our society is a shameful spectacle.

It's been a long way to get here and I fear we have so much further to go. People who thought they were born with a national birthright are fast discovering that not only is that not the case, but that there are psychic horrors in store for anyone who isn't with the present program. Hierarchy exists, has always existed, and will always exist. The revolutionary equalizers require a perpetual passion play of oppression being played out where those assigned as oppressors at birth are trampled down to keep the dead nation's blood agitated instead of settling in its corpse. It starts with broadcasting Trump's Red Hats being brutalized on every media platform and helpless to stop it. Power mewls, then smirks.

Every restless man wishes he lived in a time when he could die for something. Every wounded man wishes he lived in a time when he could live for something. When your world feels like a spiritual wasteland covered in a thousand invisible barriers, what is any one person supposed to do? *"Nothing to kill or die for,"* as the maudlin peace ballad goes, but what's worse is when you feel like there's nothing to struggle or live for. That is the hidden aspect of shame and humiliation. Degrade them so far that a pointless death might be preferable to a pointless, but painful, life. It won't be, but they might shame you into thinking it. They will shame you into thinking there is no hope to restore the man to what he once was and was supposed to be. They will shame you into drowning yourself for a greater good that isn't even real.

When a person drowns, they first desperately hold their breath. When the first bit of water gets in though the airway, it spasms to protect the body. There is no more air however and the body shuts down, sending the man into the black void while his heart gives out. Anyone set adrift in the cold, dark ocean will panic and die alone in these shifting tides. And if they're not alone, they might just drag another person under with them. The only way for the lost at sea to live is to find the buoys in the night and cling to them until help arrives. You may think such a thing doesn't exist but the lights in the sky have guided your wayward forefathers before and they still know the way home.

Home, past the broken fences waiting to be mended. Home, where the hearth still burns with persistent embers of a previous fire. Home, where words are no longer needed to feel restored and whole again.

The Ten Thousand of Xenophon's *Anabasis* famously cried *"Thalatta! Thalatta!"* The sea! The sea! They were mercenaries, no one they fought for would care if they lived or died. They were backstabbed, their leaders cut down and left to fend for themselves. There was nothing left for them here but to save themselves. After two years of endless death and struggle as a hated enemy in a land they were not welcome in, they finally saw the sea and knew they would be home.

"Loud were the shouts, the laughter, and the cheers."

This is not Ancient Greece and we are not those warriors. Nothing seems real with these listless flights from feeling. It's all so fake except for that constant anxious pressure on our hearts of a threatening future full of bugs, pods, and polycules. A simulation of drowning that never actually ends. It would be easier to give them what they want. Stop fighting it. They hold all the cards and they get a sick thrill from the humiliated helpless defiance.

Yet we cling.

This is not a pep talk. This is not about some fiery human spirit that prevails because it has righteousness on its side. This is not a call to action. This is not a sermon about the people who were cast out of a shining city on the hill and who will one day return. This is cultural graffiti, a marker for those who need to know their own have passed through; a buoy for the ashamed who want to cling instead of drown.

For now.

Resistance and restoration is the only way forward. Resistance in our mocking laughter, restoration in our children. Resistance in defying lies, restoration in our history. Resistance in our discipline, restoration in our truth.

Our society is a conquered one and our children and grandchildren might curse us for not doing more. That is their right. The fight should have been ours, never theirs. The haunted and humiliated live in pain and self-pity, always forgetting that pain must be passed through. We must pass through. We can't go back. We can't run. We have to go forward. We have to live without fear of being denied a mangy dog's table scraps. We have to live in truth. Go then, and give them nothing to gloat over.

I recall the words of Ezra Pound's "Defiance."

Go as a great wave of cool water.
Go like a blight upon the dulness of the world;
Go with your edge against this.
Go in a friendly manner,
Go with an open speech.
Go to those who are thickened with middle age.
Go out and defy opinion.

The Last Man of the Deep Wild

The American Sun, March 2020
One month before Pentti Linkola's death

"A man could be a lover and defender of the wilderness without ever in his lifetime leaving the boundaries of asphalt, power lines, and right-angled surfaces. We need wilderness whether or not we ever set foot in it. We need a refuge even though we may never need to set foot in it."

— Edward Abbey, *Desert Solitaire*

The dissident right loves the forlorn and forsaken; the more hopeless the cause, the more they identify. Folks of the right have been so bereft of genuine heroes and fighters in this age that they will plumb the chest of the weird and wild figures of history, looking for anything and anyone to align themselves with. It's a constant search for the real and the pure of spirit, always on the lookout for someone who has been fighting the good fight and uncompromised as they walk the walk. Most of the people who identify as a member of this restless motley crew are probably suburbanites and urbanites. I wouldn't doubt it for a second. These contradictions always come up when the topic of Pentti Linkola comes up and the love that the nascent environmental right has for him.

Right-wing environmentalism is not a new phenomenon. It has been mired in constant conflict and pushback. Theodore Roosevelt helped popularize conservation and the idea of land as a national antiquity in the United States, and conservatives rarely speak of him now. J.R.R. Tolkien synthesized the pagan love of nature with his deeply Catholic perspective, only the latter of which he is remembered for. Adolf Hitler dreamed of the *volkswagen* and a highway system that would bring Germans closer to the land as part of his blood-and-soil ideology, and we know how that's treated now. If you want to discredit an idea, point out that the Nazis once considered it and you won't have to explain why it's bad for people to appreciate the land that surrounds them without requiring corporations to more properly respect it for them.

Environmentalism these days has become a dirty word to the right who aren't familiar with their own traditions. Even Zizek has said environmentalism is "deeply conservative," according to *An Unexpected Wilderness*, seeing what they cannot. Some of it derived from skepticism toward industrial civilization's cult of progress and some of it as wanting to celebrate the greatness of the nation. After coming out of the Great Depression however and with the rise of television as ideology, celebrating the spoils and triumph of capitalism mattered more to a people who had living memories of living with so little and the fear that communism might take it all away. The strong association that concern for the environment had with the burned-out hippie movement did little to endear the post-war right-wing to it; that it was coupled with the soft men of the 70s led to a machismo backlash of over-the-top consumption in the 80s and 90s exemplified by songs by Denis Leary's "Asshole." However, in Europe there was a stronger environmentalist current that could transcend left and right, and it was one that brought Pentti Linkola with it.

Linkola, for those uninitiated with the meme figures of the extremely online right, is a Finnish environmentalist who was born in Helsinki in 1932. The Finnish are already a people more deeply rooted into the wilderness of their natural surroundings, but thanks to his pedigree Pentti Linkola seemed destined for the biological and environmental sciences. His maternal grandfather was Hugo Suolahti, a Doctor of Philosophy and the Chancellor of the University of Helsinki (and briefly the chairman of the centre-right National Coalition Party), while his father Kaarlo Linkola was a botanist who wrote his dissertation on the culture of vegetation in Southern Karelia—a place that his son would also examine and write about in his *Can Life Prevail?* collection of writings. The place where Pentti Linkola would spend his childhood summers would be where he would later take up residence once he decided to withdraw from the modern world, a place he would reflect upon in the TV documentary *Cry, Beloved (Land)...*, often in the way that it shaped his love of nature and the pain he felt from industrialization's encroachments on it. Linkola would not follow in his family's footsteps in academia, cutting his studies short and giving up a career in research to live most of his life as a fisherman though still managing to prove himself to be one of Finland's best living ornithologists, his work on the Finnish peregrine written alongside the popular nature writer Teuvo Suominen and being frequently cited in academic works.

Linkola was coming up in a time when Finland was developing a robust set of environmentalist writers, Teuvo Suominen being one of them as his 1967 book *Our Dying Noble Birds,* would leave an impact on Finland not unlike the impact Rachel Carson's *Silent Spring* had on the United States and its pesticides. Finns in the 20th Century had been among the most environmentally-conscious people in the world, its Green League having developed originally out of some of the populist and Eurosceptic currents in the Finns and would go on to be the first Green party to join the national cabinet of any state in 1995. While the Green League has betrayed many of those founding principles at the behest of neoliberalism, it does not diminish the ecological impulses of the Finnish people, an undercurrent that has been present since some of them mobilized against the Neste oil company in the early 70's. While for many Finns it seemed possible that they could find environmental solutions within the liberal frame, Linkola would remain the perennial illiberal thorn in their side.

Despite living on his own for most of his life as a humble self-sustaining fisherman in accordance with his ecological principles, Linkola has had numerous television documentaries and appearances devoted to him and his work. In 1983 he won the Eino Leino Prize, an award usually given out to poets, for his non-fiction writing. He has been an object of fear, derision, and fascination in Finland and those intrigued by cultural outsiders. His current international popularity has been a result of his embrace by ecological factions of the far-right and those who call themselves "ecofascists" (a controversial term in its own right due to its origin as a pejorative, popularization by a mass shooter, and its ill-defined concerns and conservationism) which has been ironic given that his 1979 work *From the Diary of a Dissident* was dedicated to Baader and Meinohof of the communist terroristic Red Army Faction, just two years after their group had peaked with the violence of the German Autumn. Linkola's most well-known work in English, *Can Life Prevail,* even includes an admiration for Pete Singer, a figure you will never find a single right-winger admiring.

Reading *Can Life Prevail* after seeing the memes can lead one to scratching their heads as to why Pentti Linkola has developed a cult following in the online world of the right. One could understand why an outsider figure like Ted Kaczynski who also had a singular focus on what he believed in and a willingness to accept heterodox viewpoints would develop a following. He combined the mystique that murderers have in true crime obsessed decadent cultures with the clarity and immediacy of his anti-technological writings, but Linkola is more perplexing with how his work drips in deep ecological misanthropy. Deep ecology, for the uninitiated, is an approach to environmentalism that holds no sentimentalism or special regard toward human beings or any other life form as it would put ecological stability and sustainability for the entire system above any one species' desire to be fruitful and multiply. In short, favoritism disrupts the whole ecological system. Over the course of *Can Life Prevail*, Linkola discusses the necessity of destroying cats because of the damage their population numbers do to wildlife, agrees that mankind is the cancer of the earth, bemoans war as a waste if it doesn't target women and children due to their role in restoring excess humanity's numbers, and proposes dismantling the last one hundred years of industrial and technological progress if life really has any hope to prevail. The most famous of Linkola's quotes sums up his philosophy by positing that those who hate life will try to fill a single lifeboat with as many drowning bodies as possible while those who respect life will safeguard what can reasonably live by severing the hands of those who cling to the side.

So why does Linkola fascinate some on the right despite these things he's written and said? The answer is quite simple. Some love him because he's unwavering in his principles and has zero liberal sentiments toward the suffering of the rest of the world, but the reality is that outside of fear mongering journalists and sanctimonious green neoliberals his ghoulishness is seen as the abstract thought experiments of a sensitive and wounded soul who has so much love for nature that he would do anything to protect it if he could. Both of these extremes are seen in *Can Life Prevail* as he also goes on to describe the strength of the women on the Russian side of Karelia, the sadness of chickens in captivity, and the necessity of protecting the beautiful and dark forests of Finland. Linkola writes as the type of man right-wingers most admire—the principled man of ethos who is perpetually fighting for the lost cause with all his soul and being. By any other measure Linkola would be seen as an angry old crank, and certainly his detractors are happy to portray him as such, but through the urgency of his gentle idealism, even if he lashes out with extreme solutions, he's found an eager audience in a world that has been saturated by insincerity and consumptive irony.

In many respects, Linkola the man serves more as an inspiration to the right than his writings. A Finnish-language blog post at sarastushlehti.com entitled "Suomalainen sijaiskärsijä" that I got translated gets to the heart of why there is such a strong affinity for Linkola. The author of the original post cites a recently released biography of Linkola, as yet untranslated into English, that introduces the man like this:

> *He comes from a family of learning and his good upbringing shows in his behavior and demeanor, but at the same time he is an everyman, earning a living through fishing. His speech and writings are harsh and grim, but seldom do you get to read anything as tender and touching as what he has written. He is a romantic at heart, but his engine is hatred. His opinions are hard, but he doesn't want to discuss them in person, choosing to write because he doesn't want to hurt another. He likes people but has chosen solitude. He has a tough shell, but he cries easily. He doesn't shy away from divulging his deepest feelings, his brokenness.*

Linkola's own writings bear this out, with his memoir-as-short-film *Cry, Beloved (Land)...* being full of the hopeless melancholy of a man who sees that the beauty of nature is in life's desire to overcome, even though you are fighting against an industrial tsunami. Even though the end remains the same. Even though life will kill you, the struggle is too important to avoid gnashing your teeth, kicking your legs, and clawing for every little inch that would allow you to just simply be heard and *understood*. This would be a painful exercise for anyone who is a dissident, but it becomes more resonant for those who have to compete with the manufactured truths of a hypernormalized regime. The burden becomes a thousand personal wounds that is usually too much for any one man who needs to be heard, a reality that Linkola meditates on at the end of the short film, stating:

> *Unpleasantness is surely in store. Every single one of my writings and interviews has brought with it difficulties in my personal life, both when I was understood correctly and when I wasn't. But this too loses all significance when my personal life loses its significance. And yet, beneath everything, until my last breath I cling stupidly and desperately to a smoldering, fragile hope that my writings could make the world an ever so slightly softer place.*

Were Linkola just an edgy ecofascist as some insist him to be—including those on the nationalist right who only know about his lifeboat ethics and take that at surface-level—he wouldn't have the fascination that transcends the political compass. Were Linkola only a misanthropic deep ecologist on the level of the Voluntary Human Extinction Movement, he wouldn't be dismissed as a crank by utopian liberals and leftists who retreat to hatred for humanity when minor politics and elections don't go their way. It is because there is a hidden heart to the things he says, because he's actually fought all his life for what he believes in instead of grifting off of popular sentiment or escaping to impossible idealism that he troubles and fascinates people who learn of him.

It's important to understand that Linkola is not an impossible idealist himself. He proposes solutions that he knows will never be taken seriously because there is no will to do so, but he does not set up for himself an environmentalist ideology that is impossible to reconcile to facts. Ideology often does not survive first contact with reality and this becomes evident in the way ideologues and humanists react to Linkola's lifeboat ethics, the ethics that are sometimes cited as proof of the terroristic violence of "ecofascism." Linkola's famously referenced quote goes as such:

> *What to do when a ship carrying a hundred passengers has suddenly capsized, and only one lifeboat is available for ten people in the water? When the lifeboat is full, those who hate life will try to pull more people onto it, thus drowning everyone. Those who love and respect life will instead grab an axe and sever the hands clinging to the gunwales.*

This metaphor was first presented by Linkola in his 1989 book *An Introduction to the Thought of the 1990s*. This metaphor of Linkola's is probably the most well-known and quoted thing he's ever written, something he would be surprised by as when others have mentioned it to him he has referred to it as a "momentary state of mind," an idle thought of his that wasn't meant to be a "public lecture" or the lynchpin of some complete and closed system of epistemological morality. It is enough though that Linkola has the courage of his own conscience that even rhetorical questions like that could shake some of the most well-regarded minds of the 20th century. The analytic philosopher and ethicist Georg Henrik von Wright, the successor to no less than Ludwig Wittgenstein in his Cambridge chair, was so taken aback by the idea that Linkola put out there that he even wrote to him on it. Linkola recounts in *Can Life Prevail*:

> *As you may know, I hold you in high regard as a thinker. At least in this country, you are the most lucid and profound among truthful prophets. As to what practical conclusions to draw from realising the truth, this is a different matter. Perhaps I too would strike at the hands that are clinging to the boat, but hardly for the love of life: rather, out of fear, in an attempt*

to save my own skin. Perhaps it would be a better solution for all of us to drown, a final proof of the human species' inability to survive.

For the amount that Linkola is said to be ghoulish and a crank, the reaction of Von Wright is one that's exceedingly common among the educated liberal and is treated as a perfectly reasonable reaction to have. Anyone who has had extended conversations with these kinds of people know how much their ostensibly bleeding-hearts don't drip with blood but with malice, contempt, and hatred for humanity when it doesn't live up to their ideological expectations. Anyone who has spoken to these people know how venomous they become about exterminating humanity when the world has no interest in their media-born "scientific humanism." Linkola may not have any special affection for humanity, he may be fine with extreme solutions to stabilize the ecological world as he sees it, but as a man of the wild he still sees man as a living creature with a place in the natural world instead of an empty vessel to be despised for failing to live up to the idealism of the foolishly privileged. Linkola has humanity because he is *not* a humanist. As he reflects on this in his response to Von Wright:

> *The above letter proves how difficult it is for a great humanist to let go of the overemphasis on the value of human life. I think I can sense some fear between the lines, something I have previously encountered when discussing the issue of overpopulation. I call it the fear of breaking loose and of disgrace. People fear that if any actions are taken to limit the world population, the situation will spiral out of control and human life will somehow lose its value forever. It is also thought that after similar actions mankind will forever lose its sense of self worth by sullying its ethical value, and will be unable to restore any norms and conventions.*

This is the real reason that Linkola has his admirers on the right. This is also why they fear the rise of the environmental and illiberal right.

This issue is up for the right to take and claim to be theirs. By right, it should be theirs. They've been led astray however by giant elevating lines on charts and the hucksters that have convinced them of both its moral imperative and that it's the only frontier that is real and matters. The right has been gaslighted into believing that to care about nature and the environment is a leftist phenomenon. The irony is that even where the issue has been full of leftists, these people always trend towards being heterodox in their thinking and beliefs because to engage with nature is to engage with reality, something the ideological are conditioned to flee from like the plague. The ecological issue is begging to be claimed by the right, and yet it has no one willing to do it who aren't already playing by the rules of the elites and their janissaries who fly around the world and agree that the only hope to stop the climate change boondoggle is infinity migration, eating bugs, and whatever new scheme they concoct to make themselves richer and normal people poorer and miserable.

This digs into the heart of Linkola's appeal. While the man has admirers across every iteration of the political spectrum except for neoliberals and their intersectional stooges, he found appeal on the far-right the way many strange idols have found themselves on those altars: he told the truth when no one else would and he wouldn't be cowed by maudlin and manipulative appeals to tears. He has refused to retreat to platitudes and stood his ground when shown images of suffering POC meant to push his country toward open borders. He has spoken favorably of any authoritarian regime in his essay "Time To Quiet Down," whether it was the National Socialists or the Soviets, that would make preservation of nature paramount since liberalism was antithetical to it. Linkola has said many things over his long years that even his admirers can and will find disagreements with, but he has never fallen for liberalism's oversocialized and moral preenings that seek to take every dissenter and bend their will backwards until they break. He has remained unrepentant, and there is so much to admire in that. He is the last man of the deep wild, the last truly free man. There is so much within that for the right to admire, whether or not he's just some old kook in the woods.

There isn't likely to be another man like Linkola. The frontier has been boarded up. Technological society welds people deeper into its iron bosom every day. Dick Proenneke is dead, and Edward Abbey too. D.H.

Lawrence is mostly remembered as a misogynist pornographer despite writing beautifully about nature. Children of the earth like Christopher McCandless wandered off to die for no damn good reason. Ted Kaczynski took revenge on industrial society with rapidly expanding packages and waits to die in a little box, editing his papers and becoming increasingly pessimistic that the technocapital system will ever be opposed. Only Linkola remains to watch the earth get swallowed whole.

There's a false assumption that there is no use to the wild if you aren't actively living out there in a loin cloth and digging into the dirt to munch on grubs. It's enough that it's simply there to call out to a man. Man needs to know it's there to sharpen themselves just as they needed the wolves to fear and fight. The saddest mountain is the one that's been reduced to a hill. It's only in captivity that the female mantis cannibalizes her mate. Have men in captivity benefitted from being resigned to a plastic cage?

Because American conservatism, now being exported to conquered Europe, conceits itself so much on this dream of endless growth and eternal youth, it betrays that it must die. Out of fear of the natural world it has fled from the reality that all things must die and in a manchild's tantrum refuses to plant seeds for new trees to grow. It has no sense for the tension between nature and industrial capitalism that D.H. Lawrence intimately understood in his writings and the necessity to say YES to both life and death as he did in *Reflections on the Death of a Porcupine:*

> *Because I know the tree will ultimately die, shall I therefore refrain from planting a seed? Bah, it would be conceited cowardice on my part. I love the little sprout, and the weak little seedling. I love the thin sapling, and the first fruit, and the falling of the first fruit. I love the great tree in its splendour. And I am glad that at last, at the very last, the great tree will go hollow, and fall on its side with a crash, and the little ants will run through it, and it will disappear like a ghost back into the humus.*
>
> *It is the cycle of all things created, thank God. Because, given courage, it saves even eternity from staleness.*

The young will take their lessons from grouchy misanthropes like Pentti Linkola because the new ways denied its nature and betrayed their duties. He fought for the lands of his tender childhood like no man has in the 20th century, regardless of any ideology or what it might take to defend it in perpetuity, or at least as long as any living thing can last in a world that seems like it's constantly in pain. He had to go there because no one else would, because the left's solutions were tepid, useless, and enthralled to liberalism while the acceptable right had no solutions at all. The left grows because it spreads like a virus that consumes everything, but the right dies because it never really fought for life. It never really fought for life except in the abstract principle. When conservatism finally dies its ignoble and pathetic death a right that actually loves nature, loves the necessity of dying, and loves what life needs to prevail must be born. Linkola cries because he cries alone.

Your land and all of its creatures are a gift to be cherished, to be a steward toward. The land will shape the people who toil within it if they love and fear it in equal awe. The patriotic songs that resonate most are the ones that speak of the beauty of the land. How could any man who does not worship money and power want to sell it? How could any man who loves life want to sell it to the lowest bidder?

You may not like the old hermit, but listen. You may need to hear it.

Kings of Dogs and the Soldiers of Misfortune

The American Sun, September 2020

"*Grayson spat in the dirt off to his side and rearranged himself against the tree so the cuffs didn't hurt so much. 'Why is a Zimbabwean mercenary, burned out on whores, sitting on a milkcrate high in the La Sal mountains of Moab, Utah? What series of events would bring about such a thing?' Grayson asked.*

The old mercenary gave a knowing smile and tapped his ash. 'I've been many places. You really want to know? I'll tell you. Spoils of war. Same as any man I suppose. But in this case the mighty western man and his Empire have fallen. I am given an opportunity to clean up, to take my piece, so I do. Simply put.'

'As an American let me confirm there's no such thing as America,' said Grayson."

— Andrew Edwards, *King of Dogs*

"*Every normal man must be tempted, at times, to spit on his hands, hoist the black flag, and begin slitting throats.*"

— H.L. Mencken, *Prejudices: First Series*

The novel is as dead as America itself, it might be said. An exaggeration, but not without truth as both are rather worse for wear. This is an old and probably tired debate. Even as early as the 1920s writers like José Ortega y Gasset were beginning to see the novel as a product of nation and history and entering its final stages as a medium as it had exhausted everything it had to portray. As Ortega states in *The Dehumanization of Art and Notes on the Novel*, "present-day writers face the fact that only narrow and concealed veins are left." It's a sad and difficult state as while non-fiction has always been predicating on presenting truth, fiction is the best avenue for understanding truth.

Speculative fiction has accelerated past its golden age at the speed of light and has entered perpetual darkness. The adventure, mystery, but most importantly, the ideas that used to tantalize the writers of yesteryear, both the awesome and the terrible, have no place within the milieu of fiction that is hastily spewed out as proof of cleverness substituting as intelligence. Certainly it doesn't help that many of the worst visions conjured up in the 20th century ended up coming true, albeit in the most passive-aggressive way, making it difficult to imagine what kind of future could even be painted. Who knew that dreary world of Oceania or Kafka's bureaucracy could be so brightly lit in a neon rainbow? It's a problem that contemporary writers mired in being afraid of the declining evangelical Christian while penning the next variation of some stirring tale of an ambiguously gay brown person beating the odds by getting into America and finding their true home in financial capitalism are ill-equipped to tackle.

The one arguable benefit to this pitiful state of prose has been the rise of the Extremely Online Twitter E-Book. Like all books the quality runs the gamut, with at least one book making minor political waves (Bronze Age Mindset) and another (Harassment Architecture) becoming a bit of a cult classic among those who have the entire script of American Psycho memorized. The latter is only one of two actual literary fiction novels that immediately come to mind as most of the books that have been launched in this niche publishing world have been non-fiction of one sort or another. It was for this reason that I was intrigued when the author of King of Dogs, Andrew Edwards, sent me a copy of his first book out of the blue. The book took a while to find my hands. I did not know him and had never heard of him. Edwards is not Extremely Online, he has not amassed a following enamored with pithy and ironic tweets, and so his book stands out with its utter sincerity of plot and prose.

King of Dogs is a novel set in the near-future of the United States that still feels a bit far-off but all too close now. The United States is in the throes of a "Soviet-style collapse," a place where rump state citizens would convince themselves they're just experiencing temporary setbacks as the people of the frontier states watch cartels and private military companies turn the most beautiful parts of the nation into their own private Wild West. What may be of most interest to intrigued readers is this picture that Edwards paints of America in this collapse. Edwards sets the stage early on, describing the near future:

> In these first decades of the new millennium, finished with social engineering and mere financial rapine, the oligarchs of the era turned to base thievery. They pillaged utilities, land and minerals. Water first: its ownership and its metering. And if American cities burned as the oligarch's corporate mercenaries secured trucking routes amid early outcry, and if this sent economic and regional refugees of all colors and stations to antic motion, and if small wars waged scattershot here and there, and if in all this there was still no living God to be seen anywhere from seaboard to seaboard then the next logical step, by reason of the ancient paradigm become new: the oligarchs merely asked how might this activity too be mediated and metered? But in truth the cause of collapse and decline lay not in corrupt logic but in flawed hearts. Apathy and deceit are ancient enablers. Without trust there can be no social cohesion. If this is the end, it's a personal end. Yet most persons simply ignored it all right up to their final moment of terror, loss, regret. And, so, the few were left to fight, as ever...
>
> The cities of the nation had long been engaged with manifold chaos and were becoming landscapes of contradiction where tiny enclaves of exclusive wealth were run round by burnt, wasted zones. Yet the old patriotic platitudes regarding democracy, opportunity and individual freedom wore on in every media. No better off than the cities, the rural sectors were beset with a plague of uncertainty, social disintegration, and low-intensity guerilla war. The civil, the business, and the extranational martial, now fully merged in cartels and cabals, sprawled over oceans and borders, eating states and then eating each other in fights over territory. If an area went untouched by direct kinetic conflict, there was still no

avoiding confrontation with second and third order effects: epidemic human
trafficking in the wake of mass, haphazard migrations and every associated
degeneration and sickness, be it physical or of the spirit. Sophisticated and
region-specific propaganda was ubiquitous. For the strong: lies to cripple.
And the weak were sent programming to wallow in that weakness.

We don't learn much more about this collapse of the United States after this expository setup as the nearly all the plot is an intimate story of tragedy and survival focused entirely on the character of Grayson.

For men in novels, the protagonist has always been a problem in terms of what it should mean for men with the privilege to be literate. While the ability to read is not inherently an aristocratic virtue, there is a certain privilege to being well-read in any society that doesn't have an industrial and democratic character. Novels are often reflective of those who read them, and thus you have the working-class power fantasy of men against the world in pulp novels and the intellectual fantasy of men against themselves and society within literary novels. Edwards attempts to merge the two in the character of Grayson, a martial man who has lost the family he wanted to start but who soldiers on with a samurai stoicism and a spirituality brined in Eastern Orthodox mysticism.

Grayson is a man stuck between worlds. Neither warrior nor monk, Grayson learns how to fight from his mentor while his natural asceticism and personal readings give him the insights of an undisciplined Desert Father. It evokes the tension of never really being anything in particular like the state of modern man under a system that moves without his volition or participation. His purpose comes from his dying mentor Jack giving his pupil a "righteous mission" to defend Jack's brother and his brother's wife and coming child.

What stands out about Edwards' writing is its lyricism. The story is simple. A man vows to his dying comrade that he will take care of his brother, his brother's wife, and his brother's soon to be born child, in the disintegrating Moab. He is supposed to get them to some place safer. Things go bad and they go bad fast, and that soldier-of-misfortune marches through hell to get to them and discover what can be saved in a world that has no right to be saved. Edwards composes intricate set pieces of every scene and trial that Grayson endures. When the story is not at a breakneck action pace describing the violent brutality of mere survival he often lingers on the spiritual degeneration of man and their embers of hope against the vivid descriptions of its physical landscapes. Throughout the story Edwards merges these sentiments into a dark poetry in motion:

> *Downstream Grayson saw green northern lights merging into a dark forest and the shimmering surface water where the creek widened and met another branch. Slow and coiling like a helical ladder in the margin between earth and heaven, the fluid bands of green light billowed on a sky stratified pink and blue at sunset and for an interminable, recursive moment, he knew he was not alone and had never been.*

There is a prescient quality to the novel as well as collapse is constantly on the tongues of anyone not in love with the system or its currency of clout. People debate what collapse even is, if it's happening, how it will happen, and compose clickbait articles and videos about the coming collapse, sell collapse gear and collapse lifestyles, and write collapse books and movies. It's become imbued with all the trappings of post-apocalypse fiction as to paraphrase Mark Fisher it's easier to imagine the end of the world than it is to imagine the end of your society's complexity. Collapse comes in many forms, but to the mind that imagines it a zombie invasion immediately seems more realistic.

Collapse is a process however. It's civilization just going out to get a pack of smokes. There doesn't come a day where people rubbing their bleary and sleep-crusty eyes go to their windows and suddenly realize "golly, I don't think I live in the Empire anymore!" This may come as a disappointment for many who have been trained to believe sanctification only comes from the blood of martyrs who throw their lives away or believe living within a Hollywood spectacle is something to aspire to. The disappointing truth is that we must live our lives in times of diminishing returns.

The problem with collapse fantasies is that many who have them have the dream of a better world for them and their own. That is, they will be the ones that come out on top of this mess and chaos. This is rarely the outcome. Collapses come with civil wars, foreign interference, and no end to plundering, raping, and looting with little recourse other than whatever countervailing force can be mustered for the moment. In the final days of the Western Roman Empire, the wealthy Ecdicius and his brother-in-law the Saint Sidonius Apollinaris defended the Gallic town of Clermont from the Visigoths on their own and with their own money. On the one hand it shows the will of the few when they and only eighteen horseback men defended the town but on the other how many will have real saints and rich men in their corners?

Clermont fell three years later to the Goths. Sidonius was imprisoned until he was released to finish out his life as a shepherd to his flock. Ecdicius disappears from the historical record after being recalled to Rome. Clermont, a hard fought lost cause, was then ceded to the Visigoths in exchange for Provence. Three years after that the last of the Roman emperors, Romulus Augustulus abdicated, making official what everyone already knew: the people were on their own.

According to some speculation the last emperor lived out his last days on a pension.

Collapses are miserable experiences for the good and decent people that have to live through those times through no fault of their own and no money to run anywhere else. Edwards' novel captures the spirit of this awful truth. A family who did right in a society that no longer expects it by marrying, creating life, and carrying the torch, aren't afforded any fairy-tale favoritism. Two centuries before Ecdicius and Sidonius defended their town from the chaos of that age, men of that same region had tired of the hostile imperial bureaucracy that was making their lives miserable and found no issue with joining the half-barbarian banditry plaguing the empire. There comes a point when all men must look at their brigands, look at the behavior of their capital men in response to the crisis, and contemplate which is the real enemy.

John Michael Greer in *Dark Age of America* writes of that coming inflection point for any empire—any society really—when the switch between civilization and barbarism is flipped:

> *[T]he overall attitude of American politicians and financiers seems to be that nothing really that bad can actually happen to them or to the system that provides them with their power and wealth.*
>
> *They're wrong, and at this point it's probably a safe bet that a great many of them will die because of that mistake. Already, a large fraction of Americans—probably a majority—accept the continuation of the existing order of society in the United States only because a viable alternative has yet to emerge...*
>
> *...It's not necessary for such an alternative to be more democratic or more human than the order that it attempts to replace. It can be considerably less so, so long as it imposes fewer costs on the majority of people and distributes benefits more widely than the existing order does. That's why, in the last years of Rome, so many people of the collapsing empire readily accepted the rule of barbarian warlords in place of the imperial government. That government had become hopelessly dysfunctional by the time of the barbarian invasions, centralizing authority in distant bureaucratic centers out of touch with current realities, and imposing tax burdens on the poor so crushing that many people were forced to sell themselves into slavery or flee to depopulated regions of the countryside to take up the uncertain life of Bacaudae, half guerilla and half bandit, hunted by imperial troops whenever those latter had time to spare from the defense of the frontiers.*

As romantic a notion it might be to take up the life of the *bacaudae*, and there were some French radicals who saw a proto-French proletariat nationalism in their own interpretation of this Gallic phenomenon, it must be stated that at the end of the day these were just bandits with a decent excuse. Morality often fades when the decisions of survival are required to be made, but reality does temper the mythology. Lost in the stories of collapse are the stories of people who would live modest, ordinary lives in any society, including a collapsing one. *King of Dogs* captures the brutal and harsh reality for people like that. They become survivors within dysfunctional and cobbled together communities at best, but plundered pocketbooks and pickings for the next gangs, cartels, and mercenary armies more likely. Only men like Grayson could survive in a place like this, but what does it even mean to survive? Edwards puts the dilemma square at the center of his story:

> Shorn of multiform vanity, a man must only concern himself with observation and acceptance if he wishes to go on when most give up. Observation so that he can respond to what the world presents and acceptance of the inevitability of it bringing more suffering and eventually death. This was the secret to Grayson's endurance: the worst had already happened. All that was left of psychic weight was to prepare to smile at death.

King of Dogs is likely to stay with its readers long after its haunting closing pages. The influence of Cormac McCarthy can be felt throughout the novel, initially within its depictions of an American frontier that never really feels settled but especially in its swift and harsh resolution that leaves the reader uncertain, possibly disappointed, but especially troubled. The story is over in an almost shaggy dog sort of way, but the loose ends are tied and the question mark we are left with is if life is worth preserving. Survival for its own sake strikes people as not worth enough to fight for, and it's not for nothing that if you were to ask people living off the fruits of industrial society what they would do if that lifestyle were suddenly and permanently shut off many of them would choose suicide. Ask the people you know during one of those six-whiskey conversations what their long-term plans are in a downturn and you may be shocked at how many people you know have the Ernest Hemingway Retirement Plan in mind.

King of Dogs is not a perfect book. The book sometimes feels as though it's in a mad dash to get to the end of the story while Edwards' writing pleads for a breather to take in the beautiful terror of apocalypse America. The singular focus on Grayson also prevents many of the characters outside the antagonists from being fully fleshed out. The book however is greater than the sum of its parts and Edwards shows promise in a time where heartless novels can only express themselves through the tired clichés of irony, transgression, and politics. Like its subject matter, *King of Dogs* puts a question mark on the dying of a medium and despite the decay and degeneration that surrounds it shows that there is terrible beauty in being able to survive. The purpose to it is that it must be done.

D.H. Lawrence writing in *Reflections on the Death of a Porcupine* writes on how men go mad and their souls are broken by what he calls "debacles," that is the crises and revolutions that try the souls of ordinary men:

> *Debacles don't save men. In nearly every case, during the horrors of a catastrophe the light of integrity and human pride is extinguished in the soul of the man or the woman involved, and there is left a painful, unmanned creature, a thing of shame, incapable any more. It is the great danger of debacles, especially in times of unbelief like these. Men lack the faith and courage to keep their souls alert, kindled, and unbroken. Afterwards there is a great smouldering of shamed life.*
>
> *Man, poor, conscious, forever-animal man, has a very stern destiny, from which he is never allowed to escape. It is his destiny that he must move on and on, in the thought-adventure. He is a thought-adventurer, and adventure he must.*

In ages of constant crisis, the literature of the age often turns apocalyptic and inwardly focused. This is reflective of the state of man's spirit and often an expectation of the afterlife to come. But when the actual world is a purgatory with pleasantries then what is there to say? There is nothing more to say in this society. We are all post-apocalyptic neoliberal capitalists now. In order to not turn completely inward literature needs to look outward, either with a prophet's vision of the future or a preparation of the wounds, physical and spiritual, toward death. The writers of today will need to find something to say about tomorrow and how to pass through to it, even if it they don't know what it looks like.

King of Dogs reveals this mindset in its subtitle. *Life is the training ground for death.* For Edwards, action, survival, and meditation are three synonyms for the same holistic necessity. I leave him with the final word on the subject:

> *The act of going-on, of surviving, was his religion put over against whatever else seemed true. The trick to survival was in realizing how utterly unnatural it was to give in, to cower or crumble. To complain and not act. A thousand generations of men, fathers and their sons, had faced austerity absolute in cataclysms, plague, extinctions, and exile. Murder and pain were implicit in the unity of things and while the saints had sufficiently, to his lights, reasoned out why it is so, Grayson reasoned that pain did not tell the truth but only pointed the way. The truth lies beyond the gates of pain.*

Essays published in my blog

—Race Borz—

Technocapitalism Is Making Us Autistic

Race Borz, September 2019

The brain trust known as the Original PineBros—a cavalcade of shitposting technoskeptics, radical campbois, and a Homeric cryptid named Ron—is always a very mixed bag. Sometimes you get deep thoughts that go on for hours, sometimes you get Garfield roleplay and unsolicited pictures of Stormking's ass. Fortunately we got the former this time around.

A text discussion between five people on one of the most vaunted numbers on the internet—*1488*—took a turn into why you see it so frequently in any kind of discount or sale:

1: "1488 starts to appear a lot around you when you pay attention. The old office had one urinal installed with a 1488 on a price sticker on it."

2: "I see 14.88 on a lot of Walmart prices now, to be honest."

3: "I've always wondered why that is. A certain markdown from a certain price I'm sure but I can't tell what it is."

4: "I always see 14.98, so it's like a ten cent mark off or something."

5: "They just avoid .99, but want as much of that dollar as they can, so they probably A/B test different cent values to see which works best. I imagine that .88 has a slightly higher return than others, because of people like us, so that's why they would keep doing it."

I don't know how true any of this is, but it *feels* true so we're going to go with that and assume that everything I'm about to write is correct (because I usually am). I don't think there's a cabal of Based and Redpilled merchants rubbing their hands behind the scenes because they've now tricked the Internet Nazis into buying Product. This is not a reality I am prepared to accept or believe in.

I do think there is something though to the psychological effect that a repeating number has. It's soothing, it's comforting, in the same way that alliteration is. It's repetition. It's dependable, predictable, and repeatable. Pondering this has led me to a horrifying conclusion:

Technocapitalism has turned us into autists.

The human mind has industrialized to prefer ever more structure and order. How much of that is the industrial society tapping into what was already there (certainly religion shows we find a soothing peace of mind in meaningful repetition) and how much of it is being engineered, I will leave that for people with more time on their hands to endlessly argue over.

These are effects that Kacyznski have noted as well in his analysis of Industrial Society. Kaczynski's obsession with the debilitating and controlling functions of the technocapital system led him to remark upon this about freedom (which may be better understood as autonomy when Kaczynski speaks of it in *Industrial Society and Its Future*, paragraph 114 and 119):

> [M]odern man is strapped down by a network of rules and regulations, and his fate depends on the actions of persons remote from him whose decisions he cannot influence. This is not accidental or a result of the arbitrariness of arrogant bureaucrats. It is necessary and inevitable in any technologically advanced society. The system HAS TO regulate human behavior closely in order to function...It is true that some restrictions on our freedom could be eliminated, but GENERALLY SPEAKING the regulation of our lives by large organizations is necessary for the functioning of industrial-technological society. The result is a sense of powerlessness on the part of the average person. It may be, however, that

*formal regulations will tend increasingly to be replaced by psychological
tools that make us want to do what the system requires of us...*

*The system does not and cannot exist to satisfy human needs. Instead,
it is human behavior that has to be modified to fit the needs of the
system...It is the needs of the system that are paramount, not those of the
human being. For example, the system provides people with food because
the system couldn't function if everyone starved; it attends to people's
psychological needs whenever it can CONVENIENTLY do so, because it
couldn't function if too many people became depressed or rebellious. But
the system, for good, solid, practical reasons, must exert constant pressure
on people to mold their behavior to the needs of the system...The concept
of "mental health" in our society is defined largely by the extent to which
an individual behaves in accord with the needs of the system and does so
without showing signs of stress.*

As I noted above, you have a bit of a chicken-egg situation here about
which is causing what. The details of it don't matter all that much. It's
what we're seeing and how it functions that matters. The way I view it is
that the chaotic pressures of this fast-twitch system is causing people to
seek any therapeutic and meaningful form of order, structure, and
repetition because this society produces no form of it for them. This
seems counter-intuitive, I realize, because after coming back to this post
I started to wonder if I had it backwards. When you look at society today,
you see what has to be some kind of perverted order with the systematic
way people go to school and work and chase dopamine on social media.
That is structural, is it not? You could say the same thing about prison,
and many prisoners once released still act within the protocols and
parameters they were taught to follow in prison. This is conditioning. It
is not meaningful.

I noted that on some level what religion responds to is humanity's
need for that. The physical world is a chaotic, dangerous, and insecure
world, so the answer to that is an ordered, safer, and secure world that
has predictable patterns that can be called upon in the service of a just and
loving God guiding it all. The duality of man exists as an oppositional

dialectic, highlighting the need to find a world in balance (the Hopi word Koyaanisqatsi means "a life out of balance"). The order that this society provides is chaotic and inverted. Things that are said to be one thing actually mean something else ("Racism is hatred for another race oh except that it now means power plus privilege also power and privilege are very nebulous"). Everyone repeats certain maxims, but look at the results being the exact opposite ("diversity is our strength"). Everyone's social interactions come largely more and more through technology, a medium that gets to decide how reality will ultimately be shaped for people and which frequently turns life into a dopamine-based video game that most people are losing. The results speak for themselves in this unbalanced life we are living, the pressures people live under in their daily lives that cause many people to cope in increasingly unhealthy ways.

An example of this behavior: we had a subscriber make a mistake in his subscription and instead of addressing it in a normal way an increasingly rarer normal person would with "hey something seems wrong here, it looks like I got double charged," said person launched into full invective full of recriminations and assumptions of wrong-doing and threats of taking it to the chans in order to try and destroy as many people as possible. It was looked into. He had two accounts:

> *Dear Subscriber,*
>
> *I understand that you were poorly socialized and the media and society trained you to be a self-centered megalomaniac long before you discovered edgy politics, and that over the top vainglorious rhetoric, threats and blackmail are the only way that you feel you can engage in the power process, but in fact you subscribed for an annual account and forgot about it.*

When things were not industrialized, you saw balance in the duality of this order and chaos. The need for meaningful structure and order is often expressed in the form of beautiful buildings like cathedrals. The chaotic pressures of our anxious, inverted society require a rubberband response that you see in the likes of things like Things Organized Neatly, a tumblr devoted to what could be called OCD tendencies, and the rise of very persnickety and particular people. It causes a rise in the kind of people who make histrionic threats over a mistake they themselves made. It frankly causes people to become autistic and have to be managed as such.

And when people reach that state, when they have been molded and oversocialized so severely by the technocapitalist system to be responding to so many pressures, many of which contradict themselves, they'll find nirvana in the smallest things and seek to impose that sense of meaningful orderliness back on the world. Repeating numbers feel great. Everything in its proper place feels good. It's just as it should be. It's just as they promised it would be.

Corporations are well aware of this. They aren't judgmental in the way I am and they don't have the nerdy-pants critique of society I do about it, they just see it as the way things are that will help them sell Product. They see the direction people are moving in from the inertia of this capitalist system, built upon over a century of conditioning now, and just nudge it ever so slightly in their favor. People like repeating numbers? Instead of 14.99 make it 14.88. Nice, soothing repeating numbers. Nothing ugly like 14.87. *BLEH.* What psycho in their right mind would buy Product for the ugly price of 14.87? No. 14.88 is beautiful. Look at the shape of those 8s, the way they repeat. Perfection.

I would expect more of this in the future as corporations examine more of the micro reasons that set people at ease. They're well-aware that people in this day and age are being completely wound up and no longer feel any sense of mental security. They now sell weighted blankets for the masses (one I admittedly own myself) and increasingly orient places to be more accommodating for those on the spectrum. It's a perverted order they may have helped to engineer and can now exploit and profit off of. They are responding to the changes that are happening in our society, our desperate need to feel secure and find some meaning in this world, and there to provide just a taste of it but not too much for us.

It's not personal, it's just for profit. Here, we slashed the price of the new Sonic game to 14.88. Enjoy.

Matrix Dolezal and the Simulation

Race Borz, September 2019

*This post is an expanded adaptation of my notes
for the Poz Button episode on* The Matrix.

The Matrix was a watershed movie in a watershed year. 1999. Seriously, go look at what came out that year. I have done 8 Poz Buttons on films from that year: The Matrix, American Beauty, Fight Club, Eyes Wide Shut (2-parter), Office Space, 8mm, Breakfast of Champions. I could easily do 8 more from that year alone. I often come back to 1999 as we've frequently said that the 90s were the decade where history was put on pause and 1999 was the year that people tried to make sense of that weird decade and everything that came before it because there was this hope and promise of what 2000, the new millennium, was going to bring.

As we can now see, it was the highwater mark and everything has just been receding sense as we get pulled into the undertow. I often am astounded by the prescience of the film as it remains formless enough to be enduring but memorable. *There is no Matrix,* as it were. It's only what you're willing to see and what you're willing to bend it toward that makes it what it is. That is what you get though when you take the religion, new age, and philosophy section of a Barnes and Noble bookstore and attempt to throw it all into one movie.

Baudrillard was famously ambivalent about the original Matrix film, seeing it as a general misunderstanding of his works. It's actually quite easy to sympathize with him on this point as once you begin to understand what Baudrillard means by simulacrums and simulations and hyperreality, it begins to become more apparent why a flashy action film about being inside an actual computer simulation because you're a human "battery" probably wasn't going to get quite across the notion of how images become copies divorced from their originals. In order to rectify this problem he was offered a hand in helping to shape the sequels. He, likely wisely, declined this offer.

It might be helpful to try and explain a little bit more of Baudrillard's philosophy, more than I usually have in the past. We can't talk about this movie without mentioning Baudrillard and you can't mention Baudrillard without talking about his ideas. *Simulation and Simulacrum* is the book that Neo uses early on in the film, before he has become awakened to what the Matrix actually is, to conceal the disks he keeps when he is committing his heinous computer crimes, as 90s hackers are wont to do. When Neo opens the book, the chapter facing the hollowed out other side is the final chapter of the book, "On Nihilism." I see what you did there, Wachowskis. Quite the way to close out the 90s.

Morpheus quotes the phrase "desert of the real" from it. "Desert of the Real" is from the early pages of *Simulation and Simulacrum* where Baudrillard is comparing the world to a Borges story about a very realistic map, as his preface to what is called the Third Order of Simulacra. But at the very least I will pull some quotes for you so you can get a taste for the way Baudrillard writes and why people often struggle with him without constant review and re-grounding in his ideas to make sense of what he is saying here:

> *Today abstraction is no longer that of the map, the double, the mirror, or the concept. Simulation is no longer that of a territory, a referential being, or a substance. It is the generation by models of a real without origin or reality: a hyperreal. The territory no longer precedes the map, nor does it survive it. It is nevertheless the map that precedes the territory—* ***precession of simulacra****—that engenders the territory, and if one must return to the fable, today it is the territory whose shreds slowly rot across the extent of the map. It is the real, and not the map, whose vestiges persist*

*here and there in the deserts that are no longer those of the Empire, but
ours. **The desert of the real itself.***

The Borges story in reference here, by the way, is "On Exactitude in
Science" (Translation updated by Nikos Salingaros):

*... In that empire, the art of Cartography reached such perfection that the
map of a single province occupied the whole of a city, and the map of th
empire took up an entire province. With time, those exaggerated maps no
longer satisfied, and the Colleges of Cartographers came up with a map of
the empire that had the size of the empire itself, and coincided with it point
by point. Less addicted to the study of Cartography, succeeding generations
understood that this extended map was useless, and without compassion,
they abandoned it to the inclemencies of the sun and of the winters. In the
deserts of the west, there remain tattered fragments of the map, inhabited
by animals and beggars; in the whole country there are no other relics of
the geographical disciplines.*

That's not an excerpt by the way. That's the whole story.

Baudrillard is drawing on this story to illustrate his notions because
this tension in the relationship between map and territory is illustrative
of the problem that occurs when people begin to mentally inhabit abstract
systems. In Borges' story, you have men who have given themselves over
to great, glorious projects to map the plains of their own existence that
their descendants find no use for and give it over for the animals and
beggars to live in. But it's a real problem, these issues of modeling, that
led Alfred Korzybski to remark "a map is not the territory."

Yes, this is exactly where Houellebecq got his 2010 book title from. I
don't just randomly pick things that are interesting to me. These things
are "one holistic system of systems, one vast and immane, interwoven,
interacting, multivariate, multinational dominion of"...well, it's a lot of
things.

But this remark of "a map is not the territory" has become one of those
philosophical points of fascination for people inclined to think of the

systems of complexity we're developing, especially with regard to the technological system and even more so to the information and media technological system. McLuhan drew upon this notion for his ideas of the medium being the message, not the actual content that it's delivering. Before Baudrillard came around, Korbynski and others were very concerned that the attempt to model reality could cause people to become confused and accept the map (abstract model) with the territory (concrete reality). Baudrillard building on McLuhan but especially of Guy Debord's Society of the Spectacle (a post all its own), is very much concerned with how the map and the territory blend together because of the way experiences and sensations can be simulated in ways to create an experience more real than real. That is, the map would just simply be far more preferable to live on. Those real falls just don't look as good as they look on the map.

Ultimately, Baudrillard rejects this example of Borges' map, "*[b]ecause it is with this same imperialism that present-day simulators attempt to make the real, all of the real, coincide with their models of simulation.*" What is real has been rendered into an abominable desert, and we've wandered so far off the beaten path that we've become unmoored in the seas of sand with no sense of direction, chasing only mirages that are copies of images that may only be a product of our delirium. If I am not being clear, what I mean to say is the complexity of our society has become so vast and we have become so divorced from any sense of reality through the technological lives we live that we can't even distinguish what was the original in this society of endlessly copied images. Was there even such a thing? We are lost in simulations of sensations and feelings. All we have are simulacra.

Simulacra, for those who aren't a bunch of gay dorks who read postmodern French philosophy, are copies of a thing that have lost its original or never had one. The First Order of Simulacra was bourgeois fashion in the Renaissance period to the Industrial Revolution. Because you had people who were now economically mobile, they could try to counterfeit their role in society with the signs and symbols of the nobility, in order to emancipate themselves from their bourgeois duties and elevate the appearance of their social rank. They wished to simulate being within that aristocratic milieu, that they may even one day become that. Fake it until you make it, counterfeit it until…okay I don't have a rhyme for this. At best they can only feign or falsify it and can often easily be found out. This leads to the intrigue and the ostentatious upper class cultures of this time period in order to mask a basic reality, but as I said, these things are detectable. The fashion decadence that emerged in 18th century Europe, but especially in France, speaks to this need to remain always the original, unable to be counterfeited lest the copy bankrupt themselves.

The Second Order of Simulacra we get from the 19th century. This is the simulacra that came with the revolution of factory technology and mass production. The simulacra, instead of trying to copy something with a higher social status, are now just repeating and recreating the same thing over and over again with only a serial number for differentiation. Sameness becomes the order of the day. The aristocracy continue their decay to the triumph of the bourgeoisie, as one no longer needs social rank to obtain power but simply money. Unlike the first order the signs here aren't counterfeits such as in fashion, but being a product of mass production it is indifferent to all of the other signs. This is where Marxist ideas and ideology and use value and the commercial law of value take root. The Secord Order of Simulacra gives birth to *homo economicus*.

The Third Order of Simulacra, which is where we are, is the technocapital and media saturation order of things. We often talk about this in the context of the media and its hyperreal images, but technology plays a large role in this beyond just making the movies look so good. You've got tampering with genetics, cybernetics, the proliferation and bombardment of information technology worming its way into every nook and cranny of culture and society. The rise of science fiction literature is the response and contextualization of all of that. Baudrillard refers to Ballard's novel *Crash*, where there is neither fiction nor reality any more (it's a novel about people who are sexually aroused by car crashes)—hyperreality abolishes both. And that is what is meant by the "desert of the real." Our relationship with media and technology have abolished the real and have rendered it a desert of itself. The map we have of what a sane society looks like, the one in our heads, is now completely disjointed from this desert of reality we have to now reside in.

When I was preparing my notes on all of this, I realized I was beginning to wander off the reservation of the Matrix. For all of its interesting philosophical ideas the first film plays with, it doesn't really scratch the surface of what Baudrillard is talking about other than we are moving toward simulation and that ultimately may result in living in a computer simulation but man fighting machine who imprisons man in the simulation against his will is certainly not what Baudrillard meant. That's fine. It's largely a movie that serves as one part teenage power fantasy and one part baby's first Allegory of the Cave, and I will appreciate it for that on those merits. But while typing these notes, I began to wonder what the future of our simulation looks like and a single name popped into my head: *Rachel Dolezal*

I've been recovering from a long term illness so maybe I was just having a fever dream when I had this notion, but whenever Trump is brought up as helping to usher in the postmodern, hyperreal presidency I think people are missing the book end that is Rachel Dolezal. She was unmasked in June 2015, the same month Trump descended the escalator and announced he was running for president.

I don't believe meaningful events like these are coincidental. This is our future being set in stone.

Rachel was what everyone needed her to be, right up until the moment one person pointed at her and made everyone see the African Queen has no clothes.

Everyone can hate Rachel Dolezal all they want, but they do so only because her real crime was that the truth about her simulated race came out, and so the socially agreed upon response was that she needed to be the sacrificial goat for hyperreality. Everyone would have been quite content to just go on pretending. She was doing good work for the NAACP, people loved her, and though they may have suspected that something was wrong, she was a beloved simulation of a hard-working and passionate black woman committed to social justice. That she had been a pretty white girl, a girl who probably would not have stood out in 1930s German propaganda, completes the picture of what the hyperreal society of 21st Century America is meant to become.

While they try to get more whites to embrace playing with non-white avatars in video games and identify with non-white characters on movie screens, a veritable stepping into their shoes in the visceral medieas, Rachel Dolezal was ahead of the curve. Why wait with these 1.0. Simulations of black heroism when you can become the black hero, the ultimate expectation of this society with its drive toward creating a mixed-race future for the sake of world peace and the end of the various oppressive isms—you can impress that girl who is going to accuse you of rape later if you call it the kyriarchy. This is present in the way people talk, that one day in the future racism won't matter because everyone will be mixed and that we are one race, the human race. But getting there won't be done with just breeding. It'll be done with gene manipulation, simulation, and other technologies. The Third Order of Simulacra. To find their place in such a society people will simulate being more mixed than they are or a different race entirely for the sake of the social power required to move through such a society. It's the only one way one would even be able to cope with a future where the preference is for people to be as mixed and diverse as possible and whether you just came from a happy white home or one where your parents are antiracist activists, as technology improves the temptation will always be there to *just make yourself black.*

Certainly this was a fear that Jordan Peele tapped into with his masterful horror film about white folks stealing the bodies of black folks because "black is in" in his debut film *Get Out.*

Rachel Dolezal was a pioneer, and her career martyred for it as the truth of what she represents in this hyperreal state is a level of reality that these people simply aren't ready for even though this is the world they've created for us. Like the people of the Matrix, she became a bit too cognizant of the Matrix and had to be dealt with.

For those of us who are attempting to just keep our wits in this desert of the real that has been laid out for us, it's an extremely daunting challenge. And we ain't seen nothin' yet. We are in the early stages of it all, we are Howard Carter in that hot Egyptian desert just starting the excavation of Tutankhamun's Tomb, hearing Lord Canavron call out to us:

"Can you see anything?"
"Yes, wonderful things."

You may live to see man-made horrors worse than Rachel Dolezal beyond your comprehension.

To end back around to where we started, I come back to *Simulation and Simulacrum*'s final paragraph, "On Nihilism," from which Neo conceals all of his dirtiest little secrets in this persona that has been crafted for him of Thomas Anderson, the doubting son of man (this on-the-nose symbology!):

> *There is no longer a stage, not even the minimal illusion that makes events capable of adopting the force of reality—no more stage either of mental or political solidarity: what do Chile, Biafra, the boat people, Bologna, or Poland matter? All of that comes to be annihilated on the television screen. We are in the era of events without consequences (and of theories without consequences)...*

This is where seduction begins.

What Brit Slouches Towards Bethlehem to Be Born

Race Borz, September 2019

The following post is a largely unedited version of a post I made on Salo Forum in response to a news article that revealed the FBI had documents on Lord Mountbatten's lust for boys.

The more the secrets of the British Empire come spilling out the more I begin to wonder if the British looked admiringly toward the model of the Ottoman Empire and wished to emulate it. This was my initial thought in typing what I thought was going to be a brief but nice effort post. Instead here's this sprawling insanity. I no longer think they wanted to be the Ottoman Empire but to surpass it in ways that we could never imagine in our darkest of imaginations. This whole effort has left me broken and shattered and you can trace the actual decline in my mental state through the entire post. I will never be okay again.

Enjoy.

The relationship between the British and Ottomans is interesting. You see an extremely love-hate relationship between Britain and the so-called "orient" which in this context are the territories that at that time constituted the Ottoman Empire. It's an extremely complex situation of wanting to be like them, to destroy them, to emulate them, to supplant them among some segments of British society. The Ottomans capitulated to the British more than any other European power except the Dutch whom they tied with (three times). The British sided with the Turks in the Crimean War. Lord Palmerston considered the Ottomans an essential counterbalance. One could of course just look at this as perfidious Albion, knowing how to play the long game in order to grab those juicy possessions once the inevitable fall and dissolution of the Ottomans came (and they played that well), but one cannot help but wonder how much an admiring spirit of Orientalism the British aristocracy had for the Ottomans, their decadence, and their access to young boys.

Take Lord Byron, whom we can call an early Orientalist or a proto-Orientalist. Mad, bad, and dangerous to know. We know for certain that he was bisexual and a possible pederast (his relationship with Nicolo Giraud is debated but Jerome Christiansen in *Lord Byron's Strength* seems to make some implication about his relationship with boys), and there are rumors of an incestuous relationship with his half-sister, but I raised an eyebrow when I found out that he may have been advanced upon by his mother's suitor when he was sixteen. As an Orientalist, Byron referred to himself as such and dressed the part and painted. He had been interested in the Ottomans, Persians, and Sufi Islam as a child. He was self-aware however of the Western sentimentality that went into it all when he commented on the success of his Turkish Tales. Byron's proclivity for homosexual and pederastic acts intermingled with his Orientalism, making him the godfather of all of this in my view. Louis Compton is the source for much of this, and he claims that Byron was eager to go on his Grand Tour for these purposes. At the very least, his time in Constantinople is known to have been spent seeing the dancing boys several times. As we know, Lord Byron lost his life fighting for the Greeks in their war for independence. I wondered about this in the context of Orientalism but then discovered that in 1809, Byron visited Ali Pasha of Ioannina during his Grand Tour that led him to Constantinople. Byron had extremely mixed feelings about this Oriental Despot who also managed to cause problems for the Ottoman Empire, a man who also had his own harem of men and women and whom it is rumored Byron had a sexual relationship with. This is pure speculation on my part but I wonder if Byron saw Ali Pasha as an older version of himself. The disposition seems eerily similar.

Ali Pasha was suspected of being power hungry and he was supposed to be deposed. He forged an anti-Ottoman alliance of various Greek and Albanian groups. Ali Pasha's rebellion in part helped feed the fire of the Greek uprising against the Ottomans. Despite the failures of his rebellion, Ali Pasha went down fighting, refusing to surrender until he was shot and beheaded in 1822. Upon hearing of his death months later, Byron mutely remarked "*a brave man but an infamous tyrant*" The conclusion Drummond Bone drew from this in *The Cambridge Companion to Byron* was in reading Byron's quote "*the Asiatics are not qualified to be republicans, but they have the liberty of demolishing despots, which is the next thing to it,*" sees a tenuous figure in Ali Pasha as better than the Ottomans. I can't help but think Byron had Ali Pasha on his brain when he was fighting for the Greeks. Perhaps Byron engaged in the most ostentatious lovers' quarrel fitting someone of his disposition, or saw the need to one-up the man he saw much of himself in.

Call it the Orientalist's Dilemma, and one that seems to plague certain echelons of British society. What Byron represents shockingly seems to play out over and over again throughout history. Britain was the site of one of the largest Orientalist artistic movements in Europe in the 19th century. John Frederick Lewis practically idolized Ottoman Egypt.

Nicholas Tromans writes in *The Lure of the East, British Orientalist Painting* on Lewis that his paintings depict:

> [T]he harem as a place of almost English domesticity,...[where]... women's fully clothed respectability suggests a moral healthiness to go with their natural good looks.

And one, of course, cannot forget Richard Burton, possibly the greatest orientalist of the 19th century and from whom Europe learned much about the Islamic world. Burton's sexuality was long-shrouded in rumor. In addition to rumors of general homosexuality, English society was scandalized by Burton's fixation of the sexual practices of what they called the Orient, calling the Arabs "A Race of Born Pederasts." There is apparently some fluidity to this term at the time, pederast, as in French it is just a synonym for homosexuality. Just really goes to show how it's assumed that if you're homosexual then you're into young men and boys. I call it extracurricular homosexuality. But this is neither here nor there. It's been well-known this problem in that part of the world with pederasty and an Englishman engaging in a bit of cultural flexing over another land is nothing new. What is interesting, and perhaps peculiar you might say, is just how much Burton lingers on this and how he did. Burton translated 1001 and Nights in a subscribers-only edition. Burton's version was not meant for wide release. It was not meant to be seen by the average person. It was published *for* the Kama Shastra Society, a secret book club that Burton founded to get around the Obscene Publications Act. The name Kama Shastra refers to the Indian tradition of works on sexual desire (same root as Kama Sutra, which Burton also translated). If you try searching around for information about the Kama Shastra Society, you'll find next to nothing.

Maybe it really was just a porno book mail order list.

But then when you look into another group, an ostensibly more serious publicly academic group, that Burton founded, you begin to wonder if it really was just a porno book subscription service. Burton founded the Anthropological Society of London in 1863 as a breakaway from the Ethnological Society of London. The two would merge back together 8 years later but what I find so intriguing here is the political make-up of the ASL. The ESL was overwhelmingly Liberal. The ASL was overwhelmingly *Conservative*, if Wikipedia is to be believed. They cite George Stocking's *Victorian Anthropology* for this. They also cite *Foreign Bodies: Oceania and the Science of Race 1750-1940*, which credits the split coming down to, among some things, the ESL's acceptance of Darwinian theories which makes sense that the Conservatives would be against that at the time. I'm taking this detour down to the Anthropological Society and away from the Kama Shastra Society momentarily because in doing my research I came across something about Burton's ASL that wasn't cited in the Wiki and doesn't appear to be in many books.

According to Matt Cook in *London and the Culture of Homosexuality, 1885-1914*, Burton's Anthropological Society of London had a sub-group called the Cannibal Club (of which he was a member):

The Cannibal Club—a sexually libertarian but reactionary sub-group of the Anthropological Society of London—wrote, collected, and translated a range of erotic literature. Members categorised sex and collated sexual experience rather as the soexologists did. They showed little reticence in describing extremes of sexual behaviour, and whilst Ellis felt a political imperative to normalise, deviance was their stock-in-trade.

I cannot stress how difficult it is to find information about the Cannibal Club, understandable given its secret society nature. *Sex, Time and Place: Queer Histories of London, c.1850 to the Present* says this of it:

A body such as the Cannibal Club...was a members-only purlieu of elite males. Lisa Sigel has characterized the members' interests as combining 'imperialism, sadism, and sexism'...Like the Anthropological Society, the Cannibal Club was an all-male group whose focus on male-male desire largely centered on the overlapping issues of homoeroticism, homosociality, and homosexuality. It provided an excellent opportunity for its members to investigate several forms of homosocial relational bonds, falling along a sexual spectrum that ranged from hetero- to homosexuality, including flagellation and masochism.

I cannot stress how skeptical I am of some of the speculations that are made by these people who have investigated the Cannibal Club as it easily falls under the hermeneutics of gay suspicion. I cannot stress how little I trust a name like Lisa Sigel. But this stuff isn't coming out of thin air and we *know* Burton was interested in this stuff and we *know* that the Cannibal Club functioned just like the Kama Shastra Society, engaging in the publication of pornographic materials to an elite group of people to pass around hush-hush.

Which brings us back to Kama Shastra. Burton translated the Kama Sutra for it. He translated 1001 Nights with a 14000 word essay, originally titled "Pederasty," now called "The Terminal Essay." (Incidentally, the Arab world has historically preferred poetry over prose and has never had a high regard for 1001 Nights. Orientalist Europeans are way more obsessed with it and its sexual aspects. I have no evidence for this at this time, but I suspect that the 1001 Nights, as a holistic work, is more Western construction based on Arabic folk tales that has been built upon over centuries. Take from that what you will.) This essay has long dogged Burton's reputation and legacy because of his frank discussion of homosexuality and pederasty in it. If you read the work, it doesn't make a distinction between the two as some people in the modern age have tried to do. I've pulled some choice quotes from it. No doubt I misrepresented Burton:

> *Before entering into topographical details concerning pederasty, which I hold to be geographical and climatic, not racial, I must offer a few considerations of its cause and origin. We must not forget that the love of boys has its noble, sentimental side. The Platonists and pupils of the Academy, followed by the Sufis or Moslem Gnostics, held such affection, pure as ardent, to be the beau ideal which united in man's soul the creature with the Creator.*

Burton consistently couches his frank discussion and interest in this subject under the veil that "but the Ancient Greeks did it too and you read them." I would argue Burton's obsession with writing about pederasty, finding it every culture, making sure the English elite are aware of it, intellectually defending the practice, starting secret societies to publish works about this that aren't for the eyes of the general public, seems to be a bit of vested interest. But what do I know? This is only the guy who translated the Perfumed Garden, an Arabic-language sexual manual whose final chapter is about pederasty. Burton never completed the final chapter in the first publication and withheld it, but was working on a re-release *with* the final chapter when he died. His wife burned it. Go figure.

Burton's interest in this is so thorough that in that 14000 words Pederasty essay, and remember this is supposed to be a translated collection of Arabic tales, that he posts a place called the Sotadic Zone where pederasty is prevalent and celebrated and he basically centers it on the Mediterranean Zone largely in North Africa and the Middle East,

India, China and the Far East, AND the New World. Basically everywhere that Anglos wanted to conquer. This creates a chicken-egg question I wish had never popped into my head. Did these Anglos conquer the world to get to what was already an abundance of catamites or did the Anglos invade the world in order to create the market of catamites by projecting their fantasies of endless pederasty onto everyone else? I hesitate to answer this.

I will note, coincidentally, that the American writer Williams S. Burroughs was very deep into Anglo roots himself, had some perverse affinity for Orientalism, a pederast himself who lived in the home of a man who procured boys and men for Americans and Englishmen, wrote luridly of pederasty, in a place called the Interzone which was basically Tangier, part of Burton's Sotadic Zone. Take from that what you will.

I've written so much on Burton, so much more than I intended to do on this essay on British Orientalism and its relation to decadent homosexuality but I'll try to wrap him up and move onto others. In addition to these secretly published works, in *Abeokuta and the Camaroons Mountains (1863)* Burton himself writes of African men:

> The Abeokutan, when taken at his best, is tall and well made, 'black, but comely.' When not so, he is hideously chimpanzee-like. The male figure here, as all the world over, is notably superior amongst the lower mammals, to that of the female. The latter is a system of soft, curved, and rounded lines, graceful, but meaningless and monotonous. The former far excels it in variety of form and in nobility of make, in strength of bone and in suppleness of muscle and sinew. In these lands, where all figures are semi-nude, the exeeding difference between the sexes strikes the eye at once. There will be a score of fine male figures to one female, and there she is, as everywhere else, as inferior as is the Venus de' Medici to the Apollo Belvedere.

Look, I'm hesitant to make implication noises because I despise how perverted our dialogue has become from the hermeneutics of gay suspicion, but I've already shown you a large body of evidence and that large body of evidence indicates that Burton had an interest in large bodies of blacks. And others, such as Rudi Bleys in *The Geography of Perversion*, have noted just how much Burton lingers on near homoerotic descriptions. I have nothing else to say about Burton himself but I will note some things about Burton's coterie and members of Burton's Cannibal Club:

- Edward Sellon, officer in India, writer of pornography. He was obsessed with having sex with dark-skinned prostitutes, had sex with his pupils when he was a school teacher, enjoyed "a good romp with children" in his autobiography (I checked the passage in question and he talks of preying on a 12 year old girl), and did the illustrations for homosexual James Campbell Reddie's gay porn novel "Adventures of a School Boy." I can find very little information about this work but according to the link the work includes flagellation so he did gay BDSM art for what sounds like a novel about violent pederasty. Awesome. We're off to a great start here.

- James Campbell Reddie, the homosexual who wrote the gay BDSM that Sellon illustrated. The Wiki relates a story of how Reddie's landlord seduced a 15-year old boy with Reddie's help. Possible writer of the gay porno "The Sins of the Cities of the Plain" which has the line "the pederastic game pays so well, and is quite as enjoyable."

- Richard Monckton Milnes, 1st Baron Houghton, a Conservative male feminist who crossed the bench to the Whigs to side with Lord Palmerstone, the man who considered the Ottomans an essential counterbalance and was an extreme hardliner on fighting the Crimean War wherein the British sided with the Ottomans against the Russians. Milnes also had the largest collection of pornography in Britain and possibly authored the Rodiad. Wikipedia implies it's just simply a poem about erotic flagellation, but it's actually about the joy one gets from whipping young boys on the ass. So more pederasty. Oh! And he was also one of Algernon Swinburne's earliest champions who is going to round out this rogue's gallery.

- Frederick Hankey, military man and connoisseur of pornography. Some interesting facts about Hankey. He was born in Corfu, Greece in 1823 when it was under the British protectorate and was apparently half-Ionian himself (his mother's name Catterina Varlamo, which to me sounds like the Venetian minority but who knows) and the son of colonial administrator Sir Frederick Hankey. Coincidentally (and I'm not being sarcastic this is a funny coincidence), Lord Byron arrived in the Ionian Islands the same year. Hankey shared the same taste for the sadomasochistic erotica as his friends. Hankey spent much of his life in Paris, dying there as well, so much so that he was encountered by the literary duo the Goncourt brothers who had this to say about him (quoting from the weblog Grumpy Old Bookman):

> [A] madman, a monster, one of those men who live on the edge of the abyss.' Through him, they wrote, they had a glimpse of 'a terrible side to a wealthy blase aristocracy—the English aristocracy—who bring ferocious cruelty to love and whose licentiousness can only be aroused by the woman's sufferings.

The personage of Frederick Hankey really stuck with the Goncourts. They'd met Hankey when both brothers were still alive and had written about them in their journal starting in 1862. They had suspected that Hankey had had an influence on Gustave Flaubert (a French Orientalist and sex tourist who had also engaged in pederasty) and they continued making occasional references to him up to the point that Edmond included Hankey as a character in his novel *La Faustin* that he wrote 12 years after his brother's death and 20 years after they first met Hankey. The character, George Selwyn, was a composite of Hankey, Swinburne, and historical politician George Selwyn (whom BBC History called " *a necrophiliac, gay transvestite*") and is explicitly called sadistic by Goncourt. Driving home just how much of a insane rabbit hole this has become, *La Faustin* was pederast Oscar Wilde's inspiration for Sibyl Vane in *Dorian Gray* as Wilde knew Edmond Goncourt (also note the reference to Swinburne in that link). The novel *La Faustin* has a scene where the Hankey composite George Selwyn points out two homosexual cocks in a yard. Oscar Wilde loved it.

- And that whole Grumpy Old Bookman post is well-worth reading in all honesty as he catalogs the complete monster Frederick Hankey was (and remember, this guy is *friendly* with most of these other guys): in addition to just being a general porn fiend Hankey took two girls for him and his friend to have sex with at a public execution, wished to own books bound in human flesh, told Richard Milnes (yes that one) he wanted to see a girl hanged and wanted the skin of her backside tanned so he could bind a copy of Marquis de Sade's *Justine* in it, was promised by Richard Burton (YES THAT ONE) that he'd get him the skin of a black woman, was admired by Algernon Swinburne for his pornography collection (he was quite enthused to meet him), and went to a brothel to flag 13 year old girls. The hits just keep coming.

- Henry Spencer Ashbee, the person I've mentioned the least but is from whom we've received a lot of this information as he was the pornographic bibliographer and man of letters that help tie all of these men and their deeds together. Despite (or unsurprisingly?) being a pornographer he grew more conservative as he aged. His wife was Jewish suffragette and his son was a Jewish homosexual socialist. After dealing with a monster like Hankey, Ashbee's main sins appear to be being a pornographer with horrendous friends and having a conservative's typical control over his family life. Unless, of course, Ashbee *is* the long-rumored author of *My Secret Life*, a purported sexual memoir of a Victorian gentleman. I'm not going to link to the only copy I could find as it's vile. The first chapter recounts his first sexual encounter as a child with a nursemaid with the rest of work appearing to include depictions of pederasty and seemingly every fetish this person could think of judging by the table of contents. Even if Ashbee wrote it, some scholars are skeptical it's even a non-fictional work (I saw one suggest parody) which just gets into the whole problem of trying to pretend the thing you actually want to do is just an ironic thing you're doing. I'm absolutely astounded at the depths of depravity in this project I started.

- Charles Duncan Cameron, a soldier and British consul who apparently has no record of sexual debauchery. I only note him because we are talking about very prominent, powerful, and connected men. Cameron was in the same society as all of these men I'm laying out and had served with distinction in the Crimean War, receiving medals from the Turks for his service.

- Simeon Solomon, a severely Jewish severely homosexual pre-Raphaelite painter. Arrested twice for sexual solicitations at public urinals in two different countries. Also associated with British Orientalism. Unsurprisingly he was also a pederast. Solomon's watercolor *Bacchus* depicts the wine god as a barely clothed teen, lesbianism in *Sappho and Erinna in a Garden at Mytilene,* trying to provoke his viewers into a game of gay chicken with the androgynous *Sleepers and One That Waketh.*

- And finally, Algernon Charles Swinburne. How to separate the fact from fiction. Swinburne is hard to figure out because of his propensity for seeding ridiculous lies and rumors about himself, something his frenemy Oscar Wilde was happy to dismiss one and all. That he was a homosexual was certain to Kingsley Amis. Swinburne was the spiritual catamite in this whole equation. Swinburne went to brothels for flogging after his experience of being flogged as a schoolboy (the recurring theme) and Swinburne's life and works brims with pederastic energy. His pornographic education came under the wing of Milnes who introduced him to Marquis de Sade (only to be disappointed that de Sade is less titillating and more extremely dull), he was smitten with Richard Burton, and he requested Simeon Solomon to illustrate his sadomasochistic poetry. Hard to tell if he engaged in pederasty because of his love of disgusting lies about himself, but I'm going with probably. Curiously, Swinburne was anti-Turkish.

All of that, all of that right there was King of the Orient Richard Burton and his BFFs. Utter insanity.

After this motley crew we can talk about T.E. Lawrence. I hesitate to even do so. I've been working on this for hours and Lawrence is honestly worthy of his own thread. What is there to say about T.E. Lawrence that hasn't already been said and covered? He played his role as a stooge for British Orientalism undermining the Ottomans by coordinating the Arab Revolt. The revolt, of course, didn't have the results Lawrence and his Arab allies were hoping for thanks to Perfidious Albion's secret Sykes-Picot agreement and the public Balfour Declaration pretty much guaranteeing that the Arabs would only see shaft after shaft. That work was in since the 19th century though.

Again, because ALL of this is tied together in the duality of British Orientalism, it is important to note that the same Lord Palmerston who was extremely incessant in propping up the Ottoman Empire as a counterbalance also wanted the Ottomans to let the Jews settle Palestine. This occurred in 1840, when in the middle of the Egyptian-Ottoman War, the Ottoman navy all defected to Muhammad Ali, leaving the Ottoman Empire in a state of total collapse. Europe intervened to cobble the Ottomans back together. Muhammad Ali had already occupied Palestine seven years previously in the last war, now the Ottomans having effectively collapsed meant that those lands would soon be up for grabs and the French were licking their chops. It was time for Britain to do its thing and make all of these forces converge and Lord "Respect Ottomans" Palmerston began to tack more pro-Zionist due to the insistence on his son-in-law, Lord Shaftesbury whose Christian Zionism was a precursor to America Zioboomerism. The level at which Zionism's history is British is frankly ridiculous. Looking at the timeline of Zionism and how various British people are vastly overrepresented in getting the Jews to move to Ottoman Palestine and for the Ottomans to let them. Behind every Jew is an Anglo, I suppose. The man whom Lord Palmerston succeeded as Prime Minister, Aberdeen, I should note, was a co-founder of the Palestine Association, one of the first organizations to agitate for a Jewish homeland in Palestine.

These are the currents that T.E. Lawrence was working against. I can't help but feel the most for Lawrence out of all of these characters. Lawrence seems to be the only one who isn't completely infused with a miasma of despicability that is impossible to peel off. I believe Lawrence truly did care for his Arab allies and their aspirations. But with that said we do need to talk about some things. Because as much as Lawrence was more genuine than all of the rest, he is still a British Orientalist and all of these recurring themes begin to recur here as well. Lawrence was a masochist, and flagellation once again returns, a vice so prevalent among the English that the French term *vice anglais* denotes gay flogging. One of the most famous episodes of Lawrence's career, his rape at Deraa by Turks, has been proven to be fake and likely the product of a lurid fantasy. Lawrence was warm with an Arab boy named Dahoum to the point it weirded the other Arabs out though his companion Leonard Woolley stresses that Lawrence was puritanical and chaste in this regard. Richard Aldington, the first man to really do damage to Lawrence's reputation with an iconoclastic biography, called Lawrence "*an impudent pederast*" but other than the Dahoum episode Lawrence's sexuality has been a large topic of debate because it does seem like you have on the one hand very real desires he has that he expresses in fantasy but on the other hand kept a firm puritanical hand on it outside of the flogging. However Lawrence did write this peculiar passage in *The Seven Pillars of Wisdom:*

> The Arab was by nature continent; and the use of universal marriage had
> nearly abolished irregular courses in his tribes. The public women of the
> rare settlements we encountered in our months of wandering would have
> been nothing to our numbers, even had their raddled meat been palatable

to a man of healthy parts. In horror of such sordid commerce our youths begin indifferently to slake one another's few needs in their own clean bodies—a cold convenience that, by comparison, seemed sexless and even pure. Later, some began to justify this sterile process, and swore that friends quivering together in the yielding sand with intimate hot limbs in supreme embrace, found there hidden in the darkness a sensual co-efficient of the mental passion which was welding our souls and spirits in one flaming effort. Several, thirsting to punish appetites they could not wholly prevent, took a savage pride in degrading the body, and offered themselves fiercely in any habit which promised physical pain or filth.

Take that for what you will in the wild and wacky world of British Orientalism.

I've already written 5000 words on this topic and it really feels like I've probably only scratched the surface on all of this. One should mention Aleister Crowley though, as a peculiar case of when the Orientalist focuses way more on sex and magic like a gluttonous nerd. *Mr. Crowley, what went on in your head?* Possible father of Barbara Bush, aggressively bisexual power bottom, hedonistic and irresponsible occultist who thought L. Ron Hubbard and Jack Parsons were the dangerous shitheads for trying to create a magical unborn child called the Moonchild, and borderline retarded fed and intelligence agent for the British government. So the dude is already hooked up with powerful people and has all of these connections, now I just need to rattle off the Orientalism and pederasty.

The man wanted to be Richard Burton. Need I say more?

Crowley spent two years in Algeria (once again, part of the Sotadic Zone of his idol Richard Burton) doing magic and having gay sex. I don't feel I need to add to that. Crowley so thoroughly idolized Burton that he did an over-the-top defense of sodomy and pederasty modeled on everything Burton wrote. Crowley then spent some time in Tunisia doing magic and having pederastic sex. I don't feel I need to add that. *Oh, Mr. Crowley, did you talk with the dead? Your lifestyle to me seems so tragic.* Crowley built upon the British Orientalist's lurid and pornographic fascinations with the perceived foreign sexuality and mysticism that had tantalized the men of his caste for the last 100 years and simply took it to the next level. It ultimately reached its apotheosis in that Tunisian desert with a British aristocrat engaging in magical, mystical pederasty with a boy named Muhammad.

So I guess now I should talk about Mountbatten.

British Orientalism would appear to have sputtered and died given the way men like Mountbatten mismanaged the rest of the empire, but it's been a roaring success. It is no longer policy but an assumed reality. Everything else is now superfluous. No entities need exist when the whole world now bends towards one destiny: a brown English speaking world of sodomites and pederasts who have been put here on earth to protect the Inner Jerusalem of the Jews and to build their own Outer Jerusalem. If I continued to look I could pile on more evidence but look at all this. Look about you! Everything has perfectly converged to this point, built step-by-step by the British Orientalists, the British Christian Zionists, and the intersection of imperial pederasty that runs through all of it.

So when I see this thread about Mountbatten and his own proclivities it really does just complete the picture. The last Viceroy of India, the final centurion of the Orientalists. Why wouldn't Mountbatten have had a predilection for young men? Why wouldn't he be content for his wife to have relations with brown men? Why wouldn't he squander the last of the possessions? The mission is done. The British boarding school system, its clergy, and its aristocracy inculcated for centuries the various spirits of pederasty, Zionism, and Orientalism, looking ever back toward the East for the destiny that was rightly theirs. That spirit drove them first west to the New World until the Americans rebelled and cut off the westward path to the East. Instead they had no choice but to play the long game until they could take and conquer was rightfully theirs at the center of the world as they spread the Anglo Imperium to every corner of the Earth, seeking every people and every part that would finally complete them. Do I sound insane to you?

Return to Blake. He is England's poet and he spoke in prophecies. His works were called the prophetic books:

And was Jerusalem builded here, Among these dark Satanic Mills?
                                        — "And did those feet in ancient time"

Spectre of Albion! warlike Fiend! In clouds of blood & ruin roll'd:
I here reclaim thee as my own
My Selfhood! Satan!
armd in gold.
                                        — *Jerusalem: The Emanation of the Giant Albion*

His poems were the Anglo Revelation. You needed only listen.

This is an Anglo world and we're all its brown rentboys.

τετέλεσται

The Wickedest Empire in the World

Race Borz, September 2019

The following post is a continuation of "What Brit Slouches Towards Bethlehem" as it was a response to Nic on Salo Forum who stated this:

"British Zionism needs a deeper dive as well. The Christian Zionism of certain elites combined with the fanatical Puritanism of such sects as The Plymouth Brethren, from which came Aleister Crowley. Their intermarriage with actual Jews during the Victorian Era solidified this alliance."

There were so many little threads I wanted to start pulling that I had to leave alone because I was already spiraling into madness but I am certain the intersection of pederastic British Orientalism and Christian Zionism goes deeper than we can even contemplate.

It didn't even occur to me to tug on the Aleister Crowley thread a bit more and saw what spilled out as I was so eager to get the post done and crack some jokes about Turbo-Sodomite Nerd Crowley. As Nic notes, Crowley's parents belonged to the Plymouth Brethren. The Wiki doesn't mention anything about Zionism or Israel but it's actually not hard to find if you dig about. One of the founders of The Plymouth Brethren was John Darby, the godfather of Dispensationalist theology, which for you good Catholic and Orthodox boys who can't keep up with Protestant shenanigans, this is the theology of our ardent Israel Firsters like Pat Robertson and John Hagee that you see on TV. It is from which the most ardent of our Christian Zionists in America emerged and had its highwater mark was in the 00's with the *Left Behind* series. John Darby also popularized the Scofield Bible, the source of so many of our theological problems inside the American Imperium with our relationship toward the Jews and Israel.

According to Nur Masalha in *The Bible and Zionism*:

Darby was at first a Church of England clergyman and later main founder of the Plymouth Brethren movement. Darby who believed that the church was hopelessly corrupt and authoritarian, founded what would become a widespread prophetic omvement, and insisted that these **dispensations** *were irreversible, speculating that the Church would soon be replaced on earth by a revived national Israel (Sizer 2004).*

Incidentally, one member of the Dispensationalist Plymouth Brethren was Robert Anderson, one of the investigators of the Jack the Ripper case. One of the *strongest candidates* for the identity of Jack the Ripper was Aaron Kosminski, a Polish Jew. Quote Wikipedia:

Anderson claimed that the Ripper had been identified by the "only person who had ever had a good view of the murderer," but that no prosecution was possible because both the witness and the culprit were Jews, and Jews were not willing to offer testimony against fellow Jews. Swanson's notes state that "Kosminski" was identified at "the Seaside Home," which was the Police Convalescent Home in Brighton. Some authors express scepticism that this identification ever happened, while others use it as evidence for their theories. For example, Donald Rumbelow thought the story unlikely, but fellow Ripper authors Martin Fido and Paul Begg thought there was another witness, perhaps Israel Schwartz, Joseph Lawende, or a policeman. In his memorandum, however, Macnaghten stated that "no-one ever saw the Whitechapel murderer," which directly contradicts Anderson's and Swanson's recollection. Sir Henry Smith, Acting Commissioner of the City of London Police at the time of the murders, scathingly dismissed Anderson's claim that Jews would not testify against one another in his own memoirs written later in the same year, calling it a "reckless accusation" against Jews. Edmund Reid, the initial inspector in charge of the investigation,

also challenged Anderson's opinion. There is no record of Aaron Kosminski
in any surviving official police documents except Macnaghten's memo.

Anderson's handling of the Jack the Ripper case comes under occasional
scrutiny and criticism. I won't speculate what exactly happened here, but
that he was from the extremely philosemitic Dispensationalist side of
Christianity and even preached *with* John Darby is a funny coincidence I
find supremely interesting. That it is only from Anderson that we get this
story that the only witness to one of the murders was another Jew and a
Jew would not testify against another Jew is something I find *very*
interesting (though in Anderson's defense I'll note that he apparently took
the idea of Kosminski being a suspect seriously). Take from that what you
will.

While the Plymouth Brethren themselves did not appear to be active
in any kind of Christian Zionist, on the level that other societies were at
the time, they laid a fertile and intellectual groundwork for other to
follow into the 20th century. John Darby died when Aleister Crowley
was only seven and there is no evidence to suggest that the two ever
crossed paths but the spirit of Darby's theology pervaded Crowley's being
and his beliefs. Crowley rebelled against his parents' Plymouth Brethren
beliefs like a petulant redditor on Sunday morning, but as any lapsed
Catholic can tell you this stuff rests heavy on your bones and will *always*
manifest in new and perverse ways the more you try to run from what
you are.

Jason Louv in *John Dee and the Empire of Angels* draws a very clear line
causality to Crowley's magical beliefs:

Rapture *is not a word that occurs in the Bible; it is a theological*
elaboration by Darby. Key to this dispensationalist view of biblical events
is that God requires human agents to advance the coming of his kingdom,
and that what is required of these agents depends on which dispensational
period of history, or "aion," is currently in effect, with the world now
entering the final aion, the Apocalypse. This rapture theology, which
gained brief popularity in the United Kingdom, soon became the guiding

religious myth of American, from the common people to the very halls of power, and is one of the primary reasons for ongoing American support of the state of Israel. As will be discussed in book III, another particularly keen student of Darby's premillennialism was the occultist Aleister Crowley, who was raised in Darby's Exclusive Brethren group in England, later applied Darby's teachings on dispensations or aions of spiritual development to Dee and Kelly's angelic magic, and who consciously identified himself with the Antichrist as a necessary component of God's dispensation to humanity during the final days.

This is not the time to delve once again into Crowley's personal depravity but Louv does talk about an episode with Leah Hirsig that really shows Crowley's depravity is bottomless. More intriguingly in Louv's book, he actually draws a spiritual line from the occultist John Dee *to* John Darby (which then of course gives us Crowley), which just shows how deep and interconnected the spiritual currents of occultism, orientalism, pederasty, and Zionism have been in Britain's history. Writing on this Jason Louv states in *John Dee and the Empire of Angels*:

For Christian Zionists, this principle extends beyond individuals to entire empires; indeed, it is widely believed among Christian Zionists that Britain's failure to work toward a full Jewish state, and America's urgent insistence on doing so, is responsible for the collapse of the British Empire and the transfer of global imperial primacy to America. Dee, who argued for a British Empire of Angels, would likely agree were he alive today...These premillennial ideas did not begin in the nineteenth century, however. Just as early stirrings of Jewish Zionism can be found in seventeenth-century Kabbalist and self-proclaimed Jewish messiah Sabbatai Zevi, so can stirrings of Christian Zionism be found in the Cabalist John Dee and the prior occult tradition he exemplified. Indeed, the conversion of the Jews (as well as pagans and Muslims) to Christianity as a preapocalyptic necessity was central to the plans of Dee's angels. More overt calls for Christian Zionism can be found in the decades following Dee's death [in 1608 or 1609], notably in the literal, premillennial, and

131

Cabal-influenced tract **The World's Great Restauration** *[sic] in 1621, which argued that the Jews would return to Palestine in the latter half of the seventeenth century prior to the subsequent Apocalypse.*

As for Crowley himself and his relationship to Zionism, it's difficult to ascertain the extent to which Crowley thought about it or engaged it. While Crowley definitely acted as an agent for the British in *some* capacity during his lifetime (the extent of which can be raucously debated), more than anything it seems Crowley's appetites always came first and foremost. An interesting thing about that just occurred to me though, while sexual degeneracy and depravity is one of the classic ways to blackmail and compromise an enemy agent the fact that Crowley was so depraved he was proud of the things he did creates a type of intelligence agent that may be more difficult to undermine. But that's neither here nor there. This is what I was able to find about Crowley and Zionism.

Crowley arrived in New York City in October 2014, two months after the outbreak of the First World War in Europe, aboard the RMS Lusitania of all ships. The Lusitania sank six months later. Take from that what you will.

In keeping with the theme of all of these intersections, in addition to possibly engaging in borderline retarded false-flagging to try and get the Americans into the war by acting over the top pro-German, Crowley was spending his time doing sex magic and picking up men in a Turkish bathhouse. He kept a diary of this time period, from which I found one reference to Zionism in Churton's *Aleister Crowley in America*:

In Europe, the overturning of the dynasties has usually been the signal for an outburst of every kind of art. Here, however, there is in a sense nothing to overturn. People drift from Methodism to Zionism through Theosophy, Christian Science, and Nut-foodism, without a single wavelet over their mental gunwale. If you tell a man that black is white, he gets thoughts, and says: 'Yes, stranger, I guess that is so.'

One other interesting tidbits from this time when you search for references to Jews in this book. Crowley was supportive of Leo Frank, the lynched Jew with a habit of preying on teenage girls: *"Crowley anticipated judicial opinion today by calling Frank a "harmless Jew.""*

Crowley, I imagine, sensed a fellow traveler.

Operating during the First World War, there was also NILI, a Zionist spy ring that had taken an important step of change in Zionist policy by siding with the British against the Ottomans in the war. The Jews in Palestine during the war had an extremely tenuous and ambivalent position as Zionism was still quite young and uncertain of itself, comprising Jews from all over Europe and its own small indigenous Jewish community, and everyone who lived there were subjects to the Ottomans. Undermining the empire you live under is a risky endeavor when you don't know what the future holds and many were not eager to throw in with the British NILI did, and in the long-run paid off for them as undercurrents of philosemitism and Zionism in the British Empire were coming to fruition.

So why am I now talking about NILI?

The book that really kickstarted the debate on Crowley's role as an agent for the British government more than anything else was *Secret Agent 666* by Richard Spence. For context on Crowley's alleged First World War subterfuge which I've only alluded to, this is essentially what Crowley is alleged to have done. Crowley got involved in the pro-German movement in America and was employed by German spy George Viereck for his pro-German paper *The Fatherland* whose policy was the very popular policy of neutrality. Among the things Crowley did was compare the Kaiser to Jesus Christ and declare independence for Ireland at the Statue of Liberty. Crowley's stunts during his time at The Fatherland either indicate Crowley was a genuine retarded sperg or a British agent pretending to be a retarded sperg to undermine the isolationists and those sympathetic to the Germans. My time in the Alt-Right prevents me from being certain on which one is more plausible.

In addition to this skulduggery Richard Spence makes some explosive allegations in *Agent 666*. By early 1917 it was pretty obvious the current had shifted to America entering into the First World War. Readership for The Fatherland collapsed, though Crowley continued to collaborate with Viereck when he could. Months earlier Crowley left New York City for New Orleans. Concurrently this was what was going on and I'll try to condense the events that Spence lays out to the best of my ability:

A 2 February note in Crowley's Record is significant. It reads, 'My 2 1/4 years' work crowned with success; U.S.A. breaks off relations with Germany." He was a little prescient; Washington formally severed relations with Berlin the next day..Crowley made this notation to himself and his gods...Barely a week later, with no explanation, Crowley bolted from New Orleans and headed east to tiny Titusville to Florida's Atlantic coast. Here lived his cousin, Lawrence Bishop [a citrus farmer and evangelical Christian], who hosted Crowley until the end of March...On 28 March, Crowley received a letter from Frater Fiat Pax a.k.a. George Macnie Cowie, financial trustee of the OTO lodge in London. Whatever the letter contained enraged and/or frightened the Beast and resulted in a break with Cowie. As the war progressed, recalled Crowley, Cowie became "violently anti-German" and started to "intrigue against me"...This crisis and what soon transpired at the London OTO lodge at 93 Regent Street must be related. One morning, Scotland Yard detectives raided the premises, guns drawn. Inside, according to the amused Mage, were "a dozen mild old people trying to browse the lush grass of my poetry"...Officially, the incident had nothing to do with Crowley...Crowley later admitted that the whole purpose of the raid was to "help me consolidate [restore?] my position with the Germans by heating the branding irons of infamy for me in the fire of publicity." It is also an excellent way to get back at Cowie and other perceived traitors. The Beast also alleged that [Everard] Feilding helped choreograph the London stunt. At first glance, this seems doubtful. Feilding was in Cairo working with the Arab Bureau as liaison to Naval Intelligence and EMSIB, and thus hardly situated to arrange police raids in London. In the Cairo post, however, Feilding worked closely with the NILI spy ring of Zionist Jews working for Britain against the Turks. The NILI group had political allies and financial connections to the same Zionist circles in New

York that were closely working with [William] Wiseman and Section V.
Thus Crowley and Feilding had a confidential means to stay in touch.
Feilding's invention in the London flap removed any need for direct
communication between Crowley and persons there. In any case, the ploy
seems to have worked. Viereck and others were reassured…of Crowley's
pariah status among the British. In July 1917, Viereck even named
Crowley editor-in-chief of his monthly International.

The Feilding that is referenced here is Everard Feilding. In addition to being an alleged friend and colleague of Crowley, what is certain about Feilding is that he was a British Orientalist, a researcher of parapsychology who married a medium, worked in British intelligence during World War I in Egypt and Palestine, and was familiar with T.E. Lawrence as he's referenced in *Seven Pillars of Wisdom*. That part indicates almost nothing but Feilding was with Lawrence's rival Mark Sykes of the Sykes-Picot Agreement (and an orientalist converted to the cause of Zionism) during Sykes' last visit to Aleppo to organize the Armenian relief until he went to Paris to assist in the peace negotiations where he died from the flu pandemic. Feilding took over for Sykes.

The William Wiseman referenced was head of British intelligence operations in the United States and was even more connected to the Zionists than Crowley's friend Feilding was. Wiseman's operations in the United States were a bit more professional than whatever it was it seemed Crowley was trying to do. One of the most curious operations that Wiseman was engaged in the USA was tamping down on Indian nationalism. Not American Indian nationalism, the feather people, but Indian subcontinent nationalism, the dot people. In the United States. The demographics I see from this time period indicate that the Indian population in the USA was something like 2500 people. But it was apparently part of a larger forgotten operation of history called the Hindu-German conspiracy where the Germans tried to help Indians and their diaspora engage in a worldwide struggle against the British and the Anglo world. Wiseman's role was to expose this conspiracy after British and American relations had become strained due to persistent American reticence to get involved in Britain's battles. Wild stuff.

Wiseman's main role in this was to tip the New York police off to a bomb plot by an Indian who seems to be named Chandra K. Chakravarty. This alleged incident is *extremely* difficult to research. There's scant information on it. Very curious when Americans are taught about stuff like the Zimmerman Telegram. I am extremely skeptical of the reality of an actual bomb plot. Contrary to popular belief the sinking of the Lusitania did not get the US into the war. It was a three year process to erode American neutrality and perception of the Germans through a combination of the Germans own policies and subterfuge and the way the British helped grease those skids. In addition to his role on monitoring Indian sedition, Wiseman was also a liaison to the British government for President Woodrow Wilson, who was well-aware of what Wiseman was doing and was close with Julius Klein, a Jewish spy. Wiseman was close enough to Wilson that Douglas Reed quotes him briefly in Controversy of Zion in a discussion of Woodrow Wilson.

Wiseman joined the investment bank of Kuhn, Loeb, and Co. after the war. The name gives away its obvious Jewish origin, but if the name isn't familiar to you the bank was run by Jacob Shiff, the Jew who bankrolled many of the Zionist endeavors and helped overthrow the Tsar in Russia by bankrolling many of anti-Tsar factions (it is claimed that Schiff aligned with the active Freemason Kerensky of the Socialist Revolutionary Party, not the Bolsheviks, which is apparently a very important distinction). Schiff is a matter all his own that's worthy of study, but at this point I don't think anyone is surprised that Wiseman joined Schiff's bank after the war (a year after Schiff died). Little seems to be known of what Wiseman did other than banking after the war. Perhaps he had it made for all his work he did for the British and Zionists. Oh wait he visited the Roosevelt Administration's state department literally two weeks after World War II in Europe started, as reported in *Desperate Deception*. And his activities continued. William Wiseman was also part of a secretive group called "the room" that included Wild Bill Donovan (future head of the OSS) and recruited corporate agents to engage in covert operations as the Second World War was brewing in

Europe.

These are the people who are just the slightest degree of separation from Aleister Crowley. Or vice versa. And the evidence that Crowley was friendly with Feilding and worked with him seems strong to me.

Other things Crowley said about the Jews according to Spence:

"Israel has corrupted the whole world, whether by conquest, by conversion or by conspiracy." In 1922 he proposed a convenient means for Jews to regain their true will and destiny—the adoption of Thelema as the foundation of a new Israel.

In the next paragraph Wiseman comes back into the picture with this quote:

Closer to Crowley, New York's Section V received and circulated many reports describing the insidious collusion of Jewish revolutionaries and bankers. In March 1917, for instance, Wiseman himself cabled to London that Trotsky was about to sail for Russia backed by "Jewish funds...behind which are possibly German." Later dispatches from Russia, including Maugham's, described "Jewish socialists" as the main tools of German intrigue in Russia, financed by Jewish financiers such as Max Warburg.

I haven't dug too deep into later Crowley, when he got fatter and stupider, and I'm sure I'm missing some real gems there. I'll probably need to read the entire Spence book. I do know that Crowley sounded off on the Spanish Civil War however. The famous 1937 publication, "Authors Take Sides," is an intriguing artifact on where the loyalties of the British literati and other assorted commonwealth subjects lay. The first thing that sticks out is the overwhelming consensus that the British should support the Republican cause. The whole paper is worth reading because of how hilariously awful and cold many of the pro-Republic takes are (and how the retarded hysterical way liberals and leftists talk of fascism has never changed). The picture continues to get clearer when you look at many of these pro-Republican names and realize just how many of them were homosexual. Many of these names in this list were among the Bright Young Things, the in-crowd of London, who were written about by journalists like Tom Driberg who is going to be talked about in this post. One of them in his pro-Republican list, for instance, is Edward Sackville-West, the rumored lover of future Prime Minister Anthony Eden, whom is outed as homosexual by the article that started this thread. Both of them were Bright young things.

Aleister Crowley is among the numerous pro-Republican voices in the questionnaire. His response is well-worth reprinting:

DO WHAT THOU WILT shall be the whole of the Law.
Franco is a common murderer and pirate: should swing in chains at Execution Dock.
Mussolini, the secret assassin, possibly worse.
Hitler may prove a "prophet"; time will judge.
Love is the law, love under will.

It really begs you to ask "what did he mean by this?"

After the overwhelming pro-Republican support you come to the woke centrists who gave their Neutral opinions. A couple of names stand out that really leads one to speculate that they probably supported the Nationalists more than they let on but had to maintain their social connections. Among them are T.S. Eliot who felt it wasn't germaine for writers and artists to weigh on the lives and politics of another people and nation and Ezra Pound, who said much the same thing but used it as an opportunity to attack the sort of moronic dandies inclined to fill out their pro-Republican opinions on a questionnaire. Surprisingly the notorious lesbian Vita Sackville-West also staked out the neutral position while H.G. Wells went with "tfw too intelligent."

Only five had the courage to say they supported the Nationalist cause in Spain. Edmund Blunden, Arthur Machen, Geoffrey Moss, Eleanor Smith, and Evelyn Waugh. With Waugh they got their token homosexual slot filled. An arguably notable absence from this questionnaire is Roy Campbell, a poet from South Africa who was friends with T.S. Eliot and had even been on friendly terms at one point with the Bloomsbury literary circle. It might not have been necessary to ask. Campbell was notoriously pro-Franco, likely the most out of any British writer in history. What Campbell had on effetes and homosexuals whose lifestyles he detested was that he'd lived in Spain and had witnessed the Red Terror first hand. Unfortunately for Campbell, a poet whose works are largely forgotten and discarded, his life had a tendency to be comically tragic. He'd failed his entrance exams and picked up a booze habit that would stay with him his whole life, he was cucked by the alpha dyke of the Bloombury circle as his wife was having a lesbian affair with Vita Sackville-West, was successfully sued by a neighbor for damage done by his goat, fled to Spain because he couldn't pay, witnessed the Red Terror in Spain, became a war correspondent for the Nationalists and almost immediately twisted his hip, fell again in WWII and damaged his hip more, lost his home in the bombings, and finally died in Portugal when his wife crashed the car she was driving. Campbell's brash and earnest opinions about the homosexuals and Marxists that comprised the cultural power-brokers of British society and his courage to support Franco forever expatriated him and blacklisted his reputation.

Campbell's hatred for these people and their ideas and lifestyles was personal as he had more exposure to this than anyone else. That Campbell had been cucked by a lesbian is unsurprising given that his wife was one of the infamous Garman sisters. Her brother Douglas was a Marxist who was pro-Republican on the questionnaire (another comic tragedy that Campbell was absent but his communist brother-in-law was represented) and his wife had an affair with the Jewish socialite Peggy Guggenheim. Her sister Kathleen married the sculptor Jacob Epstein after being his extramarital mistress and would ALSO have an affair with her brother Douglas' wife. When Kathleen died she donated everything to the Israel Museum. Her sister Lorna, married when she was 16, had an affair with the writer Laurie Lee who fathered one of their children. Laurie Lee then married Lorna and Mary's niece Kathy. Lorna would then go on to have an affair with painter Lucian Freud, the grandson of Sigmund Freud, after which Lucian would marry another one of Lorna and Mary's nieces, this time Kitty who was the daughter of Kathleen and Jacob Epstein. One can only imagine the insane levels of Judaism, communism, and homosexuality (and these things are related) Campbell was dealing with in his wife's family.

I only mention Roy Campbell, a man who was always on the outs, to contrast him with Aleister Crowley who despite his wickedness always seemed to be on the ins. Campbell settled into Portugal at the end of his life, the homeland of a poet he most admired Fernando Pessoa. Pessoa is a connection between the two men and how I re-enter Crowley into this story. Pessoa himself was deeply interested in the occult, striking up a friendship and correspondence with Crowley. Pessoa was involved in one of the more peculiar episodes in Crowley's life: a faked suicide in Portugal in 1830. Even Spence is somewhat at a loss in explaining this episode other than as a stunt to dodge his creditors and increase the value of his books. It failed. Roy Campbell wrote of this incident in his own brash and braggadocious way. Campbell had always been following in Pessoa's footsteps unawares: in addition to their sad love lives, literary melancholy, and alcoholism, Pessoa and Campbell had gone to the same high school in Durban High School. He found Pessoa's poetry too late to meet the man he'd come to idolize, and when he learned of Pessoa's episode with Crowley, Campbell's hatred of Crowley and the type of pederastic British literati lifestyle he despised came exploding out, as described in *The Presence of Pessoa*:

> He walked straight into his own booby-trap in his adventures with the *fatuous imposter, Aleister Crowley, the diabolist, dogmatic immoralist, sadist, and black-magic expert: and if I had not (in complete ignorance of Pessoa's dealings with this idiotic monster) shortened the latter's stay in Portugal, in my role of epater de bohemiens, by planting a pair of explosive banderillas in his enormous posterior on the cliffs at Cascais, so that he beat an ignominious retreat home to England where he had to lie doggo for fear of ridicule, and to sleep face-downward for weeks—God only knows to what lengths of credulous self-mystification Pessoa might not have gone!*

But Roy Campbell is forgotten and Aleister Crowley's legend lives as large as his frame.

Crowley's peculiar echo of possible Esoteric Hitlerism in his 1937 answer to the Spanish Civil War questionnaire has some possible context. After the Portugal episode in 1930, Crowley spent some time in Germany. In 1931 he was knocking around Berlin when the National Socialists saw their best election result to date. He started up a violent relationship with Bertha Busch, apparently a communist. The relationship was so tumultuous that Crowley got beat up by brownshirts after they spotted him slapping around a German woman. While in Berlin, Crowley met up the pederast who inspired Cabaret, Christopher Isherwood and gave lodging to Chris' fellow homosexual and communist informant Gerald Hamilton. Gerry, being the chatty queen he was, was informing on his own red friends to the Germans according to Spence.

There is a mysterious figure that Spence enters into this picture. Louis Gibarti. Information on him appears to be little known. His real name was apparently Laszlo Dobos, and he was a Hungarian Comintern agent who turned FBI informant later in life, according to *American Prometheus: The Triumph and Tragedy of J. Robert Oppenheimer*. Dobos turned during faction warfare in Moscow after feeling betrayed when Stalin changed over to the NKVD instead of the Comintern. Before he turned fed, Spence alleges that Dobos/Gibarti was the agent who groomed the infamous Kim Philby of the Cambridge Five for service. The connection between Crowley and Gibarti lies in Willi Munzenberg's front group League Against Imperialism. This organization allegedly has its roots in the League for Small and Subject Nationalities which was founded in New York City in 1917, the same time Crowley was there. The full of chain of connections seem unclear when you try to dig into the LSSN's connections to Crowley and its connections to the League for Oppressed People, which replaced it but was claimed to have *no* connection with the previous league, but there does seem to be smoke of some kind that leads to Chicherin, a homosexual and one of the five chairs of the first congress of the Comintern. If we accept all the claims, it put Crowley into the same sphere as the Kim Philby and the Cambridge Five.

Crowley left Germany in 1932 after it was claimed by Richard Spence that Crowley had been compromised by a faction of German intelligence that opposed Hitler's faction. Crowley spent some time settling his affairs and rehabilitating his reputation to the best of his ability, but it was in 1933 that the fascination with Hitler seemed to begin. Six months after Hitler became chancellor, Crowley told the Sunday Dispatch, *"Before Hitler was, I am."* The paper in question was owned by Lord Rothermere, a sympathizer to fascism and National Socialism. Very intriguing, the editor of the paper was Charles Eades, who became *Lord Mountbatten's* press liaison and public relations man during WWII. Crowley disparaged Hitler a couple of weeks later as a "mad dog." Previously in 1930 Crowley had made overtures to both Hitler and Stalin, sending a copy of the Book of the Law to the former (no response) and trying to get to the latter through Walter Duranty, the reporter who would cover up the famine situation in the Soviet Union while winning a Pulitzer Prize.

By 1936 and 1937, when Crowley answered the questionnaire with the notion that Hitler may be a prophet, it began to make more sense where this fixation comes from. The magnetic charisma of Hitler and the various people in his circles who were interested in the occult had amplified the air of mystique that Hitler had (something that Esoteric Hitlerists would build off of in subsequent decades). Crowley began to believe that he was manifesting some sense of his will over Hitler. When the German OTO was banned in 1937, Crowley concluded that Hitler was engaging in black magic. *Conversations With Hitler/Hitler Speaks* by Hermann Rauschning, a German conservative revolutionary who defected is a disregarded and apocryphal work that was a bestseller in the Anglo world in 1940, full of purported conversations with Hitler that worked well for war propaganda and not much else. Rauschning, as fitting his role of a conservative backstabbing someone to his right, is the source from whom we get the most lurid mythologies of Nazi occultism. When Crowley read this, he took it as proof that he had influence over Hitler. Prior to this when the war was becoming clearly inevitable, Crowley had told his anti-semitic and pro-Nazi friend Martha Kuntzel that Jews were better than Germans and that they would genocide the Hun just to upset her. Taken altogether, it seems clear now that the peculiar message Crowley wrote during the Spanish Civil War was right during that he was most ambivalent towards Hitler and the National Socialists, seeing them quite possible of incredible occultist magic but uncertain what path they would take (the "correct path" being listening to Aleister Crowley), especially since they weren't fascists with allegiances to the Roman Catholic Church like Franco and Mussolini were.

Crowley does not appear to have any involvement in the Spanish Civil War. There is however an allegation that has been made by the Guardian and a book called *Writers, Lovers, Soldiers, Spies* that needs to be addressed. What is true is that Franco was flown out of the Canary Islands by British Intelligence. What is not true is that Hugh Pollard, one of the men involved, was a friend of Aleister Crowley. I can find no evidence at all for this and Pollard does not fit the profile for a friend of Crowley. Pollard was a brash military man and a devout Roman Catholic, not the type of man that Crowley was likely to be friendly with. One could speculate they were friends through intelligence, but not even Spence mentions Pollard at all in his work.

After all of this I decided to see if there were any connections between Mountbatten and Aleister Crowley. *I found one.* I already noted the working relationship with Charles Eades. Crowley and Mountbatten also had somewhat of a mutual friend in Tom Driberg. Driberg himself was a member of the communist party and a homosexual who married a Jew. Driberg had been turned to a Soviet agent as a result of being compromised in a KGB sting when he tried to solicit gay sex. Driberg had bonded with Burgess of the Cambridge Five over their shared homosexuality, and it's already been established that Crowley had proximity to the Cambridge Five. Driberg and Maxwell Knight, a member of MI5, also shared an affinity for Aleister Crowley (again, according to Spence), and Knight used Driberg as a double agent to keep tabs on some communists.

Supposedly Driberg impressed Mountbatten enough to be given an unofficial advisory position in Burma, but even before the FBI files confirmed Mountbatten's pederasty, there was speculation that Driberg and Mountbatten had a shared predilection, according to *Prince Philip* by Philip Eade.. That a Supreme Allied Commander was a pederast and quite possibly in a sexual relationship with a Soviet spy and double agent who admired Aleister Crowley and was friends with him, that there were likely pedophiles in his circles of friends, that the allegations that Robin Bryans, a friend of Evan Tredegar whom was close to Aleister Crowley, made that "Lord Mountbatten, Blunt, and others were involved in an old-boy network which held gay orgies in country houses and castles on both sides of the Irish border, as well as at the Kincora Boys' Home" seem the most plausible reality of all, that both Crowley and Mountbatten owned copies of "My Secret Life" (the vile piece of Victorian pornography I mentioned in the last post that was likely the product of the Cannibal Club), that his wife Edwina Ashley was a quarter Jewish, that Mountbatten and his butt-buddy Eden oversaw the embarrassment of the Suez Crisis, that Mountbatten himself was the picture of the Oriental that Edward Said argued Westerners had created and imposed on others, that all of this was going on while Mountbatten was mismanaging the end of the empire and having sex with boy, truly does go to show how everything in the history of the British empire—its Christian Zionism, philosemitism, occultism, Orientalism, pederasty—just feels like it was all meant to converge into a single point at the end of it all.

There is no bottom to this hell we reside in other than Mountbottom.

40/F/Looking Down the Barrel of a (Wine/Pill) Bottle

Race Borz, September 2019

Like any good dilemma, the one I'm in is one of my own doing. I have over ten drafts of posts (or just mere ideas of posts) sitting in my queue, and never really sure which one I should try to complete. I stand in the middle of my own blog like would-be roadkill standing in the light that conveniently goes to them instead of them to it. But on the thought of the cute creatures of God's paved earth I was recently thinking of one of their dilemmas, the hedgehog's dilemma, which leads me to the fable's author, Arthur Schopenhauer.

European thinkers after the Enlightenment were perplexed with question after question that they attempted—and frequently failed—to solve, but two stand out the most in the way they've shaped the last two hundred years. The first is the more well-known Jewish Question, the second is the lesser known Woman Question. Some of you, I imagine, are surprised that this is a real thing and not just a meme. If you look at the Wikipedia page, you'll discover that the WQ is actually older than the JQ and the idea of woman's liberation and patriarchal oppression has a longer pedigree than most people realize. There's a rich history of scholarship I would love to get into here, but the history of the WQ is a post for a different time. There are two thinkers who stand out in their own thoughts on the WQ, and that's Otto Weininger and the aforementioned Arthur Schopenhauer. Otto Weininger's book, *Sex and Character*, and the man himself, are all worthy of their own post but before him was Arthur Schopenhauer and his essay "On Women."

There is very little you won't find in the Manosphere that wasn't first found in Schopenhauer's essays. Anything the Manosphere developed in its ideas that weren't first found in Schopenhauer's essay can be sorted largely into commentary on technological developments, commentary on the dominance hierarchy among men, and seduction techniques, all of which inevitably spiraling out into a supremely nerdy wilderness of jargon and categorization. It's an interesting essay, but its role as the ur-manifesto for internet misogyny before the first man who screamed the C-word into the electronic aether was a twinkle in his bitch of a mother's eye means there's not much in it you probably haven't heard if you've been marinating in the crimson juices of the redpilled cyberspace for the last ten years. Still, it is worth it just to quote him once since all masters are owed their due. On women and their sense of time, Schopenhauer writes:

Then again we find that young girls in their hearts regard their domestic or other affairs as secondary things, if not as a mere jest. Love, conquests, and all that these include, such as dressing, dancing, and so on, they give their serious attention...This is why women remain children all their lives, for they always see only what is near at hand, cling to the present, take the appearance of a thing for reality, and prefer trifling matters to the most important...The advantages, as well as the disadvantages, that this entails, make woman, in consequence of her weaker reasoning powers, less of a partaker in them. Moreover, she is intellectually short-sighted, for although her intuitive understanding quickly perceives what is near to her, on the other hand her circle of vision is limited and does not embrace anything that is remote; hence everything that is absent or past, or in the future, affects women in a less degree than men.

We see aspects of what Artie's talking about in women's short-sightedness play out time and time again in the realm of the career woman. Every year there's at least one article that comes out that really highlights the trouble career women are in and the Rube Goldberg contraption that society is going to need to set up to make sure all of these women would be able to get the happy ending they hope is waiting for them at the end of it all. The latest one is from Hannah Frishberg, one of the innumerable Millennial dumpster fires of Jewish descent that consistently watched Lena Dunham's fat girl fantasy, *Girls*. And true to form, Frishberg delivered us the latest round of Deep Concern for women in the patriarchy.

"Broke men are hurting American women's marriage prospects," according to the NY Post

There's nothing revolutionary in the article. Women prefer men who make more money than them despite the religion of Progress and Equality that we've all been inculcated with as children. It's a mark of this age that fundamentally lies about everything that what everyone knows has to be learned.

Women won't settle for less and they won't marry down. A man has to make more than them—significantly more—and it certainly matters a great deal what it is they think. It's not the deliberate way the labor market has been constructed, the numerous incentives to get more women into these high status careers (necessitating that there will be fewer of these high-performing men), or economic disparities so stark that gig-hopping is all people have; it's these men not doing their due diligence as men. And now these broke men who haven't manned up have gone and ruined the marriage prospects for these thirty-something women who are finally ready to settle down!

This story has been going on for decades. It's just getting faster and dumber now. That's just how capitalism works ladies, I don't know what to tell you. If, in those sleepless 4am moments, you ever find yourself wondering why things are the way they are, just understand that in capitalism if you can't see who the sucker is it then it's probably you.

It's also interesting seeing articles like this and seeing how much they've entrenched the two flavors of ideologies they'll allow you to have. You can have Neoliberalism With Tactical Libertarian Elements or you can have Neoconservatism With TradCath Paypigs.

The latter is pretty self-explanatory, Neoconservatism does as

Neoconservatism does and with the American public's general Protestantism so degraded and degenerated that it's a controlled, albeit chaotic, state all that remains is to catch anyone hungrier for something more serious and transcendent and real and shepherd them into an ineffectual camp of intellectual thought games while the Neocons use them as front puppets. It has an added bonus of keeping people serious about their faith docile by convincing them they have no actual role to play except to shut up and accept the subversion that's going on within the church (something LeftCaths, who are more adept at playing the power game, have been laying the groundwork to make sure traditionalists are hoisted by their own petard). That's not germane to this post though and, for the third time here, should be a post all its own.

Neoliberalism With Tactical Libertarian elements has been the more recent creation and is intriguing in the way they're appealing to modern women. Women, being how they are, love the power and status process and to be able to have higher stakes than their little circle of friends is something they're deeply inculcating into the modern woman. We mock it by pointing out they're trading spreadsheets for families and babies, but like how internet pornography is engineered to overclock men's brains and short circuit their dopamine receptors and mess with their natural instincts (especially the sexual one) by building a constant need and dependence for escalation, getting women into the workplace is meant to work in the same stimulating way by overclocking women's sublimated need for power and status. Women leaders are often atrociously horrific in their disposition and policies for this reason.

Neoliberalism is thus designed to appeal to the white woman more than anyone else. It has all the right elements for them:

- Neoliberalism prefers a complex level of capitalism that requires a high level of bureaucratic tricks for institutional stability and requires a lot of internal compliance to function. Women are well suited for this.

- Neoliberalism encourages a high level of diversity in order to break up worker solidarity and get footholds into new markets. White women will thus be the biggest beneficiaries of this due to their comparatively higher level of competence than other groups.

- Neoliberalism establishes complex hierarchies to maintain system ideology and promote continued compliance. Through this the ultimate goodies of power and status manifest, which women want.

- Neoliberalism, being capitalistic, comes with a lot of trickery and subterfuge in the realms of competition. Something women are prone to do to their friends.

- Neoliberalism, in order to function in this level of complexity and requirements to always expand, needs to embrace surveillance capitalism. Woman is the natural snoop.

Where Tactical Libertarianism comes in is to patch the cracks that inevitably form in such a system. With the modern white woman winning, it meant the modern white man had to lose. The material world is ultimately a zero sum game. Tactical Libertarianism, to suddenly become libertarian when proposals that would limit the power and reach of private companies and institutions, takes care of both the free speech issue and 'giving aid to white men' problem. The power that business has to control conversation and discourse can't be limited because "*muh private company*" (just ignore all of the subsidies and welfare they get or how they almost never built the infrastructure that all of this is working off—Obama wasn't wrong, *they didn't build that!*). You can't help white men in this system who are very clearly falling behind and have no future prospects because you don't give handouts to losers (unless of course they're the helpless and oppressed brown clients of the system). Plus many of those white men had libertarian ideas themselves once, so it's just desserts, nevermind the fact that libertarianism was always meant to be a trap for white men to be lured to and fall into. That the trap was sprung and that it's now being used against them reveals its true insidious purpose. If you don't understand what I mean by trap, here's a rule of thumb for you: if you're encouraged to believe something out of "principles" to the detriment of your own security, it's a trap.

Modern women largely cannot see this for what it is. They want and need a partner higher status than them because biology fits them with different necessities. They've been left holding the bag by their masters who are well-aware of the implications of having depressed and degraded men at the bottom of the social hierarchy. The high-status male is now an even rarer commodity, one worthy of going to war over and keeping the fighting internal instead of external. And these women cannot see the end that is waiting for them. There will be no men for a significant percentage of my generation, the Millennials, as many Millennial men who realize the raw deal they were given are going to follow their own natural inclinations and compete with Zoomer men for their women instead (if they aren't just checked out entirely, another depressingly common tendency).

I know some who became somewhat cognizant that there was no light at the end of the tunnel for them and have adjusted their expectations in the most depressing ways possible. The rest will not fare too well in the coming alcoholism and pill epidemic that is going to rack up a body count of 40-59 year old women on a level not seen at any other point in human history, except for perhaps the phenomenon of the WWI spinster who lost her sweetheart in the war. The trauma of the First World War has usually been viewed in the lens of the European men who were senselessly grounded into fertilizer for poppies in the great tragedy of the 20th century, or in a Spenglerian view as the downturning of the West, but there was a woman's component to this as well. Two million women were singled out in Britain alone, leaving women in a status of being *"nothing but a piece of wartime wreckage living on ingloriously in a world that doesn't want [them]"* as the writer Vera Brittain put it.

The beginning of the career woman is often erroneously attributed to the results of WWII but it actually had its roots in the trenches of the Western front. You can follow the path of the millions of ghosts that lead these women with no prospects now to have no choice but to take up positions outside of hearth and home. Financial security? Gone. Love? Gone. Children? Gone. From that many women would begin to trailblaze paths for career women and for many firsts, leading to where we are today. It's been a hundred years since that deposition began and the results are calcifying.

Meanwhile for the men, while they will always have more options than women at attracting younger girlfriends (and if they're smart marrying them), the picture on the ground for the youngest boys isn't looking too rosy. Even that advantage of age is not something they may find they'll know how to use. Lisa Britton courted attention with a tweet that read:

> I talk to many parents of young boys who tell me their sons have asked them questions like:
>
> Are boys strong, too?
>
> Do boys have a future?
>
> Can I be powerful?
>
> Can boys be awesome?
>
> Am I bad?
>
> It's obvious we're sending a bad message to boys & I worry they'll grow up resentful.

It really just brings up right back to Arthur Schopenhauer and the hedgehog's dilemma. I'll end this post with a meditation on that. The text of it from *Parerga & Paralipomena* (using porcupine in place of hedgehog) goes like so:

> One cold winter's day, a number of porcupines huddled together quite closely in order through their mutual warmth to prevent themselves from being frozen. But they soon felt the effect of their quills on one another, which made them again move apart. Now when the need for warmth once

more brought them together, the drawback of the quills was repeated so that they were tossed between two evils, until they had discovered the proper distance from which they could best tolerate one another. Thus the need for society which springs from the emptiness and monotony of men's lives, drives them together; but their many unpleasant and repulsive qualities and insufferable drawbacks once more drive them apart. The mean distance which they finally discover, and which enables them to endure being together, is politeness and good manners. Whoever does not keep to this, is told in England to 'keep his distance'. By virtue thereof, it is true that the need for mutual warmth will be only imperfectly satisfied, but, on the other hand, the prick of the quills will not be felt. Yet whoever has a great deal of internal warmth of his own will prefer to keep away from society in order to avoid giving or receiving trouble and annoyance.

Modern society as it is creates a warped tyranny of distance with millions of hedgehogs left out in the cold. There are those who are very fortunate, they had the wits about them to not fritter away all their time with stupid expectations or they were blessed and lucky from the start, finding someone to love and share every prick of the quill together, producing litters of children to cherish. A toast to them.

For the sake of this sick society I hope the ones out in the cold can find that internal warmth, because between the men and women it now produces without any prospect of the future, no society can handle the weight and danger of a million cold hands with their own sharpened knives.

Grim Omens of the Cyber Legion

Race Borz, September 2019

Demonology is a curious thing. After the Enlightenment, the Christian world had little use for demons other than the demons of the past. A curious phenomenon that has occurred is that renewed interest in demonology frequently goes hand-in-hand with the media, and I think it may be the best predictor for belief in it. I couldn't find an exact source on the book and film of *The Exorcist* being a specific cause in its resurgence (some sites I read said that the rise of Charismatic Christianity helped fuel the resurgence), but I simply cannot believe that it wouldn't have played a large role in it. Exorcism was demonstrably on the decline post-Enlightenment, and it was only as mass media technology became more powerful that belief in it began to creep back into the world. The technological phenomenon of hyperreality—that technology and media create a projected reality that is more real than reality—has always been, in my view the gateway of demons.

I'll let you decide if I'm being metaphorical or literal.

The decline in belief in demonology didn't mean it simply faded away into the great nothingness, however. The human mind bends toward the supernatural, and wherever orthodoxy is slain something will fill the vacuum. While the 20th century gave us the televised exorcism, the 19th century gave us Spiritualism. The Boston Brahmin Ralph Waldo Emerson was himself fascinated by these spirits of these times, but brought to it his pseudo-Quaker sensibility and lectured on it in Boston in a talk he titled "Demonology." Despite Emerson representing a spirit of America that would eventually be exhausted—and if you wish to understand the America that ultimately buried itself at Appomattox Courthouse, read *Moby Dick*, for America was once a ship of colored savages following insane Quakers on doomed quests—he was correct in this lecture to be puzzled by dreams.

He first opened this talk by noting this definition of demonology that he was applying:

> *The name Demonology covers dreams, omens, coincidences, luck, sortilege, magic and other experiences which shun rather than court inquiry, and deserve notice chiefly because every man has usually in a lifetime two or three hints in this kind which are specially impressive to him. They also shed light on our structure.*

This covered the Spiritualism that Emerson was meditating on. Emerson saved his greatest astonishment however that we would dream at all because it flies in the face of reason:

> *T is superfluous to think of the dreams of multitudes, the astonishment remains that one should dream; that we should resign so quietly this deifying Reason, and become the theatre of delirious shows, wherein time, space, persons, cities, animals, should dance before us in merry and mad confusion; a delicate creation outdoing the prime and flower of actual Nature, antic comedy alternating with horrid pictures. Sometimes the forgotten companions of childhood reappear.*

For a Unitarian Yankee like Emerson to see the touch of the spiritual in dreams as he does over the course of the essay speaks to the presence that human beings feel for the preternatural and the supernatural in their lives. Dreams are the ultimately the land of the preternatural and the playground of demons. And there is a place on the west coast of America, that transmits its own dreams across the world and where the technology of tomorrow is being built to make those dreams come true.

This is where my thread on demons and technology comes in. Demons are real, but the understanding is incomplete. Before the industrial revolution their warfare was almost entirely spiritual as this was the weakest vector for them to impose themselves upon the world without active summoning.

Things are about to get a little weird, so strap yourselves in.

I promise I'm not *completely* crazy.

Technology is not understood by 99.9% of the people that use it. Yet it is given freely with zero thought to its consequences. This isn't even getting into the issue of how the average person is only given tools of little social consequence compared to the levers of tech. Technology does truly amazing things and we are at the point where we are actually messing around with the molecular level of things. The actual fabric of material reality.

The working title of CERN's FAQ on this stuff was "Surreal FAQ."

It is acknowledged that a lot of weird stuff begins to occur when you get to this level of technology. I will not get into the topic of CERN itself and the beliefs around them. I cite them as the simple acknowledgment that reality becomes insecure at that level of technology. Downscale that to the technology that any regular person is allowed to use. There's nothing to say that reality also doesn't become insecure at the smaller level. Postmodern philosophers have noted perception and experience takes a beating as society moves toward Ellul's Technique. The science of technology's effect on the human body is still nascent. It's just assumed that it's all harmless. People resort to hyperbole from either direction to avoid the discussion of the effects technology has on human biology.

We've known though that it affects our dreams. Over a decade ago a paper came out that saw a connection between black and white TV and the color of people's dreams. Those who grew up primarily with grayscale television had grayscale dreams.

12% dreamed *only* in grayscale.

Dreams have always been one of our connections to the spiritual world, the pathway as it were. I can't think of a single major group of people in humanity or a tradition of some kind that didn't put weight into dreams and their connection to a world beyond us. Such is their power that as the seat of prominence that religion once held in societies became weaker and weaker, the psychology of Freud and Jung had no choice but to address it and the deep resonance dreams have for us. Prophecy especially, but you find as well commands within them and to this day people who put stock in their dreams will often see them as commands. The Old Testament is rife with these stories (fifteen to be precise, with six in the New Testament).

Past the testaments however, and the fulfillment of the Covenant in Christ, dreams become a much trickier thing. Saint John Cassian, from whom the Western monastic tradition owes much, warned in *The Works of John Cassian* of the spiritual power and character of dreams:

> *It is a long business too to tell the story of the deception of that monk of Mesopotamia, who observed an abstinence that could be imitated by but few in that country, which he had practised for many years concealed in his cell,* **and at last was so deceived by revelations and dreams that came from the devil** *that after so many labours and good deeds, in which he had surpassed all those who dwelt in the same parts, he actually relapsed miserably into Judaism and circumcision of the flesh.* **For when the devil by accustoming him to visions through the wish to entice him to believe a falsehood in the end,** *had like a messenger of truth revealed to him for a long while what was perfectly true, at length he showed him Christian folk together with the leaders of our religion and creed; viz. Apostles and Martyrs, in darkness and filth, and foul and disfigured with all squalor, and on the other hand the Jewish people with Moses, the patriarchs and prophets, dancing with all joy and shining with dazzling light; and so persuaded him that if he wanted to share their reward and bliss, he must at once submit to circumcision. And so none of these would have been so miserably deceived, if they had endeavoured to obtain a power of discretion. Thus the mischances and trials of many show how dangerous it is to be without the grace of discretion. (Emphasis mine.)*

Before we go any further into the spiritual realm however, let's talk about the philosophy of technology. Jacques Ellul speaks of a concept called

Technique, which is the totality of methods that are used to achieve the most efficient end. This is how society becomes technological. Technology doesn't shape to humans but humans shape to technology. An object to be shaped. As he writes in *The Technological Society*:

> *This new sociological mass structure and its new criteria of civilization seem both inevitable and undeniable. They are inevitable because they are imposed by technical forces and economic considerations beyond the reach of man. They are not the result of thought, doctrine, discourse, will. They are simply there as a condition of fact. All social reforms,* all social changes, are located wholly within this condition of fact, *unless they are purely utopian. When social change is truly realistic, it accepts this condition buoyantly, vindicates it, and exploits it. Only two possibilities are left to the individual: either he remains what he was, in which case he becomes more and more unadapted, neurotic, and inefficient, loses his possibilities of subsistence, and is at last tossed on the social rubbish heap, whatever his talents may be; or he adapts himself to the new sociological organism, which becomes his world, and he becomes unable to live except in a mass society. (And then he scarcely differs from a cave man.) But to become a mass man entails a tremendous effort of psychic mutation.* **The purpose of the techniques which have man as their object, the so-called human techniques, is to assist him in this mutation, to help him find the quickest way to calm his fears, and reshape his heart and his brain.** *(Bold emphasis mine)*

I point to all of this to make my case that it is acknowledged that technology can have actual effects on the human body and brain, that it shapes people, and that it has the power to affect dreams, the place where Church Fathers have recognized demons can establish dominion. It's an open secret that many in Silicon Valley limit their own children's access to technology that they help develop. Note that it's the educators serving high income children who do not want young children exposed to it.

I find this image to be the most troubling even if it clearly makes the most sense. Being addicted to distracting technology was always meant to be a condition for the lower castes. The brahmin have to keep their wits about them, to be plugged in but not *too* plugged in. Admittedly, part of this discrepancy in how much technology children from different socioeconomic stratum should be using has the element of educators who are deeply concerned about the state of the poor being able to close the gap and catch up. I wouldn't prescribe purely malevolent motives to those who want young poor children to be exposed to technology early and often like they're cackling in a mirror and saying to themselves "I think I'll do *EVIL* today!" No, it is the same as it ever was, with the best intentions leading us down to the deepest pits of hell. And within the pit of hell that is this relationship to technology, you find new studies such as "Phantom vibrations among undergraduates: Prevalence and associated psychological characteristics" in ScienceDirect that show 89% of undergraduates reported "phantom vibrations" and brains can become noisier from the techniques that are used to do smartphone and social media posting, as reported in "The details of past actions on a smartphone touchscreen are reflected by intrinsic sensorimotor dynamics" in *Nature*.

Again, all I am pointing to is that we are shaped by tech. I've so far avoided the obvious talking points of the effects digital pornography have on the brain. It's not anecdotal that digital pornography leads to more fetishes. They are studying it and seeing it creates a greater risk of being into child porn, according to "Is Internet Pornography Causing Sexual Dysfunctions? A Review with Clinical Reports" in NCBI.

"Born this way" is propaganda to avoid having people look into the environmental ways conditions can be induced. No one wants to believe a pedophile can be made by technology. They must all just be born that way or touched by an uncle, right? But technology can shape people. Gay pornography is disproportionately represented in pornography. According to "The Effects of Pornography on Gay, Bisexual, and Queer Men's Body Image: An Experimental Study":

> *Gay male pornography constitutes a disproportionately large share of the pornography industry; it is estimated that 20-30% of pornography produced is gay male pornography, and this pornography creates 30-50%*

of the pornography industry's revenue (Thomas, 2000). Several studies have indicated that gay men consume pornography at a higher frequency than heterosexual men (Duggan & McCreary, 2004; Træen & Daneback, 2013). In addition, gay male pornography is ubiquitous in gay male culture (Thomas, 2000), and some argue that it serves as a form of cultural and sexual validation for gay men (Escoffier, 2003).

And even at being an average of 25% of the industry, it makes up 30-50% of the revenue. Gay men consume porn more than straight men.

Are we to believe this is simply all nature?

Studies into the role pornography plays, such as "Self-perceived effects of Internet pornography use, genital appearance satisfaction, and sexual self-esteem among young Scandinavian adults" reveals that sexuality is influenced by pornography. This is not a matter of "just have a wank," there is evidence that sexual behavior is shaped by digital pornography (SEM here means Sexually Explicit Media):

In 2013, young men reported using SEM more frequently; and as compared to women, they regarded the effects of their SEM use as more positive and uncomplicated (Træen & Štulhofer, 2013). Most of them reported that SEM had motivated them to try out new sexual positions and acts, increased their understanding of their sexual orientation, and made them more aware of what they like to do sexually. A recent study of men who have sex with men (MSM) in Norway, also concluded that the frequent consumption of gay SEM seemed to play a positive role in MSM's sexuality in a similar way (Hald, Smolenski, & Rosser, 2013).

I don't think I need to keep connecting the dots here. Technology shapes human beings. It doesn't just exploit human biology. It has the ability to shape it. It has the capability of altering humanity in many of the places that the mystics and clerics have warned people to guard for. There is obviously no uniform or universal consensus view on demons. I will try to avoid getting into the weeds on this. The common view by 16th century theologians however was that demons were preternatural, not supernatural.

The preternatural occupies that twilight zone between the natural and the supernatural. If the supernatural breaks the natural, then the preternatural simply bends the reality of the natural to its will. This is what I meant earlier about the realm of demons being spiritual. Demonic possession being the most well-known form of the preternatural demon. If you believe in possession, then you believe a preternatural force is imposing its will on a human, shaping their perception of reality and making them mentally ill. The demon shapes the human. Occultists of all stripes view magic as an element of the preternatural. This is why magic is defined by some as a form of bending and shaping reality to your will. The preternatural also pertained to portents, which created a tension the church had to manage and balance.

I joke about technology allowing the interdimensional technodemons, or the Cyber Legion, to take possession of people and steal their soul. But the levels at which humanity is tinkering with the very fabric of reality and the effects that smaller scale technology have on human beings should be considered. In Japanese folklore, the Tsukumogami are tools that have acquired a kami or a spirit. One can imagine technology transcended into having preternatural qualities itself.

Let's mention a few other cultural things going on, however. Drag queen story hour, Billie Eilish (at the time a a seventeen-year-old) singing about seducing your dad in "Bad Girl" and seeming like a demon in the music video for "All The Good Girls Go To Hell."

This is emulation and simulation of demonic behavior.

The accusation can be thrown out every which way that I'm misrepresenting what we see here or that I'm just being the latest in a line of fuddy-duddies who just don't get how expression works, but there is no bottom to this well that the 21st century has fallen into. And it is not as if painted boys and pederasty are some new development in culture. It happens again and again and again and again. If you're going to tell me that you truly believe this is benign and you're not seeing what anyone with eyes see, *I don't believe you.*

I will believe though that you're fine with acquiescing to the new normal.

And the new normal is being created by the effect technology has on reality.

Like television inducing grayscale dreams, all technological media create the phenomena of hyperreality. The very fabric of reality is beginning to tear thanks to technology. One could interpret this at the preternatural world beginning to bleed into the natural. Some of my Catholic friends view it as just demonic possession. Hard to say. There's no consensus on anything like this. What's simply being mirrored and what's guided by some malevolent force is all debatable. But people's reality and biology is being warped by technology. Technology is not inherently demonic. Then again as Clarke said, any form of significantly advanced technology is indistinguishable from magic. By contrast, collapsitarian John Michael Greer, who has taken a catabolic collapse view of society through the lens of Oswald Spengler and Joseph Tainter, has long posited that the technology of today will be, in a sense, the magic runes of a failed tomorrow.

Either way, whatever the future of technology I choose to believe that it can be a vessel by which demons and the preternatural enter the world as it erodes the foundations of our reality.

Go ahead and call me kook. Call me a nut. Call me whatever name you want in the book. But human beings have long understood the veil between worlds isn't as strong as we'd like to think and we are messing with that delicate fabric.

And it's really only just begun.

Goodbye to All That

Race Borz, May 2020

America has never been an easy place to love. For many of us that relationship has been rife with co-dependencies because when you feel there is no there *there*, you quickly learn that for you there is no *anywhere*. You cling to it like a feral child that can't bear to leave his mother's dessicated corpse because there never was any life outside of her even after you were born. Life in the most diverse nation on earth is simply a force majeure. Identify with the hurricane if you can, though you may not like what the whirlwind has to say.

Minneapolis is burning. It's the type of line you'd expect a hipster to write, but the land of big waters is finding a fire that has been lit that's more barbarian hellstorm than it is the warming hearth of Norwegians seeking their Oleanna. It's just as well. The purifying waters of Lake Minnetonka are infested with invasive zebra mussels now. Loring Park may hold a statue to Ole Bull but the old boy never made it as west to the head of the Mississippi in Minneapolis, chasing the dream of utopia that his poor Scandinavian brothers would seek there. His fell short in Pennsylvania. New Norway it was called and the unfinished castle was for the clouds.

The chaos is boring now. It seemed like something, anything, could happen, but it's reality television without the catharsis. If you want to find the fascist in America, look for the ones who are expressionless or even smirking. The outraged still believe they live in a country. They still hold onto a memory that was never theirs and from someone else they borrowed.

So goodbye to all of that, whatever that was we came of age in. What context is there anymore for castaways. There's a few hundred million of them now, floating. But there's still tomorrow and the promise that might bring. The hope it might be different, even if it won't be.

There's always hope in Oleanna though, even if we do have to say goodbye to all that.

Support your wife and kids? Why, the county pays for that, Sir,
You'd slap officials down and out if they should leave you flat, Sir.

And if you've any bastards, you're freed of their support, Sir,
As you can guess since I am spinning verses for your sport, Sir.

I'm off to Oleana, I'm turning from my doorway,
No chains for me, I'll say good-by to slavery in Norway.
Ole—Ole—Ole—oh! Oleana!
Ole—Ole—Ole—oh! Oleana!

Does She Love You?

Race Borz, July 2020

For my wife

*"The world ought **not** to be a harmonious loving place. It ought to be a place of fierce discord and intermittent harmonies: which it is. Love ought **not** to be perfect. It ought to have perfect moments, and wildernesses of thorn bushes. Which it has. A "perfect" relationship ought **not** to be possible. Every relationship should have its absolute limits, its absolute reserves, essential to the singleness of the soul in each person. A truly perfect relationship is one in which each party leaves great tracts unknown in the other party."*

— D.H. Lawrence,
Studies in Classic American Literature

Men with mystic mindsets are a superstitious sort, especially when it comes to women. As they well should. Had we a little more scrutiny toward Eve in Eden or a little more responsibility to God after, we might still be in the garden naming wondrous beasts. We fear that power however, as to name it is to claim it. McCarthy says the same in *Outer Dark*, for to name is it to claim it and if you don't name it then "you cain't talk about it even." Modern men, being gnostics of another notion, can't even name their own relationships with women, and thus cannot claim them.

The name, of course, is love but even to name it means nothing if you do not *know* it. Woman is always the esoteric of the sexes, to love her is to always be initiated in some peculiar and personal mystery cult. Woman gatekeeps the darkness, woman is the goal of a man's nightfall. Home and hearth will always belong to her, when she is still within her nature. Everywhere that clerical man now walks he sees a life out of balance, nature inverted, and blood-consciousness denied.

How does a man love a woman? He just does, in spite of himself. In spite of herself. Call it the eighth sacred mystery.

Men do, women are, is the fundamental premise of man vs. woman. Men are exoteric, women are esoteric. Man is the sun, woman is the moon. And so on and so forth. But for man to even be doing anything he first must *be*, and that for the postmodern man is a nearly impossible challenge. He has to cobble together a personality made out of several damaged fractal selves and then attempt to succeed at anything in a rigged and high-stakes system where the expectations are so out of proportion they should be treated as satire. Man cannot live on bread alone, nor can he live on the *search* for a purpose. He must have one and believe in it. He certainly cannot marry without it either, unless he is a *lumpen* who has embraced the queer energies of total self-destruction.

It's hard enough to fail, but it's worse to fail so hard you lose feeling after ten years of floating through the miasmic haze of modernity. Men after a certain point accept that they probably won't find love. Sex and love are separate things though both wanted at the same time. Sex does not embarrass this age but love does, so no man will name it as to name it is to claim it. You can't talk about it even. *What does it even mean to be loved*, they ask after a certain point. Within just a few years of being exiled into the outer dark of emotion's arctic tundra men will begin writing manifestos born out of their unrealized sensations, or delve so deeply into the mysteries they try to discover quantum complexities in love, women, and sex.

What a stupid miracle that people can even live in a society that breeds these idiot philosophies.

I never got so far as this, despite my own forty years in the desert. I was an early adopter of breaking yourself so they can't break you. It cushions the blows. It sounds melodramatic when all that is being described is a long dry spell of being alone. Talking about it will always take the form of coping, but that is what man has done since the gods breathed language into our mouths: made noise to cope.

Society's greatest purpose now is to produce novelty forms of anaesthetic for a broken and disjointed population to take. Lewis Hyde notes in his essay "Alcohol and Poetry" that the word anaesthetic literally means "without sensation." An-aesthetic. To be without aesthetic. This is a place millions find themselves, which makes the literal poison pills of opioids easier to swallow for people who live in constant pain, physical or otherwise. Even when sensation returns, it can be a while for a man to notice it or to even accept it. He would need to claim it, and to claim it you need to name it.

I fell in love with a woman, and she did with me. I'm not sure who usually falls for whom first. She gave in so sweetly immediately. It took me longer to acknowledge it however as I didn't want to name it. To name it is to claim it. To claim it would mean opening myself back up to sensation, to living with pain. Romantic love was invented by the troubadours, a social construct if you will based on our ancient domestic habits. And since that time of its creation, before the greeting card industry put love on the sick path of counting orgasms and debating ages, love has always been coupled with the pain it caused. Love and pain cannot be separated, and it is not simply the pain of heartbreak. Love is pain itself and to be in love is to be in pain and to be prepared for pain for all the time it stays with you. One cannot be on an anaesthetic and be in love. Man cannot have love and be without sensation.

So I name her. I claim her. I claim her love and I love her as well. She is my future wife and the future mother of my children. I claim the pain she'll cause, as all women do. I claim her mysteries. I will beat a path onward without looking back because I know she'll follow. I love her in spite of myself. I love her in spite of herself.

I name it. I claim it.

—New Essays—

Lewis and Hitler, Parallel Lives

Published as the Foreword to Hitler *by Wyndham Lewis, October 2020*

Adolf Hitler, to quote Gustave Aimard, "is the idea whose time has come and hour struck." If one were to paraphrase a more famous Frenchman, that of Voltaire, one might say if Adolf Hitler did not exist, it would be necessary to invent him. So ubiquitous and fascinating Adolf Hitler has been that even when reduced to a one-dimensional caricature that makes the Devil look sheepish, science fiction writers of time travel stories find it necessary to spare him in their own works as Hitler is the Atlas carrying the postmodern world, its technological development, and its morality on his shoulders. Students within community college philosophy 101 classes might brag about having the bravery of killing baby Hitler, but there's no doubt they would blink at the prospect of losing the one man that defines their entire existence.

Time Magazine has earned eternal enmity for once naming Adolf Hitler their Man of the Year. Their only error was in not naming him the Man of the Century (the winner was Albert Einstein, with runners-up being Gandhi and Franklin Delano Roosevelt). Under their own rules for Man of the Year, it was meant to signify who was the most consequential person in that year, independent of morality. They rarely ever get it right, but they got it right there, even if they couched it in descriptions later discarded by the magazine's detractors that described Hitler as the "greatest threatening force that the democratic, freedom-loving world faces today." There is no argument to be had. Hitler was the most consequential person of the 20th century and if the zeitgeist is anything to go by then he should already be on the 21st century's shortlist despite being dead 75 years.

Hitler is not a man who invites indifference. The only way to have no opinion is to have no opinions. For those who shape society and sentiment however, moral disgust suffices in place of thought. What cannot be denied—not by traumatized Jews, not by agitated liberals, and not even by milquetoast critics of the right—is that the mystique of Hitler is something both ethereal and extraordinary. Savitri Devi, the forerunner of the spiritual view of Hitler that has been codified as "Esoteric Hitlerism," wrote of Hitler as the Man Against Time in *The Lightning and the Sun*. Hitler as avatar of the Hindu God Vishnu is something that will not truck with anyone other than the over-literate handful who get lost somewhere between the weeds of irony and the forests of sincerity, but it is impossible not to be drawn into this concept of Hitler as the Man Against Time.

According to Devi's work, Men In Time are the Lightning, the destructive energies of civilizational conflict that keep the world in cyclical decay. Men Above Time are the Sun, the creative and life-affirming qualities that elevate civilization above decay and create the renewal that can usher in golden ages. The Men Against Time, however, are the Lightning and the Sun, combining both of these qualities in order to create a new order and golden age of the Sun through the destructive and leveling qualities of the Lightning. To give birth to life you must also sweep away the dead. Devi writes in *The Lightning and the Sun*:

> *And in an epoch such as that in which we are now living—when, all over the world, every possible attempt is made to present him not merely as "a war monger" but as the "war criminal" number one,—it is not superfluous to stress the fact that Adolf Hitler was, not only at the dawn of his awakening as a "Man against Time" but all his life, "a bitter enemy of war" as such; the fact that he was by nature "gifted with deep sensitiveness, and full of sympathy for others;" that his programme was essentially a constructive one, his struggle, the struggle for an exalted, positive aim, his aim· the regeneration of higher mankind (of the only section of mankind*

worth saving) and, ultimately, through the survival of regenerated higher
mankind, the restoration of the long-destroyed harmony between the cosmic
Order and the sociopolitical conditions on earth, i.e., the restoration of
Golden Age conditions; the opening not merely of a "new era" for Germany,
but of a new Time-cycle for the whole world.

Many will quibble with Devi's effusive views of Hitler. Many will balk at this oracular perspective. None can deny however that Hitler has a particular quality to him that defies description and so anyone willing to broach this forbidden subject soon discovers that Hitler becomes not just a mirror to the person who approaches his subject, but a magnifier of everything that pours out of them. That same effusive view of Hitler as "a bitter enemy of war" or as a "Man of Peace" would get another writer in trouble: Wyndham Lewis in his 1931 treatise *Hitler*.

This is the quality that Wyndham Lewis wished to capture in his analysis of Hitler. He knew there was something there, but he also knew how unhappy his English audience would be at his attempt to uncover the mystery of the "Hitlerites" without screaming demons at every explanation of their growing movement. The English language is replete with thought-terminating clichés like "it is what it is," signifying that things may just happen for no reason and have no explanation. "But of course an entire country could fall under the hypnotic spell of the man with the magical mustache who could lie bald-faced to them, lie big, and make them do things that are simply against their better nature! It just happens!" Lewis understood this sentiment was bunk and wanted to understand what was really going on, no matter how offended his audience would be at the National Socialist views on everything, but especially economics and Jews.

Wyndham Lewis is not a figure you'll hear about much except from people who really like Wyndham Lewis. He was both a painter and a writer, though he is probably more known these days for his writings than his paintings. Lewis was in many ways the embodiment of the pan-Anglo experience of the expansive and fungible global empire. Born to an English mother and an American father off the coast of Canada in 1882, in some respects his life superficially paralleled his future subject Adolf Hitler and made him an effective counterpart. Both men had difficult family lives with disappointed fathers; Hitler's beat him while Lewis' wrote to his estranged wife: "Am greatly disappointed with the boy and have unpleasant misgivings about his future." Both men lived in the gray zones of what their nations were, with Lewis' pan-Anglo identity and Hitler's experience of being an Austrian with a German Bavarian dialect putting him in a world without inner Teutonic borders. Both men served heroically in the Great War and both men were artists constantly on the outs of society. Both men inevitably were drawn to fascism with a small 'f' but sought to find their own way. Lewis however is rarely connected with Adolf Hitler except in his explicit work he wrote on him, a 'shame' that would dog him for the rest of his life and would be frequently ignored by his admirers who want to admire him on his own terms. But writing *Hitler* would leave its own undeniable mark. His own scarlet A, as it were.

Prior to writing *Hitler*, much of Lewis' life followed that early fascist track. The explosive energy that informed many of the modernist and avant-garde movements that informed early fascism, as those young men were not reactionaries but a new type of man dissatisfied with liberal bourgeois society, was found within Wyndham Lewis as well. He started his own aesthetic movement called Vorticism, an Anglo alternative to the Expressionist, Cubist, and Futurist movements that had lit an artistic flame in continental Europe and were often hand-in-hand with radical politics; many of the first Fascists in Italy had risen up out of Futurism. Perhaps because England had more to look back on, and less to look forward to watching their sun just begin-ning to set, Lewis's work never quite made the same cultural, but especially political, impact as the Futurists.

Starting first as a painter, he would begin his writing career with the modernist novel *Tarr*, a typical novel about the frustrations of artistic young men angry at phonies and poseurs with money who fashion themselves bohemians. More parallels between the lives of Hitler and Lewis can be found in this novel as the two main characters are the Englishman Tarr, a ready stand-in for Wyndham Lewis, and the German

Otto Kreisler, an angry failed artist brimming with explosive creative energy and whose desire to protect his honor leads to him killing a Pole in a duel and then committing suicide before he can be properly brought to justice.

Through the 1920s Lewis would throw himself into the role of the constant satirist of the people and world he knew and positioned himself as their perpetual enemy, declaring himself as such by launching a magazine entitled *The Enemy*. There was philosophy in his writings and critiques however and he sought to find a more perfect Western world in works such as *The Art of Being Ruled* and *Time and Western Man*. At the close of the decade he would write a brutal satire of the London literary world entitled *The Apes of God* which would have been enough to keep him on the outs of 'respectable' cultural elites were it not for what he would publish next.

While Lewis brawled with the intelligentsia in the Anglo world in the 1920s, Hitler and the National Socialist German Workers Party brawled in the streets and at the polls of Germany's deeply divided Weimar Republic. Hitler and the NSDAP did not suddenly sneak up on the world, there were enough outside observers that were aware and raised various levels of alarm at their presence as the National Socialist fortunes waned and waxed. While the 1933 elections were the bolt from the brown that caused the whole world to rub their sleepy eyes and take notice of what was going on, Wyndham Lewis just happened to be in Germany during the National Socialists' meteoric 1930 rise: the May 1928 election had given them 2.6 percent of the vote while the September 1930 election netted them 18.3 percent and the second largest number of seats in the Reichstag. The Nazis had arrived under the linden trees, and Lewis was there in the midst of Babylon Berlin.

He had actually only arrived in Germany in November of 1930, two months after the earth-shattering election. His initial reason for arrival had been to seek a German publisher for *The Apes of God*, a curious mission given the limited appeal that a satire on London literary figures would have certainly had on a German public in the midst of their own deep culture war. While on this trip he got to experience first-hand this

National Socialist movement that was sending shivers down the spine of European leaders. He was certainly fascinated—how could he not be—and hatched what he thought would be a lucrative journalistic scheme: an English-language profile and explanation of this movement and its enigmatic leader Adolf Hitler. He dashed off forty thousand words on the subject, titled it *Hitler*, and sent it for publishing within months of his stay in Germany.

Lewis received only a one hundred pound advance for this timely work—6800 pounds today or 8800 US dollars. For someone as well known and established as Wyndham Lewis, this was the equivalent of a first-time and unknown author getting their first advance. That was as much as the publisher would offer even after Lewis insisted on its worth and topicality. Pennies on the dollar.

The work permanently damaged Lewis' work, but it did not bury him. Ironically what saved him was likely being so early with it, allowing him to claim being duped or foolish when it came time for international liberalism to wipe the slate clean. It was still a rather large brick that Lewis added to his own mausoleum even if antagonizing the culturally powerful and being associated with men like Ezra Pound while preferring the Black principle (Fascists) over the Red one (Bolsheviks) built that foundation.

While *Hitler* by Wyndham Lewis is as forgotten as the man himself is unforgotten, it has the honor of being the first book to study the phenomenon of Hitler and the National Socialists. Its value as a literary artifact of a time is unmistakable. First impressions are always the most fascinating and you won't find a work as nuanced, right and wrong, and complex as this work. Time capsules are so few and far between and are especially ignored by historians who require a unified picture of the past. Thus Lewis' work occupies a curious and similar space as Kerry Thornley's *The Idle Warriors*, the only work to have profiled Lee Harvey Oswald *before* the Kennedy assassination.

There is some amusement in the contemporary reaction to the work. The liberal and left-wing reaction is boring and predictable with the same kind of tut-tutting, screeching, and kvetching, while the right-wing reaction is much more interesting. *Some Sort of Genius* by Paul O'Keeffe asserts that "the Honorary Secretary of the Kensington Fascist group took issue with Lewis's assertion that Germany was a far greater nation than Italy," for example. *Some Sort of Genius* sheds further light on why this work is largely unknown to this day as "it was criticized for being biased, sloppily written, badly researched and inaccurate. But nowhere was it condemned as morally tainted. Supporting Fascism or National Socialism did not carry with it the stigma in 1931 that it would carry two years later."

Wyndham Lewis' account of Hitler and the events and environment that precipitated his rise may appear like gazing into a funhouse mirror into the past—or a regular mirror after being born and raised in a funhouse. Germany of the early 30s is both alien to our popular imagination but all too familiar in ways that are forbidden to know. Lewis reflected on that German experience first-hand, bringing the public a man-at-the-scene account of the decadent Weimar experience that has been fodder for the rulestick on how far the United States and European nations have come. His account of the Eldorado night club is especially vibrant and diverse.

Eldorado had been the gold standard for 'anything goes.' It was the pioneer of drug-soaked unisex androgyny, where if one inquired to whatever the dancer was, according to *Voluptuous Panic* by Mel Gordon, the reply was "I am whatever sex you wish me to be, Madame." Marlene Dietrich found a home there before being scooped up into American film while homosexual and possible dabbler in amateur spycraft Christopher Isherwood was a frequent customer; his experiences would inspire *Cabaret*. Wyndham Lewis writes of Eldorado's Berlin as the "Pervert's Paradise" and vividly of the dancers with the painted red rosette nipples beneath the "male-token of the chin stubble." Eldorado however is just one establishment out of one-hundred and sixty according to Lewis.

Voluptuous Panic provides lurid details of this scene that has become legendary to the discourse surrounding the rise of Hitler and the National Socialists. Gordon quotes from the Italian journalist and politician Luigi Barzini in his 1983 memoir *The Europeans* on just what sort of delights were available to those willing to seek them within Babylon Berlin:

I saw pimps offering anything to anybody, little boys, little girls, robust young men, libidinous women, animals. The story went around that a male goose of which one cut the neck at the ecstatic moment would give you the most delicious, economical, and time-saving frisson of all, as it allowed you to enjoy sodomy, bestiality, homosexuality, necrophilia and sadism at one stroke. Gastronomy too, as one could eat the goose afterwards.

While many focus on the apocryphal goose story, there was no doubt much to gander at in this night scene to the point that the name Weimar itself has become a synonym for the lowest reaches of hedonism. It is no wonder then that, according to Lewis in *Hitler*, that:

Sooner or later [the National Socialist] would desire to be at the head, or in the midst, of his Sturmabteilung—to roll this nigger-dance luxury-spot up like a verminous carpet, and drop it into the Spree. (pg. 19)

This was the moment that Lewis wished to capture. Everyone seemed to know that something historical and revolutionary was happening, that the smell of it was in the air for everyone to breathe. And no matter how much Lewis wanted to be the neutral observer of this rising National Socialist revolution, he could not help but write in wonder of it in the same way that would-be nationalists and dissidents within the dominating liberal hegemony would look back on it for inspiration.

Dominique Venner reflecting on the National Socialist revolution in *For a Positive Critique* saw it as nothing the next wave of nationalists could emulate. It wasn't a recipe you could just replicate: add one Weimar Republic, two dashes of degenerate culture, mix with street violence, bake in anger until ready. The times had changed, the tactics were now wrong. What had greatly frightened many who saw the rise of the National Socialists were their revolutionary progressive nature. And Lewis notes this in *Hitler*. These were not the staid conservatives and reactionaries that could be battered around like the straw-men they volunteered themselves to be, but a rejuvenating force that sought to capture the spirit of the times and master it to their own will by hook or by crook. Lewis saw in Hitler at the time the oneness that was so lacking in nationalist reactions. He compares Hitler to the French integralist Charles Maurras who may have been an aristocrat of the soul but lacked the Everyman touch that Hitler seemed to embody. Hitler's critics from the right are quick to pounce on these vulgar energies though many have missed the irony that Hitler could quite easily have been called the moderate Nazi.

There are passages within *Hitler* that will bring to mind the idea that all of this has happened before and will happen again. Lewis notes the hand-wringing about the energy and minds of the youth being captured by the National Socialists, decades before the word brainwashed would enter the lexicon. He notes the hypocrisy that if these young men were Marxists they would be praised but as National Socialists they are suddenly exploited and tricked. The utopian always believes himself to be in the last age, from the liberals to the Marxists to the neoconservatives and to the technological fascists. They may or may not believe that history is written by the victors but they certainly believe that history ends with them. The cycle of history and civilization has been mastered and conquered for all time. They are then promptly buried into nice little dirt plots and the eternal struggle resumes without their consent or permission.

A good portion of the book is taken up by Lewis explaining the concept of *Blutsgefühl*, or Blood-feeling. He preemptively dismisses the Anglo and American ability to truly understand what this means. Lewis certainly seems to be aware that his contemporary D.H. Lawrence, who was married to a German woman, had some understanding of this however. Lawrence, who died in 1930, had coined the term blood-consciousness to describe his own sense of essence. Where Lawrence's definition only kept an implication of race however, the German word as Lewis describes it exudes it. Curiously, this word does not appear much outside of a Wyndham Lewis context. There is no etymology to Lawrence's coining of his own English version, but that he was married to Frieda, born Emma Maria Frieda Johanna Freiin von Richthofen, until his dying days raises eyebrows at this coincidence.

There is value in contrasting these two feelings. Lewis describes *Blutsgefühl* as the foundation of National Socialism and as "a closer and closer drawing together of the people of one race and culture, by means of bodily attraction...a true bodily solidarity." Lawrence in his description of "blood-consciousness" was reacting to the popularity of Freudian psychoanalysis in his day and offered an alternative understanding in *Fantasia of the Unconscious:*

> *Sex is our deepest form of consciousness. It is utterly non-ideal, non-mental. It is pure blood-consciousness. It is the basic consciousness of the blood, the nearest thing in us to pure material consciousness. It is the consciousness of the night, when the soul is almost asleep. The blood-consciousness is the first and last knowledge of the living soul: the depths. It is the soul acting in part only, speaking with its first hoarse half-voice.*

For Lawrence there was a becoming of man in the blood-consciousness. For Lewis, he understood *Blutsgefühl* as the becoming of race in feeling. Both currents were in one form or another the emergence of essence. Become who you are, as the cliché goes. For Wyndham Lewis, however, there must be a rejection of the Exotic Sense, something he saw D.H. Lawrence and other writers indulging in. Per Lewis: *"What after all is the Exoticist, but the White Conqueror turned literary and sentimental?"*(pg. 75)

Lewis is a bit harsh on Lawrence in his explanation of the Exotic Sense, though sensing rightly that Lawrence had too much sympathy for the 'renegades' against Western Civilization even if he exhorted his readers that they could not go to the savages. There was something within England (as well as France) that Lewis notes tended toward fascination, sympathy, and engaging the exotic. Orientalism was strongest in both England and France, coupled in England's case with feelings of Zionism (and not coincidentally frequent pederasty), but there was also some affection for the Subsaharan African, both in culture (especially in its Americanized form) and as a tool in the racial subjugation of European enemies.

Simms in *Hitler: A Global Biography* argues that Hitler was obsessed more with the Anglo nations of Britain and the United States and its international and colonizing financial capitalism than he was with Bolshevik Russia. Detractors to this thesis point to the respect that Hitler had for the British, but this is not necessarily a contradiction. One can have a terrible awe for the power of a rival, and certainly Hitler saw the endgame of history as a great civil war between the emergent Aryan superpowers. Simms backs up his thesis with the shock and awe felt by the Germans at the way the supreme colonial powers had either absorbed German emigrants into their own ranks, turning volkish boys against the fatherland, or the way they deployed a dark rainbow horde from the colonies to sweep against the Central Power within European land. France in particular was known for its vindictiveness with which it deployed Senegalese soldiers to kill and then to police the Rhineland as a form of biopower and racial warfare. Though historians downplay the number of mixed race 'Rhineland bastards' that were born from the African soldiers stationed in the Rhineland, the effect of it was enough that it became one of the most prominent rallying tools for the National Socialists.

The big lie of this era is that modern men thought and behaved like postmodern men, that segregationists who stormed the beaches of Normandy did so because they were proto-Antifa. The big lie of this era is that race belief was even then the realm of cranks, or that it was so fully discredited by argument that race-thought was never thought of again. This despite *The Rising Tide of Color Against White World-Supremacy* by Lothrop Stoddard being important enough to be referenced in *The Great Gatsby* and H.G. Wells painting a world where European men are policed and beaten by black policemen in their own cities in the dystopian novel *The Sleeper Awakes*. In his 1936 novel *Absalom, Absalom!*, William Faulkner's Canadian character Shreve turns into a terrible seer about the mixed-race descendants of terrible white men swarming the earth:

I think that in time the Jim Bonds are going to conquer the western hemisphere. Of course it won't quite be in our time and of course as they spread toward the poles they will bleach out again like the rabbits and the birds do, so they won't show up so sharp against the snow. But it will still be Jim Bond; and so in a few thousand years, I who regard you will also have sprung from the loins of African kings.

Within the chapter "The Fox and the Goose," Lewis reveals much more of his intentions and his heart. A thoughtful veteran of the Great War, he knew its innumerable questions went unresolved. And like Enoch Powell he saw a deluge of blood in the river that was rising. He constantly cautions, hedging his bets, knowing it will never be safe for him to say that Hitler has some good answers to some good questions, and so he all but endorses the 'Hitlerist' position as he praises Hitler's understanding of the struggle ahead.

For Lewis this is the struggle against extinction. Perhaps as an Englishman he knew there would be no true resistance from the Empire to its conquered subjects returning home to roost. It was fitting that he would see this in animal terms as the Aryans are endangered and have been since Lewis wrote his book. It is undeniable when people like tiny Tim Wise make statements such as:

In the pantheon of American history, conservative old white people have pretty much always been the bad guys, the keepers of the hegemonic and reactionary flame, the folks unwilling to share the category of American with others on equal terms. Fine, keep it up. It doesn't matter. Because you're on the endangered list. And unlike, say, the bald eagle or some exotic species of muskrat, you are not worth saving.

These are not the only familiar feelings to be found within Wyndham Lewis' *Hitler*. The reader will find that as they are transported back to the 1930s in Lewis' writing just how little has actually changed in the discourse. The same discourses over what is white and Aryan and what about the high IQ of Ashkenazi Jews like Albert Einstein, that the idea of nation is a little absurd because it was a recent construction and these nations are more provincial and tribal than you assert, and does that not shake your confidence in your beliefs are all to be found in these writings. The non-liberal, of course, must answer ten thousand volleys to their beliefs while the project of liberal supremacy, which often withers at the merest objections made by men like Carl Schmitt, is protected from a single one. That is the struggle though, is it not? Hegemony is its own morality, especially the hegemon that fancies itself the most supreme for being kinder, gentler, and more inclusive.

Despite these nuances this is a book that is unlikely to change many minds or opinions on Hitler. Its great value is as a curiosity of its time, though not for the reasons one would expect. There are no revelatory insights into Hitler or the "Hitler movement." What the reader may find themselves asking over and over again is "why did Lewis write this when he had no expectation of changing English minds?" The work is suffused with a pessimistic tone toward the English people in their ability to understand who the National Socialists were and why they were as they were. Chapters are spent explaining just why the English will not be able to understand.

The 1930s were a turbulent decade for Lewis, especially politically. He ran into the position many of those who were anti-communist found themselves in: that you might have to take a stand against communism alongside people your enemies really hate. In *Count Your Dead*, Lewis opined on the Spanish Civil War and found himself predictably in the minority of English intelligentsia when he called Franco:

No more a Fascist than you are, but a Catholic soldier who didn't like seeing priests and nuns killed...didn't want to see all his friends murdered for no better reason than that they all went to mass and the more expensive cafes and usually were able to scrape enough money together to have a haircut and a shave.

Lewis found himself stuck in a position all-too-familiar to right-wingers in the Anglo sphere: what to do when the choices are a left-wing who provide one terrible choice and conservatives who offer nothing at all. Six years earlier in *Hitler* these same sentiments were there when Lewis wrote:

So, even if Hitlerism, in its pure 'Germanism,' might retain too much personality, of a second-rate order, nevertheless Hitlerism seems preferable to Communism, which would have none at all, if it had its way. (pg. 119)

This initial book by Lewis comes from the tradition of Anglo empiricism along the veins of Lothrop Stoddard, A.J.P. Taylor, David Irving, and Henry Ashby Turner. Lewis was the quintessential progressive artist and his draw to Hitlerism is as much novelty seeking as much as it was sympathy for the devil, the ultimate underdog. In 1930 the opposition to the National Socialists had reached a fever pitch. The Social Democrats were firmly in control of Prussia and its police force and used every opportunity to harass and prosecute the National Socialists in a manner that would be familiar to political dissidents today. Lewis was never forgiven for cataloging this in *Hitler* and the portrayal has been thrown into the piles of "bias" and "historical misrepresentation" even as he lived and saw the history himself.

The murder of Horst Wessel by a Communist street pimp, led to Wessel's door by his Communist landlord, put an exclamation mark on the violence of that era. Violence which would only intensify when the KPD (Communist Party of German) began an open campaign of assassination against pro-NSDAP bar owners in the autumn of the next year. Despite living through this history, Lewis was to later rue his romanticization of the NSDAP's early struggles.

What would cause a man who once wrote in *Hitler* "When *two nations* fall out, the armament-king and chemical-king rake in the shekels. When two men fall out, the lawyer coins money. When two *Classes* fall out, it is the same thing. Power, or wealth, passes from both to some *third* Class" (pg. 49) to disavow Adolf Hitler and take up the cause of the poor downtrodden Jew? It was not the fact that the NSDAP was no longer novel or the underdog, or they failed to uphold campaign promises.

Rather Lewis changed his tone because the persecution he observed in Germany was finally brought to bear on him.

He ran and he ran hard. He ran from his own work as he was no William Joyce, a man he had also briefly associated but who was willing to throw all in with the Germans, who at his trumped up execution stated "I am proud to die for my ideals and I am sorry for the sons of Britain who have died without knowing why." He was known to have visited the leader of the British Union of Fascists, Oswald Mosley, who reflected on him in his autobiography as a man who "used to come to see [him] in most conspiratorial fashion, at dead of night with his coat collar turned up." Wherever and whenever Lewis was asked about the Hitler book after the rise of the National Socialists he was happy to let it be pulped. "And pulp it accordingly became," he wrote.

Even before the situation with his connections to Ezra Pound and whispers of treason made him try to expunge any all memories of that turbulent period, he attempted to rectify his position and weather the coming storm. He worked hard to absolve himself by 1939 as the next European war was increasingly inevitable, publishing in that same year two works meant to give him the plausible deniability from his past that he desperately sought. The first was the complete repudiation of *Hitler* entitled *The Hitler Cult* and the second a satire on antisemitism entitled *The Jews, Are They Human?*

Even within *The Hitler Cult*, Lewis finds the necessity to invent Hitler. He recites his litany of experiences with the National Socialists in order to show that his contact with them was quite limited. The parallel prophetic powers of Lewis continue within this work—just as he foresaw the beginning of a Hitler in *Tarr*, he saw his incoming end six years later in *The Hitler Cult*:

National Socialism will die a violent death: everything points to that solution. I give it a few years at the outside. It may die in battle: it may blow its brains out: it may burst: it may merge insensibly into something else. But it will no longer be there in, let us say, six years' time. I should be sorry to assert that all those who execrate it are saints, or even honest

men. But from whatever angle you observe it, it is not an attractive
phenomenon. Hardly an intelligent man will be found who will regret it.

Meanwhile in *The Jews, Are They Human?* Lewis throws himself at the feet
of philosemitism, an easy task for an Englishman. Even within *Hitler* Lewis
was walking the edges of it, reminding his English audience just how much
they had civilized the Jewish people and entered into harmonious
matrimony with them. He continues this track in *The Jews, Are They
Human?*, writing obsequious passages to the Jews that were no doubt
meant to chase off the audience that he feared he had cultivated. Lewis
was a satirical writer who bit whom he could until he could draw the piss
out of them, but *The Jews, Are They Human?* is so craven in its self-
deprecatory humor one can't help but think of a beaten dog scuttering
around its master. Take for example this passage on the relationship
between the Jews and the English:

> *Then, even if they did decide to remain with us, the Jews are one of the*
> *most industrious races in the world; and we are one of the least industrious.*
> *They will set a high standard of hard work at least, which it will be*
> *necessary for the rest of us to live up to. That will be most salutary. It is*
> *worth paying people to come here to teach us how to work! We could not*
> *have better instructors.*

Through the 1940s, Lewis tried to get himself back into the good graces
of liberal society by praising men like Franklin Delano Roosevelt and the
melting pot and the racial incoherency of the United States. Memories
were longer than Lewis wished to give people credit for, and his brief star
never shone brightly ever again. By the early 1950s Lewis was blind and
beginning his slow shuffle into his 1957 grave. Those memories of his
flirtation with fascism lasted long enough that after he had made enemies
of all the earth more than enough of them were quite willing to let him
be forgotten, and for much of literary history he was. The man that W.H.
Auden once called "that lonely old volcano of the Right" sputtered off into
obscurity and became less of a volcano and more of a fire anthill.

Nearly 90 years since *Hitler* was first published one comes away thinking that Lewis had given up before the fighting even started. The English are as they are and they're never going to change. There'll always be an England, as the famous song went. But will there be? Vera Lynn has only passed away in this *Anno Domini* of 2020. One wonders what she thought looking around living through the years since Lewis published *Hitler* and the changes England underwent until the day she died.

While Wyndham Lewis retains a small cadre of devoted followers, largely Anglophiles, students of Modernism, and fans of the era, it is certain that interest in him will rise in conjunction with interest in his work on Adolf Hitler. The men lived parallel lives and Lewis being the elder brother thought he could keep a step ahead of the little brother and his tide. *Hitler* was pulped, its ideas supposedly supplanted in subsequent works and yet here it is almost a century later. Literary immortality, whether Lewis liked it or not.

Hitler is not going anywhere. This is his world and we're all just living in it, whether his followers win or fail. As the philosopher Søren Kierkegaard scribbled down in his journals, "The tyrant dies and his rule is over, the martyr dies and his rule begins."

In Hitler's case, it might be said to be both.

Anti-Society and Its Discontents

"Picturing others and everything which brings you closer to them is futile from the instant that 'communication' can make their presence immediate."
— Jean Baudrillard, *The Ecstasy of Communication*

"I couldn't see her face. We sat in silence, close and warm, both aware that we were close and aware that we were embarrassed by the implications of this talk about children. In our age it is not sex that raises its ugly head, but love."
— John Fowles, *The Magus*

Every man should know where his bread is buttered, and in my case I remain constantly on friendly terms with Japanese anime aficionados—"weeaboos" in the parlance of our age. It's certainly easier when one enjoys the medium themselves, though I'm casually within that world but not of that two-dimensional world. Thus, there are things that are somewhat beyond my mental grasp. The emergent phenomenon in the last couple of years has been that of the Virtual YouTubers, or VTubers for short. I knew very little about it and hit up the experts. What I found was the next generation of peculiar parasocial relationships gestating in the petri dish of our own relationship to technology.

Virtual YouTubers, for the uninitiated, create largely online video game streams where the person who is playing the game uses software to project themselves as the avatar of a cute living anime girl. These are almost entirely Japanese in origin with a recent breakout into the Anglophone sphere. The anime girl's movements are composed of the streamer's movements. Their voice is breathed through the mouth of the anime girl. They have in essence played God and made anime real. The immediate reaction from the cynically savvy is that the gamer behind the chronologically ambiguous animated sweetheart must be a male who has sacrificed his dignity for clout and shekels by degrading himself into digital cross-dressing as cyber cheesecake. This is the intuitive response, but surprisingly not the case. The hyperreality is surprisingly mundane: the most prominent of these Virtual YouTubers are women who are meticulously selected by a private company that display a range of personality, voice work, and stage presence not unlike the idol culture that is ubiquitous to Asian societies. It would seem *Bladerunner* would be a cuter world than we had previously imagined.

I tried to watch some of these videos, but it wasn't the bizarre nature of it that got to me. I just find watching other people playing video games to be boring, regardless of the person's dimensions. I'm not one to dismiss a medium just because I don't "get" it, however. From the expert opinions I sourced on this, the general sentiment is this:

VTubing is some "kayfabe," a lot of behind the scenes positioning, and most likely some scripted scenario writing. At its heart however it's a cute girl simulator without the perceived annoyances and burdens of "three-dimensional girls" who bring all the baggage that anyone known for being a girl online is going to bring. It invites an amusing suspension of disbelief.

They are not there to politic, they are not there to sell foot pictures or bath water. Their only focus is on the personality, banter, and the activity of the game. It could be viewed as a digital hostess bar, providing/ selling pleasant conversation and personality within a mutual suspension of disbelief.

The unspoken elephant in the room unfortunately is the company which owns them. It's rather cruel that these characters are simply that. The company builds the brand and monopolizes their ability to perform. They're utterly disposable. It's also worth pointing out that the relationship is less terribly parasocial than with normal streamers, because there's a knowledge that it's an avatar. It's still kind of dystopian though, but at least all parties understand what they're in for.

*Except when it comes to talking about Hololive. Some of the Hololive
Japanese girls claim to hang out in real life but nobody knows if that's real
or just part of the bit. With hololive, they have to trial and be selected like
an idol with a persona. The company then gives them an appropriate rig
which works with programs like "Live2D" to track and imitate faces in real
time which is overlayed into the stream instead of a webcam.*

One could describe VTube as a cross between Asian idol culture and
professional wrestling as simmering just at the surface is the same tension
as professional wrestling's kayfabe culture, where everyone pretends this
isn't deliberate entertainment as the masquerade is just more fun. That's
the sell, at least. Kayfabe is an intriguing concept. For those unfamiliar
with its origins, while its etymology is unknown (though speculated
upon), it came out of professional wrestling for wrestlers to signal among
themselves that the facade of the ring needs to be maintained at that
moment, lest some fan learn the truth. Professional wrestling,
surprisingly to some, is a worthy topic of study, as being part of carnival
culture it mingled with those elements and developed its own cant—that
is, its own secret language. The linguist Michael Halliday called this
phenomenon an "anti-language," a type of language spoken by an "anti-
society," that is a separate and nebulous community within a larger society
that is often in resistance to it, having to maintain its own separate identity
within it, or in need to exploit it in some way.

Kayfabe is fascinating in how reality blurs, because the masquerade is
still a show with personalities. People with human emotions, human
flaws, human realities. The frustrations can be very real as money is
always on the table in these situations. It's the same with VTubers. So
when someone is wearing masks for paychecks, the various realities of
these situations and the unstated assumptions can't help but blend into
one another. Even inform one another. The various drama inside
professional wrestling is well-known enough to people that follow it—
the situation of Triple H and the fallout of the Curtain Call which I
couldn't even begin to explain being a prominent example—and it
follows that VTuber culture has its own niche insider followers; the

people intrigued at how the masquerade works. The interpersonal relationships of actors performing the same play night after night and what happened backstage subtly influencing the show doesn't really hold a candle to these newer stages where fluid scripts are more at play. The creep factor, however, must still set in as the seed of the parasocial relationship is ever present.

Professional wrestling's masquerade, however, is overall benign, simply being an entertainment business instead of being engaged in activities predicated on subverting society in order to maintain anti-society's power hold. It was an open secret for the longest time that professional wrestling was not an athletic competition but scripted entertainment, but even into the technological age the masquerade maintained a degree of mystery and wishful plausibility to it. The masquerade is all too human and speaks to what we feel requires the mask or what lies hidden behind it. It speaks to the shadows of our subconsciousness.

For example, I've personally been gaming with the same online group for four years. I've never met them, don't even know what most of them look like. Some of them I don't even know their actual names. I would never want to peer behind the curtain on that one. There is nothing I could learn that would improve the gaming experience for me. It is in this way that many people will cling on some level to the masquerade. The reasons for it are rather simple. It operates on the same level we used to see staged plays and why we watched movies, at least until the movies became so hyperreal they became our reality. On a bizarre level we do know subconsciously that the truth will never be as fulfilling as the fantasy. Fantasies are enticing. It's why we live to dream and daydream. We find ourselves thinking about what we would do if we won the lottery, what our perfect home might be like, what it must feel like to live in an actual society and not an anti-society. The intrusion of reality is never a pleasant experience, but a healthy mind knows how to keep these two worlds separated. So what does it matter if a person just wants to relax and watch a cute anime girl play video games, watch heroic men in flashy costumes body slam one another in an ongoing storyline, or play role playing games with people we don't even know?

It matters when the fantasy is parasocial.

The word "parasocial" might be unfamiliar to some. The term surprisingly dates back to the 1950s, right when mass media was emerging into a new globalized spectacle that humanity would overcook within several times over. The term was coined by Donald Horton and Richard Wohl, with the "para" part of "parasocial" being rooted in the Greek word meaning "beside, or next to" (like the word parallel), though one could be forgiven for immediately thinking it's a portmanteau of "parasitical" and "social." What it effectively describes is the one-sided relationships that are cultivated by audiences and viewers towards the people and media that are beamed at them on a daily basis. Every person has an intimate relationship with a famous celebrity, the celebrity just doesn't know it yet. This is especially difficult for Americans as we are the epicenter of a massive media machine that bleeds dreams; we're the only zone that could have produced an Andy Warhol. George W.S. Trow wrote of this phenomenon in his aphoristic way in *Within the Context of No Context*:

> *Celebrities have an intimate life and a life in the grid of two hundred million. For them, there is no distance between the two grids of American life. Of all Americans, only they are complete.*

The parasocial phenomenon was more cohesive when it was just restricted to Hollywood and television celebrities, however. Media is the ultimate craft, and it requires ultimate craftsmen to present the best possible image and picture to the public. I don't just mean in the director's chair, I mean the publicists and public relations people who carefully cultivated the image of an idol for an eager and adoring public. There is an art in and of itself to it, to present what is often the molested mass of an aesthetic ideal in a way that not only scrapes off the miasma of perpetual psychoactive product and shameful jobs for better work, but elevates it to the aspirational. It's a dirty trade reminiscent of the Jewish *kiras* who did the secretarial work of the Ottoman sultan's harem, but the decrepit work earns its keep. Hollywood is a localized cancer though, even if it's metastasized the world.

The disaster in the parasocial phenomenon is that it has leaked out from the centralized hub of Southern California's nightmare factory. The easy access of frivolous technology and DIY media has greatly expanded the capabilities of the average person to project their image and essence without having the ability or wherewithal to see and manage the parasocial relationship. All it takes is a clever social media account or a few funny video for a person to suddenly find themselves in a relationship they never knew they had. The relationship can manifest in so many forms, from the typical romantic obsession for a conventionally pretty e-girl, to the rather benign interest in the lives of a virtual YouTuber or online personality, to the troubling culture that develops with killers and true crime.

In this way everyone is now having a one-sided relationship with a bevy of often unaware entities. Content creators and public figures are increasingly becoming aware of this phenomenon, even if they don't have the names for it. They adjust the way they perform, speaking more personably to cultivate an intimate bubble often out of a sense of obligation that this person has taken their time to engage. Separation becomes more difficult, especially if the engagement becomes necessary to the experience. Sex is even more difficult to remove from this reality, being so vital to the human experience even as the rates at which younger people are having it are plummeting. Largely one-sided intimate and sexual relationships are created within the parasocial environment through content subscriptions, videos, and podcasts. The weirdness of it makes the idea of consent a nebulous concept and almost impossible to pin down. Most have the wherewithal to stay within the masquerade, knowing the party has to end at midnight. Not everyone knows when or how to leave though.

The case of the Björk stalker provides a window into how far this collective descent into madness goes. Ricardo Lopez was, fittingly enough, a pest exterminator who came into the orbit of Icelandic musician Björk, or so he thought, and desired nothing more than to burn up in her atmosphere or crash into her world. A Hispanic obsessed with an Icelandic pop star while living in the US who kills himself over it—what a majestic thing internationalism is.

As of the writing of this essay, one of the top comments on *The Video Diaries of Ricardo Lopez*, a home video chronicle of his final days, reads:

> *There is something about psychotic people and VHS tapes that go together. Seeing a stalker today in 1080p just isn't the same as the good old days of these weird underground basement tapes. You need tracking lines, poor color, and grain to get the full effect.*

The full movie length diary is disturbing in and of itself if the various parallels to online parasocial relationships weren't already apparent enough. Lopez, an eerie foreshadowing of the "Alt-Right is a Latinx movement" meme, opens cognizant of his deteriorating mental state as he seethes about Björk "fucking a nigger" and resigned that he will only be free from this "relationship" by killing her. Anyone who watches the full video sees over the course of months his rants about being born into this world, his dismissals of anyone who would help him, his strange plans to kill the pop star of his dreams, and finally his last day of madness as he works up his courage to kill himself (and eventually does).

Anyone watching it would be hard pressed to feel anything about what they saw after the initial shock wears off. The novelty is in having a window into another human being's cataloged self-destruction. One man's parasocial relationship can then become a parasocial relationship for someone else. All one needs to do is read the various comments under any reproduction of his diaries. Between the jokes and memes you will find people attempting to empathize or get inside his mind. Some wish they could have been his friend, or there to witness. His actions become memetic as people indulge in the aesthetic terrorism of his final hours and the disfigured human soul laid bare. Like Yukio Mishima's final act of artistic annihilation at his own suicide, Ricardo Lopez goes beyond being a seemingly isolated incident and into culture itself.

Reflecting how the heart of life tends to beat in rhymes and echoes, as

Ricardo Lopez's descent into madness was nearing its inevitable conclusion, Japanese animator Satoshi Kon was producing *Perfect Blue*, an anime that draws on the themes of star obsessions and the roles that a consumer society inadvertently causes us to play. Satoshi Kon was a master of his craft, with many of his works playing upon the importance of the medium of animation being its own message and the obsession, paranoia, and trauma that accompany us with having to live in a media-driven consumption society. Kon, in contrast to the kitsch and flash that often accompanies Japanese animation, delighted in making audiences uncomfortable with the way he could bring ugliness onto the screen and make it impossible for the audience to ignore. The Lopez parallel in *Perfect Blue* is a character known by his own subculture name, Me-Mania. Me-Mania is one of the more striking characters in animation as his ugliness is never played for humor not even as just a visual representation of the reprehensible. There is humanity in him even as he dangerously obsesses over a pop star, reminding us uncomfortably that there are millions of people in this world with unfortunate circumstances whose only positive outlets are to be in a state of parasocial consumption. Even as he fantasizes about holding an idealized beauty in the palm of his hand, a nervous thought may creep into the back of our minds that we can understand why these unhealthy lives are lived this way, we just hope we can stay out of their way.

That seems increasingly impossible however. The choice is to be connected or completely disconnected, and the latter is increasingly a luxury. If someone's employer requires them to maintain a social media presence to be hired and remain being hired, that person has to become an artful liar or be capable of getting employment and keeping it, as more and more companies begin to move toward this model. Even small businesses aren't immune as there is an expectation that there be a way for the snitch class to monitor and contact anyone in order to flex that one iota of petty power the system affords them. The allowed excuses for why a person is not plugged into the social media panopticon are running out as quickly as the highway exits that white suburbanites are taking their U-Haul trucks down.

One can't help but wonder about the lives of people who will mostly be remembered as replyguys for Donald Trump's Twitter, entering into his orbit like a busted satellite transmitting everything it has left to give before it gracelessly goes out or burns up. For some of them this is just fun and profit, a grift that helped buy them a new McMansion by catering to the psychological needs of the developmentally retarded who never grew past the desire to be a child within "The Emperor's New Clothes."

It is worth returning to the notion of anti-language and anti-society. There are nine criteria to what forms a linguistic anti-language, though relevant to this topic is that the anti-language's anti-society must be a conscious alternative to society, that grammar and syntax remain the same as anti-language is just a re-skin of old words with new, that the communication of the language remain inaccessible to the layperson, and that the anti-language is a vehicle for re-socializing the people who communicate within it. It is difficult to look around at this society and argue that the United States is not in the grip of an anti-society that is not only ascending, but has developed a strong foothold into the echelons of power. Academia serves in many respects as the primordial soup from which members of the anti-society are burped out after being boiled in the jargon of their academic anti-language. The first oozings of this were seen in social media, leading to the perennially hapless conservatives and disingenuous liberals to dismiss what they called "Tumblr culture." It was presented as something so fringe that it could easily be ignored. One wonders how the people under the autistic tyranny of the pronoun people must now feel about the luxury to ignore this creeping culture of contrivance. People have memed on the phrase "we live in a society," but answer this question: *Do you?* Are you certain about that? Are you sure you don't just live under the capricious whims of an anti-society?

Once robbed of simple language, once forced to speak in the fluid anti-language whose definitions change as suddenly and as easily as the river's current, people of society can't help but inevitably turn parasocial. There is no longer any security in the relationship of language, making the one-way relationship with the idealized much safer to pursue. Young people are having sex at lower rates contrary to the media depictions of the youth being ravenous sex fiends that can't keep their hands off each other or any animal, mineral, or vegetable. It's not the celibacy that's troubling but the lack of intimacy—if sex is down then intimacy has certainly cratered. Culprits are plenty, but ask the young men, as invariably the clueless questions always ask "what's wrong with them," and the most common answer you'll get is the minefield of anti-language's esoteric rules and the crushing feeling that a rape accusation is inevitable. The latter has become a passion play more and more men have felt has become impossible to ignore. Dig deeper and you'll find more reasons to count such as smoothing of the brain and body by an inescapable addiction to internet pornography and an alienation that has rendered millions into cultural mutes.

The obsession with two-dimensional girls becomes inevitable in this way. It's low stakes in this way, and for some it becomes enough to simulate a sense of intimacy with the girl on the screen. If it needs to be deeper than that, perhaps an ASMR artist simulating the sensation of hair brushing or kind whispers will do the trick. If that doesn't work, well, the parasocial rabbit hole is always deeper if you want or need to dig down. Most know where to stop and how to contain their fantasies. It's a way to blow off steam. Others are not capable of this and once aware of them others will work to avoid or obsessively neutralize them as they do in our present moral panic over incels. Parasocial relationships aren't a symptom so much as the only seemingly sane response to a dangerously fake and intolerable anti-society enmeshed into every waking moment of a person's life. Where there is no security in the concrete world, even behind a literal closed door, the spirit has no choice but to flee toward the abstract.

The parasocial relationship can and often does lead to self-destruction. Before the advent of social media, its extreme cases manifested in random acts of violence, often perpetuated toward the self but sometimes ending in murder. Last year an "e-girl" was murdered essentially for being what she was. Her murderer killed her because he is what he is. Anyone who has conversed with someone deeply within their own parasocial reality knows there's almost no penetrating that secret world. Oddly, the best death to a parasocial relationship is through boredom, when the fire goes out and interest fades. The masquerade comes back into view as the lights are flipped back on, the masks are casually removed, and the soft doughy bodies come much more clearly into focus.

It would be nice to know that this is the banal epiphany reached by people trapped in an extremely online spiral. I don't think anyone doubts however that there won't be more "e-girl" bodies in the pursuit of the parasocial absolution. The cult of progress is such that even people who are skeptical of any actual convenience of technology and its interconnectivity can't foresee a future without it and its necessity. Dehumanization, demoralization, and destruction of the individual's wellness is inevitable according to these prophets. Mark Fisher called this "capitalist realism," but "technological realism" might be a more apt description.

Now with technology, people who die but whose images have reason to persist can be remade into something that moves and speaks like them. It's been happening with the kids who died in the Parkland shooting. Had they not died in the schizophrenic tank that makes up America, they would have likely gone on to live lives of no note, accruing a social media trail of good memories and connections with friends and family. That's no bad fate, but how can that be balanced against immortality in being remade for a political purpose? More perversely, grieving parents can now see their children growing up in virtual reality and interact with their image in that limited, simulated way. If parasocial relationships can lead a person obsessed with a pop star down a violent, self-destructive path, what's to make of the human condition in this parasocial scenario? With this in focus, with the Trump replyguys, the Ricardo Lopezs of the world, and the exploitation of the unspeakable grief of parents, a relationship with a Japanese cartoon girl seems downright benign.

We die but our images live on. Some die and hope their image lives forever. But what will document our lives when the image is gone? Where do we go when the masquerade ends?

McGulag

Picture two scenarios.

The first is you, walking down the street. All around you are propaganda posters commanding you to accept that oppression is freedom and to trust and never question the inscrutable leader of your country. His jaw is strong, his eyes are piercing as he appears to be staring through you even from the distance of the printed page. You don't know anything about him other than what is within the sanctioned pages of the party documents. You don't even remember exactly how long he's been in power. You don't remember elections—did you even have any? Life goes on because you keep your head down, hoping you won't be targeted next. People have disappeared in the night. No explanation given. It's like they were never even there. Men in dark coats with black cabs appeared but you try to forget that you ever even saw them. You fear they may have already found a way to monitor the thoughts within your brain. You know there's a place where they take away people and they are never seen again. The very few who somehow get back are never the same. Not even human. Just broken husks. Such is life in the regime that never ends.

The second is you, walking down the street. All around you on lawns, in storefront windows, and on poles are posters and stickers making content-less declarations about "love" being good and "hate" being evil, pithy slogans that signal correct opinions that are ill-defined. You encounter another person, visibly different in skin or dress. You say nothing, uncertain if the two of you are even capable of conversation as you're not even sure how to address this person or what the two of you could conceivably talk about together. And at any rate you're not feeling talkative after a stupid social media post got wildly out of hand. Now you're looking for a job as rent is due soon and the company that owns the property is known for being quite litigious and unforgiving when it comes to rent. If you even get an explanation for why you won't be hired, it's some bizarre combination of overqualified and underqualified. Even manual labor has turned you away as lowering your quality of life as much as you have is still too high for what they're used to paying. Sometimes the social media post comes up, but for the most part people are just avoiding you. In a weird way you feel like a ghost. You're living in constant insecurity. Your job is tenuous, your health is tenuous, the friends and family you were already seeing less of are making sure that less is now none. You don't know anyone. You don't have anyone to go to. You're just...there. And even that is becoming intolerable.

The former will not likely feel real unless it's been washed in grayscale and drab lighting. The latter will not feel like oppression because the former is oppression, as you are taught and programmed. How a person understands oppression is generally visceral and not verbal. The meaning of a word is in a picture, not in its definition. In an increasingly illiterate society—that is, that they are *not* reading, not that they *can't* read—the definition is tertiary if it matters at all. Hence why appeals to dictionary definitions of words like "racism" is a fool's errand. What is oppression? Would you define it as "prolonged cruel or unjust treatment or control"? That's how the dictionary defines it, but be honest with yourself. Admit you would never have explained it like this, because thanks to school and media you think oppression is looking sad in a black and white photo while an authority figure questions you harshly with the looming threat of violence just around the corner of his wicked smile. There is no other conceptualization of this that you were allowed.

It's the same as the word "occupation." To you, occupation would imply a foreign army marched in and took your capital by force. What is an occupation, if not rule by non-native populations enforcing their hostile will on a population whose interests they disregard, bully, and subvert, to the point of transforming it if it cannot (or will not) be annexed to another power? If you agree with this definition, then what do you think about the fact that in American democracy voters get what they want from elected officials 0% of the time while lobbyists get what they want 100% of the time?

And yet despite all this, even people who know better about how this system works will sometimes throw all their weight into voting for a party whose chief purpose is to root them out and waste their time. Whatever debate there might be had on the efficacy of voting against a party that is perceived to be even worse, there is no objective argument that can be made that anyone is voting for something or that they will benefit from it, unless they are a member of said party of course. People can be motivated quite easily however by a looming fear of the gulag making its American debut. There's a problem with this fear, as illustrated by the paradox of neoliberal oppression (that oppression does not seem real unless it's aesthetically correct).

The gulag of the 20th century doesn't work as a tool of repression and control in the 21st century. Its implementation made sense in an expansive environment that had room for a controlled exile. The effect of being isolated from those you knew and relegated to hard, killing labor within intolerable conditions "worked," as it were, in a system that only needed its population to accept its lies and legitimacy. The hypermodern situation of being constantly plugged in, constantly propagandized, constantly deconstructed to the point of simply being a brainstem of signals and receptors makes the gulag into a deterritorialized antiquity. It's useful for scaring the easily spooked, but superfluous, especially given the prison system's policy of punitive interracial rape and sodomy, of which the American public is overwhelmingly in support—the original meaning of "rape culture." Even there the threat and reality of prison rape is vastly overstated and its instances murkier; the public desires rape more than the rapists.

There's an interesting thing that occurs when you read *Industrial Society and Its Future* in its most recent and likely last to be published edition. It's not often anyone ever gets a chance to revise their own manifesto as those who write them normally die within hours of it being released. Kaczynski in his time behind bars has continued to read books and has revisited things he wrote, leaving behind a number of footnotes where he's admitted he was wrong in what he previously wrote. In one note he disavows anarchism, explaining he had no idea what anarchists were really all about at the time he had quasi-aligned himself as one. In a very pertinent letter he wrote after his imprisonment he explains that the Soviet Union wasn't nearly as repressive as he had been led to believe, especially when compared to the way the System of liberalism terrorizes:

*I've changed my mind about [the Vietnam War] because I've concluded that I vastly overestimated the danger of communism. I overestimated its danger partly as a result of my own naivety and partly because I was influenced by media propaganda. (At the time, I was under the mistaken impression that most journalists were reasonably honest and conscientious.)...At least through the 1970s, I accepted the image of communist countries that the media projected. I believed that they were tightly regulated societies in which virtually the individual's every move was supervised by the Party or the State. Undoubtedly this was the way the communist leaders would have **liked** to run their countries. But it now seems that because of corruption and inefficiency in communist systems the average man in those countries had a great deal more wiggle-room than was commonly assumed in the West. [Robert] Thurston's [Life and Terror in Stalin's Russia, 1934-1941} is instructive. On the basis of Thurston's information, one could plausibly argue that the average Russian worker under Stalin actually had more personal freedom than the average American worker has had at most times during the 20th century. This certainly was not because the communist leaders **wanted** the workers to have any freedom, but because there wasn't much they could do to prevent it.*

The 20th Century liberal conception of what a person is supposed to fear in totalitarian societies (which they were taught by nature liberal societies simply cannot be) permeates literature and culture and provides a security blanket where someone can assure themselves they live in a free society, because as long as you shut up, you can earn a meager pittance to buy frozen pizzas to consume in between marathon gaming sessions and

Tinder hookups within a studio apartment for singles. Liberty is an LLC, the freest people in the world say. Repression is having the leader you never voted for on propaganda posters all over your city. Liberation is a corporation you are allowed no meaningful stake in giving you opinions on your family, relationships, and livelihood through giant advertisements 24/7.

These conservatives, libertarians, and reactionaries still speak in fear of gulags with updated post-ironic verbiage like "FEMA camps." No tool is off the table for power, but this outdated concept will never concentrate the millions of people that wannabe elites have no idea what to do with. The amorphous quality of liberalism makes it such that beyond nebulous and abstract concepts of rights and equality, it must work constantly to avoid definitions. The esotericist knows that to give definition to something allows you to finally name and see it. What demon or spirit would ever want to operate anywhere other than the invisible world? In a sense liberalism may be a poor word to describe it as its evolution has made its political theory defunct. It has shed its carapace and become power itself, embodying the 48th and final Law of Power, Assuming Formlessness (*The 48 Laws of Power*):

> *Power can only thrive if it is flexible in its forms. To be formless is not to be amorphous; everything has a form—it is impossible to avoid. The formlessness of power is more like that of water, or mercury, taking the form of whatever is around it. Changing constantly, it is never predictable. The powerful are constantly creating form, and their power comes from the rapidity with which they can change. Their formlessness is in the eye of the enemy who cannot see what they are up to and so has nothing solid to attack. This is the premier pose of power: ungraspable, as elusive and swift as the god Mercury, who could take any form he pleased and used this ability to wreak havoc on Mount Olympus.*

It is in this way that it's obvious that the gulag or the camp has no place nor purpose, it is from a time when great armies moved across the earth and governments corralling wild and unconquered lands and people needed to keep them concentrated in order to watch them. Some might bring up camps in China or North Korea, but whatever the full truth of these places are, these are the results of countries that are still balancing the liberalization of the world and the evolution of their own antiquated systems. Being spread out was a strength in those brief days, now it is a weakness. That old form has nothing to accomplish here when anyone anywhere can be watched at any time. Forced labor was meant to break the spirit, but for many that spirit is already broken. Some came pre-broken.

It's better for the system to have nothing for you to own, to rent everything while co-workers and managers reify narratives for the purpose of compliance, especially when the technological system aids, abets, and allows for this. The gulag is the world. There's nowhere else for you to go. Those golden arches are the gateway to this brave new world. You can find some peace perhaps but what are the chances your grandchildren will have no choice but to work in the McGulag and keep their mouths shut for fear of being cast into the outer darkness and in constant, smothering anxiety because basic health, basic security, and basic wellness are constantly just out of reach.

The future is not a difficult one to predict, because without black swan events, the path moves in a rationally evil matter. Communication, technology, and media companies will be owned by a few who are engaged in human engineering projects through the use of consumption-based incentives. Their money-power in the legislative bodies and courts will unfetter them even deeper under the principle that their "free speech" is paramount. Meanwhile the masses will be at their mercy, especially as the few companies that own everything will be engaged in their own engineering of them as employees through similar but negative incentives—participate in this humiliating, sexually and racially abusive seminar, or lose the wage. This financialized system will print and pass whatever it needs to stay afloat while squeezing blood from the stones of Americans, all the while talking about the beauty of democracy and diversity and the liberation of its so-called freedoms and opportunities. The human body will continue to be commodified in every form while every drug will be called a cure. Children will be treated as having the wisdom and consent of adults while adults will continue down the path of infantilization. It's hard to imagine it anything more than a technological *120 Days of Sodom* while the victims of this very long and very dark winter will constantly be haunted by the spectre that the Powers That May Be might suddenly decide to put them in camps. How grim that must be!

Don't kvetch or whine to me about the picture I paint. Don't cry to me that I'm saying "all is lost." *You* think that. Men take the facts as they are and face them head on.

I can't for the life of me think of any ancestor that moped about how difficult things are and always have been, about the struggle that seems insurmountable but must be fought. Many fell into the bottle or fell under way too soon, but these were not regretful lives. For me they were Yorkshire and French men seeking better lives in the colonies and the new frontiers, Quebecois that heard there were better jobs that awaited if they'd just move and lose their language, and Russians who wanted out of the chaos of becoming the new Soviet Man and found out decades later there was nowhere to return back to. I'm smarter and much more fed than all of these men, but like many in my own generation, I feel like half the man they were. Should I cry about this? Wail? Gnash my teeth?

You're never really going to have control of it all except in those rare moments that quickly reveal themselves and then are gone. You can be depressed about it as much as you choose to indulge in it but remember that no matter how much you worry about the gulag, you're already in the spiritual one. Is life any different? Surely you've heard someone shrug their shoulders and say "life's a bitch and then you die." Is that good enough for you? Is that sufficient?

Orwell for all his faults was simply never taught correctly. There is truth in knowing that evil extinguishes the human spirit. There is wisdom knowing that Little Brother is more resentful than Big Brother. There is weight in remembering what you are and speaking, acting, and living in constant defiance of the petty totalitarianism of the soul.

Whither, American Futurism?

Back to blood. Blood in, blood out, that's the only way being an American will ever matter again. America, as it is, is an economic zone. The amalgamated stock of its founding peoples and European newcomers scarcely know what they are, but they believe that the American government was good to them and so they should be good to it. They believe that loyalty to traitors should count for something, even as they pay for it with blood, treasure, and children. What they believe are their symbols they find they must share or rent. Flags and totems on lease from entities that own the rights and want to see them doped and dropped. These are sentiments that will not do. These are not beliefs that will last. It is time to push forward.

Americanism is dead, but American Futurism can win. American Futurism will win, but not without its people. I come not to praise Trump, but to bury him. I come not to go back, but to go forward. I come not to save America, but to create her. There is nothing you should not be willing to cast aside or destroy in order to take that essential first step.

The name may be confusing. Futurism was best known as a 20th century artistic movement, popular in Italy (almost non-existent in America save for the Italian immigrant artist Joseph Stella). It most famously prefigured the Italian Fascist movement (with some of Mussolini's most infamous architecture being influenced by it). The writer of the *Futurism Manifesto*, Filippo Marinetti, also co-wrote the *Fascist Manifesto*, although Marinetti's very modernist and progressive views put him at frequent odds with the reactionary wing of the Italian fascists. This original Futurism found itself perpetually in conflict with the past, seeing an extinguished creativity and no ability to press forward within its mournful sighs of what has been. Worshiping the past was clasping a corpse; the deed was done, and people could look wide-eyed in horror at what they've done like Ilya Repin's *Ivan the Terrible and His Son Ivan* or they could leave the wake and face the sun. *"Let the dead bury their dead: but go thou and preach the kingdom of God."* (Luke 9:60)

Whatever Futurism could be said to be, it sought a necessary vitalism as ancestor worship without transformation is worship of grave sites. Its first maxim was "We want to sing the love of danger, the habit of energy and rashness." It ends:

> *Your objections? All right! I know them! Of course! We know just what our beautiful false intelligence affirms: "We are only the sum and the prolongation of our ancestors," it says. Perhaps! All right! What does it matter? But we will not listen! Take care not to repeat those infamous words! Instead, lift up your head!*
>
> *Standing on the world's summit we launch once again our insolent challenge to the stars!*

The tragic irony of America is that it has wanted nothing to do with Europe since its inception, but in order to understand itself it has always needed Europe. Perversely in its darkest of hearts it also meant it would need to enslave Europe. D.H. Lawrence saw it himself when he penned these words from *Studies in Classic American Literature* in 1923:

> *For the American spiritually stayed at home in Europe. The spiritual home of America was and still is Europe. This is the galling bondage, in spite of several billions of heaped-up gold. Your heaps of gold are only so many muck-heaps, America, and will remain so till you become a reality to yourselves.*

The miracle of America in the 19th century, prophesied by Benjamin Franklin and seen so clearly by Lawrence, was its engine of production.

Whatever one might say about Christian America, deeper there in the country were the eyes of machine rationality and the Puritan's cleansing fire of spirit. Calvinists of America asked for a spiritual shredder and got it. They and their subdividing kin gathered up colored savages to lead them on tragic, doomed quests to complete America. All that was left in that religious flotsam was the chief business of America: business. Knut Hamsun, in his disastrous American adventure, was horrified at how America chewed up and degraded its white children, the Old World's progeny. America starts and ends for most citizens on July 4th for a reason.

The best attempts to revitalize the 20th century away from liberalism's corpulence came from avant-garde artists with sharp politics. It wasn't enough to win. Now 100 years later who can even speak of art when the Spectacle is everything and irony's slave coping reigns supreme? Something must push things forward. Something must form. Something must become truly American and not beat a sad, tattered war drum for victories that mean nothing to its drummers. The future must be ours, by hook or by crook. All else is death.

We need a return of frontiers in the 21st century, and it *will* happen. Not the same way as before, as the maps are already drawn. The maximal war of all against all was already declared. Better to know it now than have to catch up. And though the borders to the wild frontier feel like they were closed before we were born, new spaces will be born outside the Empire. Our goal, our American Futurism, is to have our minds and souls ready for this new reality. The war is maximal because the enemy works from inside.

The enemy holds up the past like some kind of medieval folk monster wearing the bloody skinned face of your grandfather.

You have to look into that face.

Know it isn't anything but a flesh marionette and destroy it.

This is the emotional hurdle and it's there for a reason.

The Lost Cause is a noble one and they are numerous. I do not begrudge anyone who retains attachments to them. Our ancestors fight valiantly and our ancestors fight honorably. Our ancestors also die. They die like men, and death is as noble as poverty. Death is as noble as the state of America. I don't begrudge the Lost Causer and those that mourn. But if we become the Lost Cause then we are done. It's over.

This is not an easy topic since it's not easy to see any path forward in the American ideological desert. It is pretty clear what needs to be thrown out, which is nearly everything. Doesn't matter which president you like or how you feel about the founders. The house is burning and you can pick through the rubble later if you want. The fundamental truth is many that came before might have walked in some step with us, but they aren't us. They were men, men with their own dead ideologies and selfish motives. There is no anger here and they are not betrayers. Anger is for men in tears who beat the futile ground with fists.

What are our symbols? We'll create them.

Who are our people? We'll create them.

What is our credo? We'll live it.

Even if a year zero is necessary, then so be it. No shackles. No looking back. Theatre politics are not going to be good for us. There is a strand that places way too much value on symbolism and appearances, which is a losing formula in America. These sentiments are not connected to an actual power struggle. As tempting as it is to cherish symbolic victories, and I am certainly guilty of this several times over, we should not believe in them. Only real victories, however they look.

Those who are inclined to think of themselves as American Futurists have a long road ahead of them, a long road filled with obstacles, sinkholes, and dead-end detours everywhere. But it's the only road. Cop cults and its various expressions (ironic given the very ethnic origins for why cops even needed to be a thing) will stay as long as the rest of the foundations of American myths do. Perhaps they'll be revised, but until the average American actually understands they're living under an occupation government, it will stay. There will be little bits of progress here and there towards deflating the myth, since at the end of the day, myths don't put bread on the table. That's how things can happen real quick. Things do turn on a dime, despite how the small and slow death might feel.

Certain people carved space on the North American continent for the white man. Then a bunch of bad things happened and now here we are. Now weirdos make up new myths because America is the world empire and people want in on that hobo pie. Simple tragedy happened here, though maybe it's not so simple because everything is complicated now. America is money-power. For now.

It is ironic now that the Bidenist Imperial Order is in fact nominally Irish Catholic (though you probably wouldn't know it or realize it unless someone else told you). Then you have many of the remnant descendants of those original Anglo elites, those with ancestors whose views would have passed from suspicion of the Papists seamlessly into white racialist sentiments or even Nordicism, endorsing the rotting neoliberal Jewish-oriented imperium with an ethnic Catholic as its puppet emperor. What even is this? America? Whither, America?

Doesn't really matter which of the European blood ended up here though. They're here. And these mixed up identities, what are they? They're nothing. I could crunch the numbers and tell my son that he's something like 33% Irish, 12.5% Russian, 25% French, and fractions of other identities that I have the genealogical roots for and so on and so forth. What good does that do him? He'll be white, and that will be real and true, but for him white will not be enough. Not that white isn't enough for other people to pass their muster, but white simply isn't enough for *him*. He deserves more. He deserves to be American, and that's an identity that must matter. That is why I'm an American Futurist.

I've been known to say that whatever America once was, it died at Appomattox Court House. So many descendants of those original settlers bled out on the fields, hills, and mountains, and already the plan was set for new immigrants to bury those corpses and take their place. The next fifty years left Americans with trying to solve its questions of blacks and Indians and what it meant for them to be American with the different European newcomers. It seemed like something was beginning to form, but the Second World War rendered that moot as liberalism and money-power triumphed, and for a pretty penny the American was endlessly deconstructed and reinterpreted until emerging into its current form.

Despite its dying, nature abhors a vacuum. Something will need to rise up out of its corpulent husk.

I don't have a plan or manifesto that sets the American Futurist agenda. That can only be determined by the men who create the future. It's a monumental task, but America has never been an easy land. It was always a frontier, and despite attempts to touch the stars, America is the final frontier. Its children have nowhere else to go.

It's not enough that the future belongs to those who show up. The future belongs to those who take it and create it.

Pine and Graph: A Collapse Story

"Ours is essentially a tragic age, so we refuse to take it tragically. The cataclysm has happened, we are among the ruins, we start to build up new little habitats, to have new little hopes. It is rather hard work: there is now no smooth road into the future: but we go round, or scramble over the obstacles. We've got to live, no matter how many skies have fallen."

— D.H. Lawrence, *Lady Chatterley's Lover*

"I wish I had anything poignant to add, but the end of the day I'm just a gay retard nerd."

— Pikraft, PineBro

Most civilizations die, but very few of them are outright murdered. And while the murderers may have their own justice that waits for them, it doesn't change the fact that you have a body lying on the slab at the morgue. Victims have to cope with living in a world that they were violently plunged into by no fault or wish of their own, and while this is never a fair thing, it is nonetheless a thing that must be accepted and lived through. Denial serves no one except for vampires and monsters that feed on the tears of false hope. This society is a trough that we have begun to feed from at the moment of our birth, and we know no other way than to participate in it. The learned helplessness inside of this system of control is where the worst ideas on how to save the world—as if such a thing were possible—begin to emerge.

Online ecosystems should only be frivolous things. John David Ebert in his work on Hypermodernism—the post-postmodern era he argues we entered into after the popular adoption of the Internet in the 1990s in the midst of globalization and the financialized economy—noted the difficulties of this atomization and hyperindividualism. In his work *Hypermodernism and the End of the World* he writes:

> *The Hyperindividual has no connection with history, community, or any kind of idealistic, utopian projects. Those all characterized the past. The Hyperindividual is a world unto himself...On Facebook, the Hypermodern individual becomes a unique presence in cyberspace, with his own website and his own YouTube videos; the technology now enables him or her to gigantify out of all proportion to any relation of scale that would connect him or her to any group or social formation whatsoever...The Internet— with its satellized connections to the Exosphere—unplugs and deworlds the individual, putting him into orbit about the planet.*

It should be noted that the word autistic comes from auto, meaning the self, and originally meant or signified a notion of "morbid self-absorption." We are men without time. There is power in this exploitation. Liberalism is a key component to this power as it puts no limits on what technology and capitalism are allowed to do to the human being. Liberalism considers the individual's defenselessness to be a moral imperative, allowing more ethnocentric tribes and sociopathic strivers to exploit this design feature within technocapital. What meaning could one possibly derive from existing extremely online in this way? And what these forces were doing to the individual it was also doing to the natural world in its ceaseless drive to liquidate and digitize everything in the pursuit of production and control. Those who began to pay attention to what was happening searched for any explanation and answer to the questions these insurmountable forces were posing. It wasn't just about the technology. It was about the trees and animals, the transformation of society, the destruction of cultures and dehumanization, and the state of civilization.

This analysis of ecology, environmentalism, technology, collapse, but most of all a desire for togetherness and camaraderie culminated in the curious creation of a niche Twitter phenomenon first called Pine Twitter, later Graph Twitter. The origins of it are quite muddy due to the ephemeral nature of Twitter accounts in dissident, radical, and right-wing spheres. After the energy of the 2016 election was beginning to wear off, there began a general convergence from different ideas and currents that had begun to percolate. Interest in Ted Kaczynski, the Unabomber, and an interest in right-wing environmentalism began to crop up. The reading of *Industrial Society and Its Future* past its frequently memed upon first sentence was the first coagulation, as a number of Twitter accounts began to take a deep interest in Kaczynski's ideas and developing a robust skepticism towards the system of technology (what Ellul called in its totality Technique). Many of these users began to identify each other through the use of the Pine Tree emoji. Interest spiked so quickly that a birthday card was even arranged to be sent to Kaczynski with well-wishes from various Twitter issues (I was among those who participated). Contrary to the libels of hack journalists like Jake Hanarahan, the Netflix movie about the hunt for Kaczynski had nothing to do with the renewed interest. The fact is that anyone who has been on the Internet and following its "darker" or weirder side has known that since the day the Washington Post published "the Unabomber Manifesto" that people have been debating his ideas and that this is a current that has ebbed and flowed for twenty years. Kaczynski resurgence among Millennials and Zoomers came about at a time when these hopeless generations who grew up on media that talked about terrorism, shooters, and serial killers were experimenting with this edgy aesthetic ("terrorwave"). A political killer was always going to generate interest, especially one that already had memes attached to him. It's understandable though that a journalist would imagine that someone would get their ideology from whatever is on Netflix since that's where they and other aspirational elites get their beliefs.

On the appeal of political and stochastic killers for the hypermodernist generations, John David Ebert writes:

The spree killer, disconnected from all social formations whatsoever, wishes
to leave a mark on the socius because he feels somehow disincluded from the
larger project of Modernity. The irony is, however, that in actuality, there
*is nothing that he is disincluded **from** since Hypermodernity has melted*
down all coherent social formations. The modular individual as world
*island unto himself is the **only** ontological self that exists in*
Hypermodernity.

Kaczynski, of course, is not a spree killer, but his impulse toward
wrecking the industrialized Technocapital system that makes a Modern,
Postmodern, and Hypermodern reality possible is one in which the
extremely online, the autistic, and the atomized would find
understanding. These are similar impulses. For those in edgy politics,
who appeared to face insurmountable problems, especially with how
plugged in they were to social media environments, with an inability to
truly escape them or the other machinations of the increasingly powerful
tech giants, Kaczynski's words in *Industrial Society and Its Future* were a
bolt from the blue:

138. Thus it is clear that the human race has at best a very limited capacity
for solving even relatively straightforward social problems. How then is it
going to solve the far more difficult and subtle problem of reconciling
freedom with technology? Technology presents clear-cut material
advantages, whereas freedom is an abstraction that means different things
to different people, and its loss is easily obscured by propaganda and fancy
talk.

Though there was nothing codified about Pine Twitter at the time (called
Pine Tree Gang by some), the most unifying factor within them was an
interest in Kaczynski (with deep ecologist Pentti Linkola being quickly
adopted) and the development of a right-wing ecology. As people came
and went, a core group of posters who were connected through mutual
friends became the face of it, and despite many of them being originally
from the far-right, they drew in people from the left and even people who

were non-white and became a group of vigorous shitposters who were interested in ecology and technoskepticism. I joined in around this time when the group became more known as the PineBros. What struck this sort of second wave of Pine Twitter was that the future isn't left vs. right or blue vs. red. It's up and down, black and green: those that believe we have a future in the stars, in the blackness of space and those that believe our future is rooted in nature and to the green earth. The label "ecofascism" was frequently rejected due to its nebulous history (the term being an ill-defined pejorative that was later adopted by right-wingers who wanted an edgier online fascism that appeared to have good optics).

There were many precursors to this phenomenon in the form of men like D.H. Lawrence and Edward Abbey, men whose politics don't make sense in the paradigms that were and are assigned. Edward Abbey was a self-described anarchist, but was wholly unique in being anti-immigration as he saw it as a capitalist tool for growth that would wreck the natural world he loved so much. As he most famously stated: "Growth for the sake of growth is the ideology of the cancer cell." Between *Monkey-Wrench Gang* and *Desert Solitaire*, he developed a quirky but passionate defense of humanity and nature against the technological system.

D.H. Lawrence's stated politics were all over the place and generally anti-democratic, but his true politics were his art, and he died just as the 1930s kicked off. Lawrence wrote of the little creatures of the earth in his books and poems, of the beauty of the cycle of life and death in the world, of the struggle of machine against nature. He wrote of the natural beauty in places like New Mexico and the savage and strange energies these unmolested places can stir in a man. On what machines do to a man he wrote in *Studies in Classic American Literature*:

> *The more we intervene machinery between us and the naked forces the more we numb and atrophy our own senses. Every time we turn on a tap to have water, every time we turn a handle to have fire or light, we deny ourselves and annul our being. The great elements, the earth, air, fire, water are there like some great mistress whom we woo and struggle with, whom we heave and wrestle with. And all our appliances do but deny us these fine*

embraces, take the miracle of life away from us. The machine is the great neuter. It is the eunuch of eunuchs. In the end it emasculates us all. When we balance the sticks and kindle a fire, we partake of the mysteries. But when we turn on an electric tap there is as it were a wad between us and the dynamic universe. We do not know what we lose by all our labour-saving appliances. Of the two evils it would be much the lesser to lose all machinery, every bit, rather than to have, as we have, hopelessly too much.

Pine Twitter's edgy origins unfortunately made the kind of associations that would develop after the 2019 Christchurch shooting almost inevitable in a way. It also attracted people who hadn't actually read any of the works the PineBros were discussing or had any interest in vitalism. It was essentially racist or white nationalist prepperism with nice professional photos of Cascadia. There's nothing inherently wrong with that, but it isn't Pine Twitter. More problematic though was that not only were these people calling themselves ecofascists, but they were also calling for accelerationism. Accelerationism was a technological and capitalist concept that was frequently associated with the writings of Nick Land but then developed through the connotation that if stochastic terrorism occurs and bad things happen to society, it'll quickly accentuate the contradictions and lead to swift revolution and collapse of the System. These were juvenile notions.

Messing with the iced coffee, slut environmentalists who believed that you could save the earth by getting a reusable cup for Starbucks, two of the Pinebros (Garden and Redux) started posting memes of the World3 graph from *The Limits to Growth* in various memes to remind them that these fads were stupid; you cannot prevent a catabolic energy collapse with the same mechanisms that was used to create this consumptive civilization. For anyone who cares deeply about the environment, every social media post about going green or "one weird trick to help the environment" is another day of excruciating agony. Ecology is a delicate balance, and if an ecosystem could be saved by careful purchasing decisions then it would have evolved Madison Avenue marketers on its own.

This was when we had started to read John Michael Greer and other "collapsitarians." The interest in figures like Kaczynski and Linkola were maintained, but it now synthesized with the analysis of figures like Joseph Tainter and Ugo Bardi in trying to understand the process by which civilizations and societies collapse, with the concern for the environment and nature now being baked into this.

Some people reject the model out-of-hand as the Club of Rome is an institute full of some of the worst users and abusers of the financial global elite. It is certainly possible that every bit of data that extrapolated for it is an unmitigated lie with its sole purpose to control and trick the populace about what remains. Either position you take is the existential gamble we all choose to take.

We rebranded into GraphTwitter regardless, and with memes like "Learn to Cobble," "Look at this Graph," and "Collapse is a process," the rest became microhistory. While that is essentially the history of GraphTwitter, these ideas did become codified:

The environment will not be saved by an equitable rainbow coalition on the board of Woke Capital.

The environment will not be saved by welcoming in as many climate refugees as you think your nation's body can hold.

The environment will not be saved by feeding the masses bug protein bars until they finally learn to accept your enlightened rule.

The environment will not be saved by using recyclable plastic cups while being an Iced Coffee Slut.

The Industrial Revolution and its consequences have been a disaster for the human race.

Our technocapital society is destroying our ability to even be free, autonomous human beings.

Our resources are finite and precious and are being wasted on frivolous things for frivolous people.

Collapse is a real phenomenon, a rot that sets into every great civilization and takes it down a long unwinding to the end.

We are living through an interminable end of days.

While many are in denial, many elites know and simply don't care or are pursuing malicious actions.

All we have is each other and our will to survive.

This is why The Graph became our totem. *Memento mori*, a reminder that our technocapital industrial society has its own obsolescence. And while you may be enjoying your midlife crisis with your shiny new Porsche and younger Asian wife, the grave still looms somewhere off in the middle distance. You can shut your eyes from it if you'd like, but we are still going to put the colorful spaghetti of doom in front of your face.

Pentti Linkola famously titled his collection of essay and thoughts "Can Life Prevail?" The Finnish deep ecologist is known to be quite pessimistic about the future, once writing:

> *The coming years will prove increasingly cynical and cruel. People will definitely not slip into oblivion while hugging each other. The final stages in the life of humanity will be marked by the monstrous war of all against all: the amount of suffering will be maximal.*

To answer the late Linkola's question if life can prevail, I answer with the affirmative and eternal Yes. Life can prevail. Life must prevail. Life will prevail. No matter the great pains of the coming centuries, no matter the fields of fertilizer that are left behind because of the selfish altruists who doomed millions, no matter the decades in the wilderness that will be required to make it through that darkness and back into the light, the crucible of Life will prevail.

This thorny path is not an easy one, and it will not be for the ones who thought they could have a good life. You may not have a good life, but life's still good. The future will not select for the detached and cynical, as trials and tribulations require men who can believe in something, whether that's gods or righteous causes, and it requires women who can give those men life. The future requires a people who have a purer strength of heart.

As for the immediate, the only sensible path I see at the moment is dissensus. Dissensus being the deliberate avoidance of consensus. In dissident thought and politics, from whatever is approved by this malicious technocapital system, consensus can be dangerous when numbers are too few and people too disparate in location or being. That's assuming consensus could even be reached as every man vies to be the king of a single fiefdom. Better to go our separate ways, but in touch, to work our own way until something finally seems to work or something changes that makes unity much more viable.

They were wild days. In between actual discussions of Baudrillard and Kaczynski, we were quick to call one another or ourselves faggots, expelled people for actual homosexuality, marveled at Ron's ability to kill hogs, puked at the sight of Pikraft's mutant toes, were forced to change our personas to monkeys before monkey-posting came into vogue, were nearly torn apart over *Garfield* erotica, and were eventually torn apart by the application of cartoon breasts to avatars. It was in its heyday a real brotherhood that believed art, beauty, and nature were worth fighting for in the online arena of metairony and anhedonic nihilism.

While as an online phenomenon it's largely over, the guys are still around and have become living proof of its life-affirming ideas. Many of the guys have gone on to start families, myself included, while others continue to spread many of the ideas and humor that made it feel so vitalistic. For all of the memes, esoteric philosophy, and occasionally terror wave aesthetics, it was just a group of guys confronting that things were fucked that couldn't easily be unfucked and wanted to fight that spiritual war together. In the words of Stormking, who brought all of us together: *"I don't know what to say, it was a good time."*

It was a good time. Only love, art, and brotherhood will redeem life within this world. Only men willing to carry the torch for their children, who can show them it is a beautiful thing to have honor, respect nature, and fight for life will see it through to the end, somewhere down their line.

—For my brothers and the ones who came first—

Nishiki	Garden
Menaquinone	hbdnrx
Stormking	Hexroth
Altdeath/Tesla	Hiker
Ashkenazbol	James
Bill Marchant	Jesse
Biologic	Levi
Blake	Mfckr
Bradshaw	Nomad
Calamity	Otto
Chef	Patroc
Clark	Pikraft
Cor	Ras
Crisprtek	Redux
Daedalus	Ron
Dasein	Rory
Deep Eco Rider	Serpent Mound
Dharmaking	Skeef
Dogbot	Spook
Doomist	Tech Support Ted
Dwarf	Trash World Citizen
Eight-Eyed Eel	White House Counsel

The Protestant Way of QAnon

QAnon will probably be with us for a very long time, albeit in a diminished form. Cults don't die easily, and the future for those who want a future will be to be part of a cult or a community (and as many have pointed out, cults are a kind of community). QAnon would not be possible without the collapse of Protestant churches in the United States (and I would argue that the Catholics in the USA were also very Protestantized as their view of cultural Christianity is very informed by it). Boomers were the first generation to grow up in that collapse of Christianity in the country, which is why they had the Moral Majority, then the megachurches, and now Q.

Trump functioned a lot like a new John the Baptist in the way die-hard Q people talk about him. The language is very theologically similar to what is within the Gospels, right down to the importance of faith and that you're lost without that faith. Many of them will eventually give it up, but the belief will persist, helped by Dems making this all very theatrical too with their hysterics.

Discussing Christianity within the overly analytical and utterly powerless right-wing outside of personal spirituality is pointless, especially if it's involved in American Christianity. The demographics of Christians in the more intellectual and heady aspects of the American right-wing are largely out of step with American demographics (QAnon speaks to those demographics much better). Catholics are 20% of the population, white ethnic Catholics only making up 11% of that figure. Eastern Orthodox are 1% of the population. Protestantism is vastly underrepresented in the online right. Put all of these people in the same room and see how long it takes for them to be at each other's throats over history and theology.

I go to a Traditional Latin Mass. We talk to people in and outside of the church. Most of the people who go to services are suburban people who drive in, and within their own suburbs they are scattered, living nowhere near one another. Most of the community we live around and talk to don't go to church, any church. There's a thing to be said about not antagonizing people and there's a thing to be said for wanting to attract people of good moral character and good standing which Christianity can help attract, but the institution itself is a rather meaningless concept in the context of America, which I think can be credibly called a post-Christian country.

This is why QAnon thrives and will continue to thrive in mutated forms.

Irony, Seduction, and the Shakes

Irony, despite being utterly played out, presents one of the greatest challenges to anyone who wishes to pursue something with more meaning and more transcendence. It fills the vacuum of the God-shaped hole, and it's not for nothing that those infected by it pursue performative religion, especially sects they perceive to have the most mystical trappings and accoutrements. The problem is the inherent misery and deceitfulness of the ironic. Many people who have tried to confront them, especially on the level of pointing out their hypocrisies and contradictions, find their shot hitting nothing but a wall. There are no happy warriors among ironybros, just angry, spiteful people chasing status and a real moment in a sea of interconnectivity.

When the *Joker* film first came out there was a bizarre online debate that flared up and raged over it. What has made it funnier is how little it even mattered. The movie has gone on to be as mainstream as it could possibly be, entering simple pop culture lexicons and becoming one of the most profitable movies of all time. But the fears of it being an "Incel" movie, the talk of astroturf campaigns to get young right-wingers to identify with the character of Arthur Fleck, didn't amount to anything. All of the blustering arguments about how it's a subversion of Hollywood values that you can find if you trawl the depths of Twitter and disparate forums never amounted to anything but flash and avatars. It was what everyone who is grounded in reality said what it was the whole time: just a movie. The anger and fighting must have felt more real than the movie itself.

It's one of the things that draws out the way people's minds are poisoned by irony and media consumption. People got worked up over it while furtively reaching for the irony mask so they can then pivot to "I don't even care" or "why do you even care about getting mad about a movie. That's cringe."

You care.

And we care because you care.

David Foster Wallace is probably the most well-known figure to have written on irony and media, with his focus being on television and writing. Wallace killed himself before he saw how internet culture would have an all-encompassing consumptive effect with media, destroying the ability for many people to even be literate on a meaningful level. Wallace wasn't the first to talk about what it meant to be ironic, and many of his ideas were influenced by the writer and literary critic Lewis Hyde. Hyde laid out a rather enduring description of what irony functionally is in his essay "Alcohol and Poetry: John Berryman and the Booze Talking," as things get confusing when anyone tries to talk about it. First there is irony as a tool, which Hyde doesn't get into except obliquely, but it bears explanation. Irony does not inherently have issues as irony can be used to highlight contradictions and absurdities through the lens of expectation. This is the longer history of irony and its literary and dramatic applications. Irony developed where there were gulfs between actors, audiences, and personas as what is known and what is not supposed to be known by whom is permeable, and fundamental truths, comedy, and tragedy can be found in those emergent gaps. By stating the opposite of what everyone knows to be true and insisting upon it, by engaging in insistent falsehoods, real and known truths begin to bubble up to the surface.

Lewis Hyde in his essay likens irony to a slave dialect, which is fitting in that the behavior of the irony-poisoned amounts to little more than slave copes. Hyde explains the way of this "slave shuffle":

> In a power structure, dialect is the verbal equivalent of the slave's shuffle. It is an assertion of self in an otherwise oppressive situation. It says: "I'll speak your language, but on my own terms." Baby talk works the same way.

It is the speech equivalent of the child's pout. Both are signs that there is a distance between real personal power and desired personal power...When the slave shuffles he has been baffled into the myth that he has no internal power and his only hope is to cajole a piece of the action out of the master. The cloying voice depends on the audience it hates. It is divided, identifying with a power not its own and hoping to control that power through verbal finesse. This is the style of the con-man.

Later, Hyde pens his possibly most famous passage on the usage of irony, illustrating how dangerous it is when irony is adopted as an identity marker. Its copes are no different from those trapped in the addiction cycles of substance, though in the culture of the internet, substance is substituted for content. Irony is the music of a songbird that loves its cage, as Hyde explains:

Irony has only emergency use. Carried over time it is the voice of the trapped who have come to enjoy their cage. This is why it is so tiresome. People who have found a route to power based on their misery—who don't want to give it up though it would free them—they become ironic. This sustained complaint is the one of active alcoholism.

With the analogy to alcoholism, Hyde connects the culture of irony to one of self-pity. Certainly when one looks at the ironists of the far-right, they're frequently less the jester and more the tough guy alcoholic quietly crying into his cups, bemoaning what the world has done to him and deprived him of. There's no shortage of memes in the far-right that, when considered for half a minute, strike the tone of cloying detachment and esoteric self-pity. What tries to mask itself as too-smart and above-it-all reveals itself as revels of the ugly.

Every position the ironic take is just a tactical position, in the same way that every excuse the addict has is tactical to its core. This is its fundamental dishonesty. This is a tyranny of lies. Media goes to the heart of it all. For many deracinated, wounded people, media is the only culture and outlet they have, so they must defend it like the rebel who becomes dictator. Media however is practically impossible to avoid, because we are all tainted by the Spectacle. Naturally the media environment, sensing marketing opportunity, will put a price tag on miserable feelings and identities. It takes the commodification of opposition and suffering and culturalizes it. Burger King helps create the conditions of a fat and depressed society (often depressed because of the fat) with their food. Now they are selling you Unhappy Meals, giving your misery a brand with a price tag. Is this not a culture of irony?

Irony is re-adapted from its chief purpose as a tool. It pairs with humor because humor is a vector for truth. The problem is tools can be used on you. Whoever you are can be repackaged and sold back to you. And when your society is so atomized and deracinated that you no longer have culture, you look to the people who broke you for how to act. This is the problem of culture-jamming.

They *do* study you and how you engage with brands, positive or negative. This is Advertising 101. "But how does the product make you *feel*?" Advertising and marketing rules by pathos, not logos or ethos, and production adapts to that. And if industrial capitalism persists itself by managing and creating how people feel, then the media industrial complex persists itself by managing and creating how people feel in relationship to the images they transmit. As David Foster Wallace wrote in his essay "E Unibus Pluram: Television and U.S. Fiction":

> *TV has gone beyond the explicit celebration of commodities to the implicit reinforcement of that spectatorial posture which TV requires of us.*

This relationship of images is the essential thesis of Guy Debord's *Society of the Spectacle*. Whatever one thinks of turgid neo-Marxist analysis, there's something to be said for its main point on what the Spectacle is. According to Debord:

> *The spectacle is not a collection of images; rather, it is a social relationship between people that is mediated by images.*

That is, it's not the image that matters, it's what your relationship to that is. This is a similar theme in the vein of Marshall McLuhan's that "the medium is the message" (though *ironically* enough Debord had a great disdain for McLuhan, or at least some of his points, in his *Notes on The Society of the Spectacle*). The Spectacle is a phenomenon of technological mass media and its totality and power over us. As Debord would likely note, the issue of ironic consumption and culture-jamming is that it's baked into the totality of the Spectacle. Debord explains in number six of the work:

> *Understood in its totality, the spectacle is both the result and the project of the present mode of production. It is not a mere supplement or decoration added to the real world, it is the heart of this real society's unreality. In all of its particular manifestations-news, propaganda, advertising, entertainment-the spectacle is the model of the prevailing way of life. It is the omnipresent affirmation of the choices that have already been made in the sphere of production and in the consumption implied by that production. In both form and content the spectacle serves as a total justification of the conditions and goals of the existing system. The spectacle is also the constant presence of this justification since it monopolizes the majority of the time spent outside the modern production process.*

David Foster Wallace also realized how the Spectacle worked in this way. It would use irony to reify itself. Media saturated every aspect of our lives to the point where we think in media and become media (*"wow! he's just like…!"*). The logical thing for them to do is pitch that it's better to be inside the TV than out. Media becomes the oracle we have no choice but to go to. Wallace traces this genealogy of television's hegemony and consumption imperatives:

> *[W]hat makes television's hegemony so resistant to critique by the new fiction of image is that TV has co-opted the distinctive forms of the same cynical, irreverent, ironic, absurdist post-WWII literature that the imagists use as touchstones. TV's own reuse of postmodern cool has actually evolved*

as a grimly inspired solution to the keep-Joe-at-once-alienated-from-and-part-of-the-million-eyed-crowd problem. The solution entailed a gradual shift from oversincerity to a kind of bad-boy irreverence in the big face TV shows us. This in turn reflected a wider shift in U.S. perceptions of how art was supposed to work, a transition from art's being a creative instantiation of real values to art's being a creative instantiation of deviance from bogus values.

It positions us in a very atomized way where we feel both alienated but also satisfied by what we see. Ironic enjoyment often derives from coping with that contradiction. It is worth quoting Wallace at length on this.

Irony, entertaining as it is, serves an exclusively negative function. It's critical and destructive, a ground-clearing. Surely this is the way our postmodern fathers saw it. But irony's singularly unuseful when it comes to constructing anything to replace the hypocrisies it debunks. This is why [Lewis] Hyde seems right about persistent irony being tiresome. It is unmeaty. Even gifted ironists work best in sound bites.

Make no mistake: irony tyrannizes us. The reason why our pervasive cultural irony is at once so powerful and so unsatisfying is that an ironist is *impossible to pin down*. All irony is a variation on a sort of existential poker-face. All U.S. irony is based on an implicit "I don't really mean what I say." So what *does* irony as a cultural norm mean to say? That it's impossible to mean what you say? That maybe it's too bad it's impossible, but wake up and smell the coffee already? Most likely, I think, today's irony end up saying: "How very *banal* to ask what I mean." Anyone with the heretical gall to ask an ironist what he actually stands for ends up looking like a hysteric or a prig. And herein lies the oppressiveness of the institutionalized irony, the too-successful rebel: the ability to interdict the *question* without attending to its *content* is tyranny. It is the new junta, using the very tool that exposed its enemy to insulate itself.

People, through irony and posture, reinforce the necessity of watching media. Whether it was the *Joker* film or whatever comes next, he is vindicated because people will fight on behalf of the Spectacle over the efficacy of watching this movie or that as a cultural touchstone. People can say they'll pirate it all they want, but the media has still created attachment to the product so that people attack detractors on the battlefield of cool. This is why you cannot culture-jam televised media. You can adapt it, embrace it, make memes about it, but that was always meant to happen. Better to just admit that this is what you're doing, because denial is sad to see.

If you're watching, it's for you. It was made for you.

People having a moral-panic about incel shooters and the *Joker* movie is by design. The music industry took a moral panic about Satanism in heavy metal music and sold being part of a transgressive and "dangerous" culture back to them as product. Why do you think you're so special? The system absorbs these things and frequently applies them as tension and conflict to create exploitable divisions in people that they can profit off of and secure further control over every aspect of a person's life; even what they will identify with. The day is already coming when society will become so desensitized to terrorism and have no value for human life that not only will terrorism not matter, but it will become corporate sponsored entertainment. It's already on the verge of happening. Baudrillard writes of this seduction—seduction for Baudrillard being what does not subvert or transform social relations, but is a play with appearances, arguably similar to how irony functions—in his "On Nihilism" chapter of *Simulacra and Simulation*:

> *Against this hegemony of the system, one can exalt the ruses of desire, practice revolutionary micrology of the quotidian, exalt the molecular drift or even defend cooking. This does not resolve the imperious necessity of checking the system in broad daylight. This, only terrorism can do. It is the trait of reversion that effaces the remainder, just as a single ironic smile effaces a whole discourse, just as a single flash of denial in a slave effaces all the power and pleasure of the master...The system is itself also nihilistic, in the sense that it has the power to pour everything, including what denies it, into indifference. In this system, death itself shines by virtue of its*

absence...the dead are annulled by indifference, that is where terrorism is
the involuntary accomplice of the whole system...

Joker has a control function. The superhero/supervillain dichotomy is a
superficial expression of the duality of man. By making a supervillain
movie they invite the people who see themselves as supervillains to reveal
themselves. This, again, is the seduction of irony. A clown supervillain
who blames society forces you to engage with it in an ironic way and
defend it in an ironic way, because if you sincerely say "wow he's just
like..." with that, you out yourself as a cringey dork.

Thus they already have you controlled, and you can't culture-jam that.
You may think that your rebellion to social taboos is more unique and
impossible to be commodified and created for you because you've created
this absurdist culture of being an online racist joking ironically about being
an online racist who says the N-word, but you're wrong. It can be
created, commodified, and sold back to you. The way you try to jam it
can be absorbed (and even engineered).

And in the end, you still derive who you are from their images, not
your own. You're their creation, and ironic posturing won't protect you
from exploitation. What is the way out of all this, however? The answer
is not an easy one. Without power to enforce better norms—in fact the
system predicates itself on enforcing abnorms—it leaves mostly the
epiphany, the spiritual, and the self-reflective as the only possible way for
someone to discharge the slime of irony's poisonous culture. Movements
cannot be built on individualized developments of consciousness
however. Go outside. Log off. Just don't look at the screen, or any
screen. This won't save the world but it just might save your soul. It's the
best we've got right now, so the final word lies with Lewis Hyde:

The way out of self-pity and its related moods is to attend to something
other than the self. This can be either the inner or the outer world, either
dreams and visions which do not come from the self, or other people and
nature. The point is that the self begins to heal automatically when it
attends to the non-self.

Never the Twain

There's a journalist outside of my apartment door. He looks like he sweats a lot and that the salty beads mix in with dirt in his unkempt beard. He's fat in the face and fat in the belly, and he knocks on my door with the anticipation of a child's Christmas.

"James Foust," he calls me by my real name. He speaks with authority but I see the nervous twitch in his eye through the peephole. He strains to look back at me through the little glass, but I lean to the side and let the light through. I can hear his heavy, rasping breathing through the door, like an elderly beast feeling the thrill of its final hunt. I close my eyes and listen to my pounding heart. I listen until I hear the steps move back down the hallway and until all I hear is silence. I slump down and sit with my back to the door. I feared this day for five years, but it still feels unreal.

I was Ethnoskate1488. I never had an actual show, despite all the jokes that I should start a racist skateboarding podcast (I've never skateboarded). I just sometimes showed up on other people's shows and streams, quick with a few edgy jokes and regurgitated points I cribbed from much more succinct but shyer posters. They called me Ethan for short. Podcasting was a way for me to blow off steam, and despite not having touched a microphone in five years, it's about to ruin my life.

Years ago the only people interested in unmasking anonymous posters and podcasters were the few journalists who received NGO money and a legion of extremely online superhero film superfans who did it for free. A lot changed in the Biden and Harris administrations, and with a combination of public and private funds, the Justice League changed the game. Many people were surprised that DC Comics and WarnerMedia would work with an organization whose sole aim was to dox "anyone of interest" who had supported the Trump administration or helped get him elected. We weren't surprised in the least. Their full mission statement should be framed in a museum just for its brazen banality:

> The Justice League is a catalyst for racial, sexual, gender, and religious minority justice in the United States and abroad and beyond, working in partnership with communities and businesses to dismantle white supremacy, patriarchy, and all manners and forms of kyriarchy and strengthen the intersectional movement in order to advance the human rights of all people. This necessary task is impossible without a truthful audit of the fascist element of the Trump administration toward anyone of interest. This is the moral imperative toward a more perfect union, and the Justice League is proud to partner with conscious businesses and organizations committed to doing the work.

Instead of having radical liberals who weren't talking to each other because of various polyamorous and molestation dramas and the clout they wanted to horde, the Justice League cut a swath through the personalities by paying for all of the information disparate actors had collected, collating it, and offering bounties for anyone who had information on personalities they wanted to know about. There was no personality, no commenter, they weren't willing to put on blast as they were flushed with cash, and people quickly became addicted to the flash target of the week once they figured out how to gamify the process. They easily bought out the people who at first bristled at this new competitor, as most of them found a new home in the organization. They fundamentally found no disagreement working for a quasi-corporation with the cushier lifestyle it afforded antifascists who had struggled during the previous years' intense lockdowns.

The journalist trailing me was a particularly odious example. Everyone simply called him The Blob. This was his full-time job, and he did it despite the debts it put him in and despite the money that the Justice

League threw at him never doing a bit of good. The devil deserves his due however, and no matter what people said about his physique, his physiognomy, or his life, he was relentless in the pursuit of his own satisfaction. He himself had been doxed and exposed multiple times, but no amount of shaming him about his hovel and filthy lifestyle ever dissuaded him from the satisfaction he got at getting people fired. I have friends who keep tabs on him and the sad, pathetic details of his life. It's never done anyone a bit of good.

I was shaken out of this reflection by the annoying sounds of my smartphone's notifications. It was across the apartment, charging. My body simmered in nervous anxiety at what could be on there, but I pushed myself up off the ground and walked over. It was not a long distance in my apartment, with the computer pushed to one side, the kitchen on the other, and my bathroom right next to the exit door I had rested against. I didn't need to look at the phone, and I often planned ways of never looking at it without ever following through. After all, it could be my girlfriend, my mother, or my job needing me to do something. There were always a thousand reasons that I needed to stay plugged into the electric cloud.

I picked up my phone and started swiping away all the garbage. Game notifications, special offers. There was an AMBER alert I paid no attention to as it was almost certainly a custody issue. I saw a story about Trump, teasing that maybe his daughter Ivanka could run in his place and become the first legitimately elected female president of the United States. Swipe. Swipe. Swipe swipe swipe swipe swipe. I just wanted it all gone. There were three missed calls and two texts accompanying two of those calls. The first was from my uncle. No text. The next was from a guy from the same political milieu who knew who I was, and the other was from Katie, my girlfriend. My buddy's text said "bro, call me." Katie's notification said "we need to talk."

I knew who to call first.

I went to the kitchen to fix a snack while the phone rang. Eventually the voice of Derek, formerly, Resaxutionary, came on the speaker. I chopped carrots and boiled water as he spoke.

"Hey. Sup."

"The Blob found me."

"Wow, that sucks. Do you need anything or any help?"

"I didn't answer the door. I don't know what he knows. But like I told you before, these people will need to post everything as I'm not saying anything. I'll deny it's me even if they have audio of me saying 'I am Ethnoskate.' They get nothing."

"That's rough. Well, call me if I can do anything."

"Right, but obviously this is not why you called me."

"No, did you see the latest thing with Trump?"

My knife pressed down through the carrots, hitting the board with each slice.

"I saw something about his daughter. I don't know. It's all fake and gay and it has been for a very long time. I haven't been following it. Please tell me you aren't following it."

There was a pause. Derek replied half-laughing, half-apologetic, "well who else are we supposed to support? I get that some guys are really into Hawley, but we can't split the vote."

I set the knife down. "That's not what I'm talking about."

"You mean the whole thing about Trump teasing that maybe he won't run and he'll support his daughter instead. I mean, it's a bit of a funny troll and a way to poke at how nobody really voted for Harris, but there's no way he's serious about that. Trump is going to be the guy in 2024.

"Trump is 77 now. He's looking a lot worse for wear, this can't be anything more than a grift to keep the money rolling in."

I grabbed the sliced up carrots and dropped it into the pot of boiling water.

"They're destroying his life, man, no one asks for all that pain and trouble just for a grift. And just look at who has betrayed him and the comments he made about Netanyahu and the people who have betrayed him since the last election was stolen from him. He knows the score and he knows this is his last chance to deal with these people once and for all, otherwise it's all over for him. Guys like you just had too high expectations for him. You wanted a Hitler and that's not what he is. But he can still do a lot of good for us, at the very least by not being one of these neoliberal shills."

"I haven't done politics since 2018 and I never asked for that. God damn—" I stopped myself before I said what I wanted to say. I wanted to say "you lost your wife and she has custody of your kid because your support and online comments led to your doxing, stop making excuses for a con-man." But I couldn't. I'll take whatever friends I can get these days. "Sorry, I'm just tired of hearing stuff like that when that's just not true. You tell me what the benchmarks are for Trump to be good for the cause or the movement or whatever, and I'll point to where he's failed and failed time and time again. It's just how it is, and not being President Harris isn't enough for me to care. Aren't there any groups or chats you can discuss this in?" I asked, somewhat exasperated as I tossed the block of ramen noodles into the boiling water.

"Which? Can you name me one? They're all gone Ethan and none of the new ones are trustworthy. I'm not discussing this with anyone who didn't go through what we went through."

Then why do you keep hoping.

"At least promise me that if for some reason Ivanka gets the nomination, you won't support her."

Another pause. This time it was longer.

"We have to buy time, and the Trump name is useful."

I didn't know what else to say anymore. I sighed and finally told him, "It was good to talk to you again, Derek."

"It was good to hear from you Ethan. Let me know if the Blob causes you any problems. I've lost touch with a lot of the old crew, but I could see who is still around and who I can scare up."

"Thanks, bro, but I think we're all on our own now." I poured the ramen and carrots into the bowl, keeping most of the salty broth in the pot. I applied a smidge of mayonnaise and bacon bits and stirred.

"Ain't that the truth."

I sat in the silence of my apartment and ate my concoction. I didn't boil the carrots long enough and so I ate around them. I wasn't even that hungry, the stress was far too overwhelming. I looked out from my window and saw Indian children talking to each other outside. These were the bulk of my neighbors. I've lived here a couple of years and have never learned any of their names. Eventually they ran off, doing whatever it is immigrant children do with each other in this country. I looked at my phone. I had more calls I needed to make.

I decided to call my uncle on the way to Katie's. I hit the pavement of the exurb, walking out of my apartment complex and heading towards the little downtown area where she worked that looked like a cozy little town surrounded by a sea of industrial parks. I was never close with my uncle, but a few years ago I worked for him and we'd always talk politics. His instincts were good even if everything he believed was wrong.

"Uncle," I said once he picked up.

"Jim," he called me. "How's it going? What's that noise in the background?" He was referring to the zooming traffic outside as I walked the sidewalk near the road.

"It's traffic. I'm walking into town to see Katie since I don't have any work today. I'll move a little bit away from the road so that you can hear me better." I moved down into the grass that sloped down away from the road, walking beside the remnant trees that were once part of whatever massive field or wooded area this exurban area once was just a few decades ago.

"What happened to your car?" he asked with concern.

"Couldn't afford it anymore. Had to choose between that or rent."

"Call me again tomorrow, I can scrounge up some work for you if you need some part-time work."

"Sure thing, but I know that's not why you called me."

He chuckled a bit and began to draw out what he had to say like a child that had a surprise he wanted to show his parents. "What did you think about what Trump said?" It was always politics with my uncle. He knew I had supported Trump in the past, and so whenever we talked in the last three years it was about that and always that. About how the election was stolen from Trump. About the court cases that were brought against him, his family, and supporters. About the schemes to support him that came and gone; every few conversations there was always a new one. From schemes to overturn long done election results, to schemes to help Trump out, to schemes to help Trump take back the White House, there was always something new to put some cheapened hope in. I stopped him before from donating money, and he still helps me out. The least I can do is hear him out.

"I didn't really see, what's going on?" I half-lied, I thought. I always pretended not to follow what was going on, just to hear it from him, but there were often times he knew about stuff I had never heard. Some of it was from the online group he had found, sometimes it was just because I was that checked out.

"Well, Trump is teasing supporting Ivanka running for president instead of him, but it's obvious he's just trying to bait the media. I'm not really crazy about her, I think her husband Jared caused a lot of problems, but like I said that's just not happening. He's going to run. He has to run. All of these bozos that have been making his life a living hell since he left office, I'm sure he's licking his chops waiting to go ham on them. He won't be so nice this time around."

"If they stole the election from him last time, why wouldn't they do it this time? More and more Republicans are even talking about using rules to keep him out of the primaries."

"Yeah, they can try. They'll look stupid when they try. But they can try. No, I will admit that we were a little naive in 2020, but things are different this time. You have Patriots now who are infiltrating the party and the Deep State to make sure the election is run fairly, and against Kamala Harris, Trump is going to win in an absolute blowout. Pretty sure that New York will be in play because of how bad that state has gotten."

I wasn't sure what to say at first. My uncle was a good man, but my family tells me all he talks about now is this, all he watches is the new "independent" news sources that have popped up in the last two years. There's always plans and theories as to what's going on, but the new administration just keeps rolling on with what they're doing. Life just keeps getting harder.

Sensing my silence he filled the air. "Trust the Plan, Jim. *Be the Plan.* That's all we can do. That's all we can be. Patriots are in place. We're going to get those bastards this time."

"You're not doing anything with them, are you?" I asked, worried that he was operating in some kind of fed-monitored online group now. I pressed him further. "You aren't in any of those QAnon groups or off-shoots are you?" While they were mostly harmless, enough of the splinter groups had been rolled up on fears of shootings from some of the members. I wasn't sure what to believe about that as I don't trust the government to identify an actual terrorist.

"No need. Just enjoy the show. But I will admit that if things get too hard for me, if I get something terminal, I wonder about who I should just go and take out."

"Yeah, well, let's not talk about that on the phone as I'm pretty sure someone is monitoring us."

"I hear that, I hear that. Well, thanks for calling me back, I was just curious what you thought."

"I guess we'll just need to wait and see."

I hung up the call. I was tired of politics. I was tired of politics five years ago when it became apparent what a dog and pony show it all was. I remember what it was like being constantly sick, being constantly made sick by being plugged into the media cycle. Despite being aware of how it all worked and how the stories were crafted and how Trump played upon that cycle, I could never get enough of it. There was always something to hope for and debate, to argue about and lose friends over. As far as I was concerned, I got out just in time.

My feet were starting to get a bit sore as I approached the small town down the street from my exurb. I had not gotten used to the walking yet. I spent most of my time in that apartment. If I absolutely needed to go anywhere, I had Katie to take me there.

I like Katie. She's kind. She's pretty. She doesn't have strong opinions on anything that even men should have strong opinions on. She's just a good person. Maybe other men want more, but this is all I ever wanted. She says she doesn't agree with what I believe or once believed, but she's still here. She worries. I tell her not to worry. I fear I've given her reasons to worry.

The town was active as I got down onto the main street. I pulled out my mask and pulled it up to right under my nose, ready to pull it up over if any busybody started to approach. I put my earbuds in to drown out their nose. This has become typical of life in the last four years. The lockdown never ended. Covid never went away. Anyone too loud about how fake the crisis had become quickly found problems in their employment. Society had already separated and atomized further, no one ever really talked to one another, but a person's employment would always remain the field of battle.

Despite the restrictions and despite the people eager to enforce them, how people obeyed it was always barely minimum, if at all. People were congregated together, looking into shop windows with their masks pulled down. Everyone eyeballed one another, wondering who could snitch, pulling their masks up and separating if they got the wrong vibe off a person. *How do people even live like this*, I wondered. We'd gotten used to it though.

I walked in and around these small crowds as I headed for the cafe Katie worked in. I probably should have just called her, but it seemed more right to just come and see her. I had a feeling I knew what this was about, and if my relationship was going to end then it wasn't going to be in some distant way, the same way it seemed like everything was ending these days. Plus I was already starting to go stir-crazy in that apartment, I would take any opportunity to get out of there.

When I arrived at the cafe, the Blob was sitting there. I should have known. His eyes look even beadier now that I was seeing them this close. If you looked at his photo on his social media accounts, there always seemed to be something off about it. Something unreflective, like a shapeshifting vampire. Whatever photo he used took off fifty pounds, and seeing him much closer he almost seemed to be bursting out of his clothes. For the first time now I noticed something that made the whole scene even more unsettling. Through his shaggy hair he was wearing some rather feminine barrettes. I recalled hearing through the grapevine that the Blob had been talking about gender *a lot*, recently. He grinned a crooked smile at me, and I felt the desire to pop him well up in my blood.

He waved at me to come over to his table, knowing that I would have to pass by him anyway to get to the counter. I walked over, intending to just pass on by, but stopped to look at him. It was time for me to do what I had been preparing for since the day I knew I might be found out. I stared at him and removed my earbuds.

"Hello James, or should I say Ethan, or should I say Ethnoskate?"

I stared at him without speaking a word.

"I stopped by your apartment earlier, but you weren't there."

I stared, utterly silent.

He furrowed his brow a bit, "I'm almost done with the piece I've written about you for Justice League," he gestured with his fat hands at his laptop, "though I would love it if you had a comment for me. Tell me your side of the story. I'm a journalist, I'm more than fair."

I could feel the anger well up in me, but I just stared. I stared right through him to the back wall and I could sense his discomfort that I was looking past him. He glanced his eyes around, slightly confused. He smirked.

"Don't you want to know how I found you?"

Nothing. I gave him nothing. I would give him nothing. Absolutely nothing. Absolutely nothing at all.

Someone tried to get around us. He seemed to be confused as to what was going on. He covered his coffee with the top of his hand as he scooted past me. The Blob's eyes tracked the man who was moving past and then returned to me, realizing that my gaze had never wavered. I left no expression but eyes that burned through his own small-soul.

Now he seemed agitated. He balled one hand up into a fist, and then tried the fake pleasantry once more. "Would you like to hear what Katie said? She had some very interesting things to say. You'll probably want to hear them before you talk to her, it might prepare you for it."

I continued to stare at him. He took a deep sigh and looked back at his laptop as though he were reading something. He glanced back at me, then back at the laptop. It was clear he wasn't really sure what to do. I continued to stand there, making it as uncomfortable as possible with the blank slate on my face. I might've stood there for ten more minutes if I didn't hear the voice of Katie calling to me from the counter. I slowly turned toward her and walked away, leaving my back to the Blob and never turning back.

I approached Katie, trying to shake the experience of seeing the Blob here off my shoulders. She bent slightly to the side, probably to look at him. I raised my head and looked at her with softer eyes. I saw her purse her lip as she took stock of me. She turned to another woman behind the counter and said "I'm taking my fifteen minute break." The woman nodded and Katie led me out through the cafe to the back behind the cafe.

She turned around and folded her arms once we were outside. "What's going on Jim? Are you in trouble?"

"Probably. Did you say anything to the Blob?"

"What?" She was bewildered.

"The fat guy, the journalist. What did you say to him?"

"I didn't say anything! I did what you said if someone asks about you and just told him no comment. He kept trying to play your stupid podcast to me and asking if I recognized your voice but I told him he needed to order something or get out of line. Then he tried to arrange a time we could talk after work. I had Big Tom make him order but he left. Then he came back and he's been sitting there for about an hour or so. Why, did he tell you I said something?"

I slumped against the wall of the building and let out a breath of air. "Yes, basically. I think he was just trying to confirm my voice for himself. Someone else who got doxed by him said he does stuff like that, pretends to have more information than he actually does. He might still publish or submit what he has anyway, especially if other people confirmed for him, but we'll just have to keep denying and operating like we don't know what they're talking about."

She rubbed her temples. "Jim, this is a level of paranoia I don't think I'm ready to live with."

"There's nothing to be paranoid about anymore. He publishes what he thinks he's got, we just ignore it. We deny everything. Let them prove I've done anything. That life is far behind me and I'm never going to acknowledge it to them."

She looked like she was on the verge of tears. "You aren't still doing that dumb podcast, are you? Don't lie to me."

I looked at her a bit confused. "Katie, I haven't had a microphone since before I met you. They're just chasing the high of being able to dox internet edgelords and combing through the archive of anything they think is notable enough. I'm a nobody. Just a white guy who wants to live a normal life with the woman I love."

She pursed her lip again as a tear ran down her cheek. She rubbed her face with her hands and snorted. She walked over to me and just put her arms around me. She rested her head against my chest and sniffled. She squeezed. I put my arms around her and just held her. She felt very warm. It felt very nice. I liked this more than everything I thought had mattered five years ago.

She looked up at me, her face beat red and embarrassed.

"What's wrong?" I asked her.

It took her a moment to bring herself to answer. My heart stopped until she said it. "I spit in his coffee." I burst out laughing. "I shouldn't have done that, it was wrong but I couldn't stand to hear the things he said about you." I squeezed her tighter.

"James."

"Yes?"

"Is there a future for us? It's not going to be like this forever, will it? I don't just mean the paranoia about our lives being ruined because you did something stupid on the internet because of Trump or whatever, I just mean all of this. I'm so tired. I'm so tired of it all. The last four years have been election, lockdown, and we're back to election again. Nothing seems to change unless it's just getting worse. We can't keep living like this."

"I promise you Katie, it won't always be like this." I couldn't be certain that would ever be the truth, but it felt right.

We stayed in our embrace until she finally said, "we need to go back inside, my break is going to end. I'll see you tonight?"

"Yeah, I'll see you tonight."

We walked back in through the backdoor and she took her spot back behind the corner. The Blob was still at the table, and he nodded at me with that same sweaty face and that same crooked smile. A flicker on a television screen in the corner near the front door caught my eye. The chyron on the television read that Trump was now teasing that he'd jump into the race but make Ivanka his running mate. I sighed. More conversations with friends and family to come. More grift, more kabuki theater, more tricks and schemes. More nothing.

I started to walk past the Blob, then stopped. I looked at him again, less staring this time. I took in his shape and almost briefly felt sorry for him and the life he lived. Almost. He looked at me expectantly, like I might finally say something. I looked around at the mostly empty cafe. Those who were there had socially distanced themselves far to the other ends. I wondered if they sat as far away from him as they could on purpose. I looked back at Katie, who was back on shift and fulfilling an order. I looked at the Blob's table and to his coffee. He had taken the lid off. He continued with that wicked smile. I opened my mouth, then spit into his coffee. Without waiting for his reaction I walked out.

I could hear him struggle to get up and I could hear him shouting angrily at me, but I walked quickly out that door without looking back again. I walked swiftly down the sidewalk and dipped down different side streets to lose him. I eventually got back on the main road and the long walk home. I walked with my shoulders broad and proud. It felt like there were no more victories in this world, but I would take that one.

I stared off into that uncertain orange sun. This was the rest of my life. Past that sun there was only darkness ahead. I welcomed it though, simply for the promise that would lie once the night was done. I thought of Katie, her warm embrace. I thought of children and their possibilities. I thought of Trump. At the end of it all, he would disappear, like he'd never been there at all. All that remained it seemed was myself.

That'll have to do.

Dear Son or Daughter

Dear Son or Daughter,

I don't know when you will read this. I don't even know what you are yet. Your mother just sent me a video of the first time I heard your little heart beating. There's many more months to go before you can even take your first breath. You're just the size of a mushroom, but the way your mother talks about you, you'd think the next twenty years were planned out. That's just a mother's way. As your father I have to be hard and I have to be honest with you about the world we brought you into.

These are things you need to know.

First is your mother and I love you very much. Love is unconditional, but this society cheapens what is given out of the highest motive by taking it as malevolently as possible. Love is not love. Love is duty and love is strength, two dead virtues in the land you will grow up in. Love does not stand by and watch a person destroy themselves with bad decisions, because love is not tolerant. Love that tolerates a child to poison themselves is no love at all.

Second is your mother and I had lives before you. It's the folly of the young to think they sprung fully-formed with wisdom like Athena from Zeus' head, but sadly you are going to learn some hard lessons in the hardest of ways, most likely ignoring our warnings. You've got the blood of stubborn laborers, it couldn't have been any other way. You will likely hurt the way I hurt, fight the way I fought, and grit your teeth thinking this is like what no one else before you ever had to do. Your challenges will be unique, and they will be yours, but know you aren't alone. Your mother and I have seen people die and watched them destroy their lives or give into despair while we were powerless to save them. We've taken drugs, fallen in love with wrong and bad people, and injured our bodies beyond repair because we thought we knew better or thought it all hopeless. We thought just like you did until we were adults and our parents opened up to us. Our parents failed in their own way, and we'll probably fail you in ours. The hardest lesson you'll probably learn is just how human your parents are.

I can't promise you that when you ask me honest questions that I'll do better than my own father, even though I wish I could. We are difficult blood. Every man who wishes to do better than his father is always shocked at just how hard it is, especially when they've got the feral touch. My father had it, my uncle had it, my great-uncles had it, my cousins had it, and you will probably have it, especially if you're a son. That's how powerful blood is, no matter what many well-meaning and also malevolent people tell you. You aren't just what's in your brain. You are our blood, our spirit, our will, our nation, and our essence. You belong to nature and you belong to time and history. You are our bite and our drive and our desire to live for a thousand years and not know why. Forgive me when I struggle to answer your questions the way I had to forgive my own father for not having the answers I needed to hear.

Third, you've probably noticed that not only your grandparents but many of your relatives believe differently than we do. Many of their morals are not our morals. Some of them are even upset about our morals. This was unavoidable. We will still love them even if they will not love us. For your grandparents, they came from a time when their morals were an affordable luxury. For your other relatives, they wanted to get on in this world and the way they were taught even made sense at first. Your mother and I could not get on like that. We would not sacrifice the truth or betray our insistent souls. We believe the things we believe and we say the things we say because we mean them. Passion moves us, and if it moves you too then say it and say it hot as D.H. Lawrence wrote. Don't keep it like a secret, but understand that family may not understand. We love them nonetheless.

Fourth, you're going to be given a lot of bad advice from good people. The average person who is simply seeking a happy life can only go off what they think *seems* to work, or they will try to fill the air with sweetness for lack of knowing any better. They'll often be wrong, but bless their hearts. You will hear things about doing what makes you happy and to just be yourself, and these are all fundamentally true statements, but they neglect to mention there's about a hundred asterisks affixed to that. They're telling you to choose a destination without giving you a roadmap to do so. When asked, they might say more nice but unhelpful things, like to use your brain or just work hard, which will not only tell you nothing, it might even tell you less.

Fifth, you're white. You will hear a lot of very confusing stuff about this, both from people who want to hurt you and help you. What this functionally means is you are an unrecognized American ethnicity and your burden is to carry it and explain it wherever you go. What you are is American, but no one will recognize that because they will "well actually" you about it until they can find a way to terminally hurt you. You don't have an escape valve however. Through your mother you're mostly Irish and a little bit Scottish, and through me you get a combination of English, French, Russian, and a smattering of German that makes up all Midwestern stock but that fundamentally doesn't matter. You cannot retreat to any of these individualized components like the way I did with overemphasizing my own Russian heritage. This is without getting into adoption as my grandfather was adopted by an Italian man and an Irish woman. There's not a single strong component for you to latch onto. You are doomed to be a doomed American.

Sixth, we've raised you with religion in contrast to the way we were raised. Your mother and I were raised non-religiously in households of mixed Christian denominations. We were set loose and allowed to explore religion on our own without any guidance. The results were mixed and in the end we only ended up in the same church to spare you the same circuitous journey. We are Roman Catholics, as most of our ancestors were. While we aren't quite as anti-clerical as some of our relatives, the institution of the church as it is does not get a free pass.

Religion is important, Christ is important, but when the truth is misrepresented, it is incumbent upon us to be loud and to be critical. There have been bad religious leaders constantly throughout history, and for us to survive in this society we must have a healthy view of how our Church conducts itself.

Finally, this society is intolerable. There is no other way to get around it. There is no other way to explain it. It is full of deceit and it is full of predators. It is full of malevolent sadists and it is full of people with no courage. It is disgusting on so many levels, and you're absolutely right to reject it. And you will absolutely be punished for that. You will need to be careful over what you say and who you trust as this society has no honor and no sense of justice. It is ruled by hostile, evil people who hate and despise the normal people who live in it. People like your mother and I. People like you.

Now you know it. So what do you do now?

Some might say this is a horrible thing to be telling a child, but regardless of when you read this, if you're old enough to understand the words that I'm saying, you'll be old enough to understand how important they are. And you'll be old enough to understand that we filled our home with love because the world is full of heartlessness. We filled your life with nature and art because there are many fine things worth fighting for, virtue most of all.

The hardest lessons are the most worthwhile. The worst lessons are the most important. Bitterness is an easy feeling and it comes on strong, so it seems impossible to even be thankful for the things you've lost. I can't imagine it sometimes. No just civilization forces its own to tell its sons and daughters to prepare for diminished expectations. But for you to succeed, and I believe you will, you are going to need to fight and thrash and get a death grip on everything that comes your way and know when to walk away when it's gone. You will have so many wonderful things come into your life, and in order to survive you will need to know how to be thankful for them when they're finally gone.

What I've learned now is that there is something in the DNA that makes you a real person once you become a father. It activates when other people see you becoming one, especially when those people are relatives or pillars within your community. Whether or not those shoulders of yours suddenly become broad, they see you now as you should be. I don't think it's incumbent upon every man to become a father. It's a lovely thing, but not everyone is fit for it, and it will not save an already failing relationship. But it is a weird miracle and it must remain sacrosanct. Your mother and I were raised by lovely, well-meaning parents, but they believed if you followed your bliss you would never be steered wrong. They taught this same lesson to us, not being taught better that every person has to be led to the door that opens the mysteries of life. They wanted us to be happy but never told us how, hoping we'd find it ourselves. We did, eventually, but believe me when I say that thorny path can be cut in half by good guidance.

When I was a younger man I told myself that I didn't want my children to grow up to be anything like me. I believed this to the point that I only wanted to adopt, seeing enough problems in our ancient history and the quiet horrors of today that it seemed wrong to make life that would be tormented by those same thoughts. These were selfish sentiments from a selfish person. There's no expectation except to make you a person of good moral character and good standing in your home, community, and country. That expectation is not on you, my child, but on us. The fatal conceit of well-meaning people is to leave a better world behind for the next generation instead of leaving behind a better people for the world. None of that is possible without the foundation. The house that is nothing like its foundation will last as long as it needs to, and then it becomes nothing.

There's a lot you will need to learn, but keep these maxims close and you'll never go wrong:

It's okay to be white and angry.
All porn is child porn.
Family is a haven in a heartless world.
Nature is balance.
The struggle is sacred.
No rights, only duties.

No one ever asked to be born. No one ever wants to die. When you accept this fundamental premise, no matter how difficult it is, the world will open to you. I know it doesn't seem to make much sense. It might even seem impossible with how grim existence can be once dread sets in, but it will open to you. I promise you it will.

This is the world I leave behind for you. After I raise you to adulthood, it's all yours. I haven't left much of a pretty picture behind, but your mother and I tried to fill your room with beautiful art and our home with beautiful music. There are challenges you will face and fights you will have to fight that I will never be able to prepare you for. All we can leave you is a faith, culture, and credo that will give you that haven in a heartless world.

Life is the mystery. I can only bring you to the door and open it. The rest is up to you.